The New ABCs of Research

THE NEW ABCs
OF RESEARCH

Achieving Breakthrough Collaborations

BEN SHNEIDERMAN

Distinguished University Professor
University of Maryland, USA

OXFORD
UNIVERSITY PRESS

OXFORD
UNIVERSITY PRESS

Great Clarendon Street, Oxford, OX2 6DP,
United Kingdom

Oxford University Press is a department of the University of Oxford.
It furthers the University's objective of excellence in research, scholarship,
and education by publishing worldwide. Oxford is a registered trade mark of
Oxford University Press in the UK and in certain other countries

First Edition published in 2016

Impression: 1

Published in the United States of America by Oxford University Press
198 Madison Avenue, New York, NY 10016, United States of America

British Library Cataloguing in Publication Data
Data available

Library of Congress Control Number: 2015944381

ISBN 978–0–19–875883–9

Printed and bound by
CPI Group (UK) Ltd, Croydon, CR0 4YY

Praise for **The New ABCs of Research**

Increasingly, the breakthroughs in research that contribute to solving the hardest problems in our world rely on collaborations among teams of experts from different disciplines. Shneiderman's new book examines how to make such collaborative research ventures productive. He builds on two key foundational principles: the importance of combining applied and basic research and the role of science, engineering and design as tools and methodologies. Building on these two principles, he illustrates the approach with further elaboration and a host of case studies from industrial research to academia to government. This book will be compelling reading for anyone thinking about building an effective research organization for the 21st century.

John Hennessy, President, Stanford University

The New ABCs of Research is a brilliant synthesis about the creation of knowledge that matters. It does for Applied/Basic Research and for Science/Engineering/Design what C.P. Snow did for Science/Humanities in *The Two Cultures and the Scientific Revolution*. The content is rich and thoughtful, the writing is crystalline in its clarity, and the chapters on Science, Engineering, and Design are each one worth the price of admission. By using captivating case vignettes to illustrate, the book expresses its own message of working in both theory and practice. I love this book.

Mark Smith, Chief Innovation Officer, MedStar Health; Director, MedStar Institute for Innovation

This is a must-read book for all those of us that want to create radical innovations and breakthrough scientific advances to solve the 'wicked' problems surrounding us in the 21st century. It also provides valuable advice for policy makers and organizations that fund basic research. It is both inspirational and pragmatic with many examples that illustrate how to achieve a productive bridge between applied and basic research – a bridge that creates a "unity of purpose, which promotes the raised ambition of doing both". To do both we need tools and mindsets that advance deep collaboration and that help us jump epistemic borders. This requires deep listening and more importantly, a sense of humility.

John Seely Brown, Former Chief Scientist,
Xerox Corporation and director of its Palo Alto Research Center (Xerox PARC)

Real breakthroughs come when applied and basic research resonate and collide. Then science, engineering, and design team up to speed the flow of innovation. Shneiderman's new book shows how.

Vint Cerf, VP and Chief Internet Evangelist, Google

The New ABCs of Research celebrates the way the Web has changed research methods and goals. It's about teamwork, community, and sharing. It's about making a better society and better lives for everyone. It's about passion, hard work, and hope. It's what we need for the next hundred years.

Dame Wendy Hall, University of Southampton and the Web Science Trust

I am in complete harmony with the theme presented. I have no doubt about the accelerated progress gained by connecting the most fundamental thinking to potential applications. Very often the big hit applications turn out to be something not initially considered, but the back and forth between utility and understanding stimulates the expanding visions that fuel all avenues.

Dan Mote, President, National Academy of Engineering

Ben Shneiderman's powerful and important new book makes the strong case that we must integrate studies of practical problems with the development of theory: each supports and drives the other. This strong, highly readable book presents well-reasoned arguments combined with powerful case studies. Academia has gone too far with its emphasis on theoretical abstraction and discipline silos: It is time to blend engineering, science, social sciences, business, and the arts.

Don Norman, Prof. and Director, The Design Lab, University of California, San Diego, former Vice President of Apple, and author of *The Design of Everyday Things, revised and expanded edition*

It's excellent … a critically important research manifesto in the spirit of Vannevar Bush's 1945 *Science: The Endless Frontier*.

Rita Colwell, Director (1998–2004) of the U.S. National Science Foundation

Ben Shneiderman's *The New ABCs of Research* presents a compelling, even-handed argument for a new paradigm for interdisciplinary collaboration that puts engineering and design on an equal footing with basic science. This well-written book is full of sound observations and sage advice for students and young researchers alike, while at the same time providing plenty of food for thought for established researchers and policy makers.

Henry Petroski, Aleksandar S. Vesic Professor of Civil Engineering and Professor of History, Duke University

Innovation powers economic growth. But how to achieve true breakthrough innovations? Ben Shneiderman's *The New ABCs of Research* explodes the myth that innovation is the product of lone inventors and shows how the key lies in collaboration and conducting applied and basic research together. It's a must read for those who are looking to spur innovation in the academic, corporate, startup and urban innovation communities.

Richard Florida, University of Toronto, author of *The Rise of the Creative Class*

I absolutely love it all! *The New ABCs of Research* captures, catalogues, and advocates for exactly what we need to be doing in research and scholarship at a major research university. It beautifully describes the combination of basic, interdisciplinary, and translational research with partners that is so powerful and so needed. I want to capture it for our strategic plan.

Mary Ann Rankin, Provost, University of Maryland

Shneiderman's message distils key learnings from the last three decades of academic research and commercial innovation. His prescription for integrated and iterative applied and basic research should be read by every student, faculty member, university president, and funding agency lead.

Deborah Estrin, Professor, Computer Science and Founder of Health Tech Hub, Cornell Tech

For Sam, Nina, Milo

We seek solutions. We don't seek—dare I say this—just scientific papers any more.

Steven Chu, *Nobel Prize Winner, US Secretary of Energy*

PREFACE

O ne of the transformative experiences of my college years was reading the work of media scholar Marshall McLuhan. His mind-expanding book *Understanding Media: The Extensions of Man* described how the hot and cold media were "retribalizing" culture as they wove together the electronic global village. McLuhan foresaw changes to accompany the shift from linear print to immersive electronic communications. He predicted the disappearance of privacy and reduction of disciplinary specialization.

McLuhan's writings resonated with me as I was trying to narrow my educational focus among physics, photography, programming, and psychology. His writing helped me to realize that I could follow more than one direction at a time and weave together diverse approaches to life. My career trajectory went from particle physics to programming to psychology, latching on to the design issues in programming, graphical user interfaces, and information visualizations. Along the way I learned about the difficulties of bridging disciplines and combining research methods.

My experiences taught me how to work within academic systems, while figuring out how to change them. This book sums up my experiences so as to guide junior researchers in how to work within their academic systems, and senior researchers in how to change these systems. I try to be respectful of current technologies, but aspire to create new environments so that researchers can contribute to a human-centered future in which conflicts are resolved, health and wealth are shared, and our planet is healed.

I'm an optimist, so I believe that these and other ambitious goals can be attained through open discussion and constructive collaboration. I believe in the unbounded creativity of humans, whose capabilities are augmented by powerful technologies and supportive social structures. I hope I have laid out my vision clearly in this book, and look forward to seeing how others apply, extend, and even challenge it.

Many people have contributed to making this book. I especially thank my wife, Jennifer Preece, who wisely pressed me to take my time with this book, to let my ideas germinate, and to develop a deeper understanding of the complex issues. Her inspiration and outlook inform and enrich me every day. Several colleagues took a strong interest in the book and gave me extensive feedback, challenging me in helpful ways. Every chapter of this book has benefitted from thoughtful comments from Catherine Plaisant, who has been my research collaborator for more than 25 years, and from Harry Hochheiser, a superb PhD student of mine who has become a close colleague. Others provided substantial feedback on chapter drafts: Jonathan Lazar, Aaron Marcus, Jon Orloff, and Seth Powsner.

Many others made thoughtful comments on selected chapters or helped with information on specific stories: Ashok Agrawala, Victor Basili, Katy Börner, Steven Brint, David Bruggeman, Brian S. Butler, Linda Candy, Marshini Chetty, Timothy Clausner, Rance Cleaveland, Rita Colwell, Lindley Darden, Nancy Dianis, Ernest Edmonds, Gerhard Fischer, James S. Gates, Ken Goldberg, Kara Hall, Jim Hendler, Bruce Hoppe, John Horgan, Norbert Hornstein, Jerry Jacobs, Shahab Kaviani, Julie T. Klein, Karim R. Lakhani, Julia Lane, Jimmy Lin, Mary Lou Maher, Sharon Bertsch McGrayne, Fernando R. Miralles-Wilhelm, Dan Mote, Judy Olson, Leysia Palen, Mihai Pop, Helen Sarid, m.c. schraefel, Sara Shneiderman, Ted Shortliffe, Mark Smith, Erik Stolterman, Hari Sundaram, J. D. Talasek, Mark Turin, Barbara Tversky, Karthikeyan Umapathy, Ping Wang, and Susan J. Winter.

Still others were helpful with the case studies, which are such an important part of this book: Victor Basili, Rita Colwell, Camille Crittenden, William Dabars, Nathan Eagle, Wendy Hall, Jim Hendler, Chris Johnson, Peter Norvig, Werner Purgathofer, Dieter Rombach, and Alfred Spector.

The Oxford University Press staff was highly professional, diligent, and supportive in this project, especially Keith Mansfield, Dan Taber, Victoria Mortimer, and Elizabeth Farrell.

My administrators from the University of Maryland have been helpful in small and large ways, especially Jayanth Banavar, Ken Gertz, Reza Ghodssi, Samir Khuller, Amitabh Varshney, and Pat O'Shea. My thanks to all who think that research projects can advance knowledge and contribute to a better world.

Ben Shneiderman (December 2015)

CONTENTS

PART IV MAKING IT HAPPEN

LIST OF CASE STUDIES OF NEW RESEARCH STRATEGIES

Introduction

T he research heroes who take on the immense problems of our time face bigger-than-ever challenges; but, if these researchers adopt potent guiding principles and effective research life cycle strategies, they can produce the advances that will enhance the lives of many people. These inspirational research leaders will break free from traditional thinking, disciplinary boundaries, and narrow aspirations. They will be bold innovators and engaged collaborators who are ready to lead yet open to new ideas and who are self-confident yet empathetic to others.

This book reports on the growing number of initiatives to promote more integrated approaches to research so as to promote the expansion of these efforts. It is meant as a guide to students and junior researchers, as well as a manifesto for senior researchers and policymakers, challenging widely held beliefs about how applied innovations evolve and how basic breakthroughs are made.

The first guiding principle for research is the "ABC principle."

The ABC Principle

Combining applied and *basic research* produces higher-impact research, compared to doing them separately.

Some individuals, teams, and managers already follow versions of the ABC principle because they have seen its payoffs. Combining applied and basic research may increase the workload, but it will likely increase the quality and impact of the outcomes. I believe that those who come with raised ambitions are

The New ABCs of Research. First Edition. Ben Shneiderman.
© Ben Shneiderman 2016. Published in 2016 by Oxford University Press.

more likely to form the next generation of research leaders. We desperately need bold researchers who are committed to both societal improvement and research excellence.

The ABC principle will be embraced by those who study the empirical evidence, stories from colleagues, and historical precedents. The 14 case studies in this book describe individuals such as Rita Colwell (Section 1.3) and large organizations such as Google Research (Section 1.5) who found their own paths to the ABC principle. These and other examples show that working on applied problems regularly triggers productive basic research that has broad impact. Increasingly, funding agencies recognize the power of the ABC principle and are requiring it in their program announcements, such as the announcement for the US National Science Foundation's "Algorithms in the Field" program.

Although "ABC" here stands for "applied and basic combined," there are other ways that it could be interpreted. As the subtitle of this book is *Achieving Breakthrough Collaborations*, it could stand for that; alternatively, it could stand for "Accept Bigger Challenges" or "Actively Build Connections." Readers might also be able to think of playful variations, such as "Ask Better 'Cuestions.'"

Teamwork is a key theme of this book, although there is always room for the lone technology tinkerers or solitary theorists who passionately pursue their dreams until they are ready to share with others. However, organizational partnerships and collaborative teamwork appear to accelerate innovation and produce more frequent success stories that reshape education, communities, business, and government (Chapter 8) than individuals working alone do. The prevalence of new tools and research strategies means that such high ambitions can be realized. Web-based libraries, open access publishing, social media engagement, visual communication tools, and other new technologies provide new opportunities for researchers to collaborate. The existence of these technologies, as well as new research strategies such as citizen science, big data analysis, visual analytics, and rigorous cases studies, means that the lofty ambitions of research teams can be achieved.

This book also encourages research teams to use all the powers of the following principle to produce more successful applied and basic research:

The SED Principle

Blending the methods of *science, engineering,* and *design* produces higher-impact research, compared to working separately.

I believe that the research leaders of the coming decades will be those who adapt the ABC and SED principles to fit their research projects. Success will require imagination coupled with perseverance, reflection amplified by collaboration, and inspiration channeled into action.

I consider science, engineering, and design to be "disciplines" rather than "fields," "areas," "topics," and so forth. The term "science" refers both to a specific body of knowledge and to the research methods used to expand that body of knowledge, such as observation and controlled experiments. Scientists seek to understand the world as it exists, while engineers build systems and services that did not exist before and which are based on stated requirements for efficiency, effectiveness, and safety. In contrast, designers gather requirements and then seek open-ended possibilities through iterative social processes that include diverse stakeholders, so as to create novel, often unexpected, outcomes. In the past, science was often associated with research, while engineering and design were associated with practice. However, there are now a vast number of science "practitioners" and growing communities of engineering and design "researchers" (see Chapters 3–5).

Researchers who embrace the ABC and SED principles and deftly apply new technologies can form highly motivated teams to deal with the challenges of our time, while inspiring their colleagues and future researchers. The quest for excellence is a noble human value, which manifests itself best in research when outcomes increase human knowledge, heal our planet, and raise the quality of life for every person.

Achieving these high aspirations requires thoughtful tailoring of the following five research life cycle strategies (described further in Chapters 6–10):

1. Bring academic researchers closer to *civic, business, and global problems*, to help ensure that meaningful problems are being addressed and that the barriers to technology transfer are lowered.
2. Apply the power of *observations, interventions, and controlled experiments* to produce clear descriptions, causal explanations, reliable predictions, and prescriptive guidance.
3. Form and manage *research teams with diverse individuals and organizations* possessing the necessary knowledge, skills, and resources to address major problems.
4. *Test ideas and prototypes with realistic observations, interventions, and controlled experiments* so as to make rapid improvements and scalable designs while collecting evidence to refine theories and practical

guidelines. Combining quantitative big data analysis and qualitative ethnographic observations in well-designed replicated case studies promotes excellence.

5. Present research results effectively to *promote adoption*, applying strategies that can be refined by using carefully chosen measures to *assess impact*.

These five strategies, taken together, provide a classic case of the whole being larger than the sum of its parts: together, they create even more opportunities than when they are applied separately, as research leaders seek appropriate partners to define problems and then work with those partners to validate theories, using traditional research methods in fresh contexts. Academic, business, and government partnerships based on genuine problems often smooth the way to successful technology transfer. These strategies emphasize the use of small research teams and larger collaborations, so that prototypes can be tested quickly to support scaling up (increased size) and scaling out (increased diversity). As solutions are found, these teams can reach out to their diverse audiences

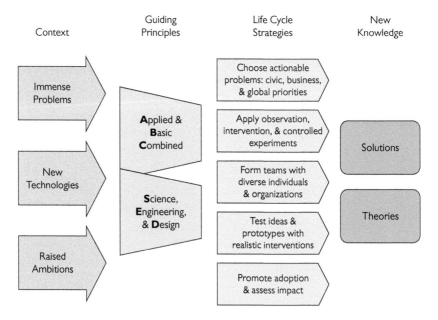

Figure I.1 The new ABCs of research are based on three contexts, two principles, and five strategies and produce two outcomes.

to promote the research results, while carefully measuring impact. The impact can be in academic terms, such as citation counts, in business terms, such as patents and products, in personal terms, such as improvements for customers, in environmental terms, such as air quality, or in global terms, such as conflict reduction.

In summary, the societal context of immense problems triggers raised ambitions from research teams. Fortunately, changes in attitudes about research, as well as access to new technologies, mean that there are fresh opportunities to achieve breakthrough collaborations in research projects. Researchers who accept these realities by adopting the ABC and SED principles can then use the five research life cycle strategies outlined above to steer their work to obtain potent new knowledge and solve societal problems (Fig. I.1). Policymakers who share this vision can change their management policies, criteria for recognition, and priorities for funding to reflect these fresh ideas.

How This Book Is Organized

Part I begins with a chapter on combining applied and basic research (the ABC principle) followed by a chapter that presents the case for blending science, engineering, and design knowledge and methods (the SED principle).

Part II reviews the disciplines of science, engineering, and design, giving a definition of each discipline and its boundaries. For each discipline, there are distinctive processes for doing research, validating results, and measuring impact, accompanied by different philosophies and ethical concerns. Each discipline also has theories and practical guidelines, although with large variations. Many earlier attempts to bridge disciplines show the eagerness to reach out to diverse colleagues, and the rich payoffs that result from infusions of fresh thinking. While administrators often encourage interdisciplinary collaboration, the realities of disciplinary traditions that favor specialists mean that the ABC and SED principles and the five strategies listed above will encounter resistance. However, change is possible. Innovative hiring practices, reward criteria, and new agendas can be realized if courageous leaders promulgate new attitudes and practices.

The chapters in Part III describe in more detail the five research life cycle strategies outlined above. These strategies represent distillations of practices that have been developed by individuals, teams, and organizations. My goal is to make these strategies understandable, well motivated, and well defined, yet pliable enough that they can be adapted to diverse environments. A key issue is choosing actionable problems and then dealing with the inevitable setbacks, or outright failures, that require revisions to theories, and changes to applied interventions. Strategies for carrying out research and then promoting it while measuring impact can help improve outcomes. These five chapters provide guidance for students and junior researchers, as well as a foundation for change for senior researchers and policymakers.

The two chapters in Part IV summarize the book's recommendations for how to promote change that will make research teams more likely to succeed. Shifting individual thinking and institutional practices will not be easy, but the potential benefits in new research opportunities and societal improvements may be attractive enough to steadily grow the community of those who believe in and apply the book's recommendations.

Each chapter ends with a "Skeptics' Corner" to address concerns and a "Summary" that points the way forward. This book also contains 14 case studies of innovative efforts that blend research methods to achieve high impact. These vignettes demonstrate that change is possible and that researchers and managers are already trying these new research strategies. Some efforts are from large or multiple organizations with demonstrated successes, such as Bell Labs, Google, the Center for Information Technology Research in the Interest of Society (CITRIS), and the Fraunhofer institutes. Some are still-emerging organizational pioneers that provoke controversy, such as Arizona State University, the Web Science Trust, Vienna's VRVis Zentrum für Virtual Reality und Visualisierung (VRVis), Rensselaer Polytechnic Institute, and Utah's Scientific Computing and Imaging Institute. Some are smaller efforts of individuals who are trying new directions, such as Nathan Eagle's social media strategies, Sebastian Seung's transformation from physicist to theoretical neuroscientist to engineer and designer, Rita Colwell's remarkable research on cholera reduction, and my classroom team projects. Finally, the shift to evidence-based decision-making for government selection of social programs shows how applied research produces high-impact solutions while collecting powerful evidence to refine theories. Each case study describes ways that individuals, managers, and teams are striving to conduct ambitious collaborative research.

A Note about Scope and Diversity

Every writing project has a finite scope. This book focuses on researchers in science, engineering, and design, but some of the same concepts would apply equally well to researchers in math, art, humanities, history, sports, entertainment, and other human endeavors. My examples reflect my experience and are largely drawn from American and European environments, especially those tied to computing. The inclusion of more international examples from diverse disciplines would help, so readers are invited to suggest them for a second edition or Web supplements.

The historical examples mention more males than females, reflecting past realities, as only 2 of the 199 winners of the Nobel Prize in Physics, 4 of the 169 winners of the Nobel Prize in Chemistry, and 11 of the 207 winners of the Nobel Prize in Physiology or Medicine were women. I give some examples of role models of women in the text and the case studies but more are needed to encourage young women. Recent books on women in science are helpful in celebrating women researchers, but integrating their stories into widely used textbooks will take time.[1] I hope the principles presented in this book, such as working on societal problems, as well as the strategies, such as teamwork, will be especially inviting to women.

Similarly, I am a proponent of universal design concepts to support the participation of researchers, especially those from different cultures and those with disabilities. Diversity representation is an important issue for the entire research community; I believe that the recommendations in this book will contribute to greater diversity in research participation.

A Note about Terminology and Concepts

The range of language used to describe research is enormous, forcing me to spend considerable time choosing terminology. My choices included:

- *Applied research* (practical, goal directed, solution oriented, mission driven, etc.) and *basic research* (pure, fundamental, foundational, theory oriented, curiosity driven, etc.).
- Describing science, engineering, and design as *disciplines* (not fields, areas, topics, concentrations, traditions, etc.). I see social sciences (sociology, psychology, economics, political science, etc.) as part of science, but put mathematics, fine arts, humanities, history, sports, entertainment, and other disciplines as beyond my scope.
- Science, engineering, and design each have *researchers* (innovators, inventors, discoverers, originators, creators, etc.) who pursue novel

directions to expand knowledge, evaluate their work, and publish their results to explain their methods, and *practitioners* (professionals, workers, entrepreneurs, managers, employees, etc.) who apply their skills reliably and productively to more well-understood problems but rarely write about their strategies. Sometimes researchers become practitioners to carry out well-understood processes to accomplish specific goals; sometimes practitioners become researchers in order to make useful innovations that result in research publications, patents, or novel business practices.

Science is often described as the study of the *natural world*, while engineering and design are devoted to creating something new in the "*made world*" (built environment, constructed world, sciences of the artificial). Increasingly scientists are engaged in projects to change the natural world or they join with engineers and designers to create something new in the made world. Made-world research also includes sociology, psychology, economics, political science, and the general term of sociotechnical systems.

I focus on *teams* (partners, collaborators, coworkers, groups, organizations, networks, communities, etc.). The broad term *interdisciplinary* research includes transdisciplinary research, cross-disciplinary research, multidisciplinary research, cross-cutting research, and so forth.

I use the term *methods* (methodologies, approaches, processes, techniques, etc.).

I concentrate on three research *methods: observation, intervention,* and *controlled experiments,* with occasional mention of other methods such as field studies, case studies, surveys, interviews, mixed methods, combined methods, quasi-experiments, laboratory studies, randomized controlled trials, natural experiments, modeling, simulation, and so forth.

I emphasize research outcomes as new knowledge. New knowledge can be in the form of practical *solutions* (devices, technologies, innovations, problem fixes, improved processes, etc.) and practical *guidelines* (best practices, do's and don'ts, patterns, how-to manuals, etc.). New knowledge can also be in the form of *theories* (laws, rules, rubrics, frameworks, mechanisms, models, etc.), which consist of *clear descriptions* (terminology, taxonomies, hierarchies, ontologies, etc.), *causal explanations,* and *reliable predictions.*

Guiding Principles

The immense problems of the twenty-first century invite innovative thinking from students, academic researchers, business research managers, and government policymakers. Hopes for raising quality in healthcare delivery, securing community safety, expanding food production, improving environmental sustainability, and much more depend on pervasive application of research solutions.

This book recognizes the unbounded nature of human creativity, the multiplicative power of teamwork, and the catalytic effects of innovation. Contemporary research teams get a further boost from fresh ways of using the Web, social media, and visual communications tools that amplify collaborations.

CHAPTER 1

Combining Applied and Basic Research

The ABC Principle

Theory without practice cannot survive and dies as quickly as it lives.
He who loves practice without theory is like the sailor who boards a ship without a rudder and compass and never knows where he may cast.

Leonardo da Vinci

Theory without practice is castles in the sky. Practice without theory creates a series of one-offs, with zero enhanced ability to solve the next problem that comes down the pike.

Mark Smith, Director, MedStar Institute for Innovation

1.1 Introduction

Thomas Jefferson's masterful mission statement to Meriwether Lewis was a brilliant example of combining an applied research goal with basic research questions. Jefferson wrote that the "object of your mission is to explore" and find "the most direct & practicable water communication across the continent, for the purpose of commerce." At the same time, Jefferson stipulated that Lewis make geographic, geological, astronomical, biological, meteorological, and other observations to add to basic natural science knowledge. Jefferson also detailed the

The New ABCs of Research. First Edition. Ben Shneiderman.
© Ben Shneiderman 2016. Published in 2016 by Oxford University Press.

social science research agenda for encounters with American Indian nations, requiring Lewis to record the languages, traditions, laws, customs, and religion. Jefferson's eagerness to learn about the tribes extended to their agricultural practices, as well as to their hunting and fishing implements. He believed that there was much to learn from how the American Indian nations made clothing, built housing, and treated disease.

The Lewis and Clark expedition (1804–1806) was a remarkable human drama of how the 33-member Corps of Discovery paddled and portaged up the Missouri River, crossed treacherous, snow-covered trails through the Rocky Mountains, traveled down the Columbia River to the Pacific, and then returned safely, having achieved many of the goals set for them. They were aided by the young Shoshone American Indian woman, Sacajawea, who accompanied them with her baby while acting as an interpreter and liaison with indigenous tribes. Their teamwork triumph, tarnished by a future of tragic encounters with American Indian tribes, helped expand commerce while advancing research, thereby creating a national sensation.

More than a century and a half later, John F. Kennedy, dealing with Cold War political realities, challenged NASA "to go to the moon in this decade" by engaging in "the greatest and most complex exploration in man's history." Kennedy focused on how "the growth of our science and education will be enriched by new knowledge of our universe and environment, by new techniques of learning and mapping and observation, by new tools and computers for industry, medicine, the home as well as the school." While Kennedy expected research contributions, he was well aware of the international excitement and broad growth of interest in science, engineering, and design that the moon landings would produce.

What is striking about Jefferson's and Kennedy's challenges is how they instinctively tied applied research goals to basic research pursuits, with the expectation that this combination would have high payoffs in business while stimulating further efforts in science, engineering, and design. These visionary leaders believed that challenging applications and basic research went well together, stimulating progress toward both goals.

However, these presidents' beliefs in synergistic interaction between applied and basic research are not universally held. There are strong voices from those who believe that curiosity-driven basic research deserves special support free of linkage to mission-driven applied research. This suggestion of the primacy of basic research has shaped research policy, government funding, educational programs, and more.

Similarly, some applied researchers differ with the presidents' encouragement to combine applied and basic goals. These applied researchers are content to solve their specific problems, without thinking about the theories that could lead to universal principles with widespread adoption.

While there are clear differences between the methods of applied and basic research, the ABC principle (Applied and Basic Combined) is based on the belief that projects that pursue both applied and basic goals have a higher chance of producing more dramatic advances in both arenas. The ABC principle is aligned with the growing ambitions of researchers and the increased appreciation for innovations that address contemporary problems. The case studies in this book show diverse approaches that provide inspirational templates for combining applied and basic research.

While national challenges such as going to the moon or building the first atomic bomb required massive teamwork (in the form of Project Apollo and the Manhattan Project, respectively), many smaller contemporary research projects could be improved by combining diverse researchers in large teams (see Chapter 8). In some communities there is a growing appreciation for teamwork, and improved collaboration tools are boosting the capabilities of research teams. These larger teams are more likely to take on more ambitious projects than smaller teams are, pursuing applied and basic tasks simultaneously. This increased ambition does not always make for an easy path. Setbacks and failures will still be common experiences for researchers, but effective processes can produce resilient teams. In spite of difficulties, the evidence is growing that larger teams are likely to produce higher-impact results than smaller teams are.

1.2 What Is Applied Research?

My characterizations of applied and basic research are meant to make both seem attractive. Some researchers may prefer applied while others prefer basic research problems. However, the first guiding principle of this book, the ABC principle, is that working on both applied and basic research aspects of a problem at the same time will yield better results for both.

Contemporary examples of applied research leading to basic research include Tim Berners-Lee's development of the World Wide Web, and Sergey Brin and Larry Page's creation of the Google search engine, both of which led to an explosion of network science research. Applied research is characterized by these features:

Applied research is mission driven: Applied research is based on researchers working closely with practitioners to understand natural and made-world problems. Taking on real problems requires taking the time to learn the practitioners' language and forces applied researchers to address problems as defined by others. Applied research is sometimes described as being mission driven, a description that suggests that it always has a practical goal, unlike curiosity-driven basic research. Applied researchers are more often attracted to solving problems that have social, health, or economic impacts.

Applied research looks for practical solutions and guidelines: Promoters of applied research are often satisfied with producing workable solutions and practical guidelines, but are even happier if the solution can achieve broad applicability. They are especially thrilled to see the prompt application of their work to goals such as increasing agricultural yields or raising manufacturing quality.

Applied research examines complex interactions between multiple variables: Applied problems are often complex, with many variables that cannot be easily controlled because of rich and changing context, and are sometimes called "wicked problems," that is, problems for which solutions sometimes work and sometimes fail, because of changing conditions. Applied researchers strive to understand interactions between variables such as a mayoral candidate's political positions, media expenditures for positive versus negative advertising, and socioeconomic variables as they influence voter turnout across the hundreds of polling places in a large city. Applied researchers like conquering complexity and learning how to deal with changing conditions. Sometimes solutions in complex situations may not come with causal explanations, and therefore these solutions need revision when conditions change.

Applied research uses realistic (rather than idealized) scenarios: Applied researchers enjoy working on realistic situations, trying multiple solutions, refining promising ideas, and getting their hands dirty. Applied researchers thrive on these challenging situations, which force them to learn more, try many solutions, and fail frequently until they find success. Simplified problems ("toy problems") may be too easy for them, not offering enough of a challenge or appearing to be merely games.

Critics of applied research argue that its narrow focus on practical outcomes ties it too closely to business needs or government programs, thereby undermining interest in universal principles in the form of theories and predictions. Critics also complain that applied research only addresses short-term goals with incremental contributions, rather than long-term problems and fundamental breakthroughs. These legitimate concerns can be reduced if applied researchers spend more time speaking with basic research colleagues, who could provide concepts, language, and methods to improve the applied research. Additionally, applied research enthusiasts should remember Kurt Lewin's comment that sometimes "there is nothing more practical than a good theory."[1]

1.3 What Is Basic Research?

Contemporary examples of basic research projects include the search for the Higgs boson, looking for evidence of interstellar black holes, and the Human Genome Project. Basic research is characterized by the following features:

Basic research is curiosity driven: Basic research is generally understood to be motivated by curiosity or a drive to understand the world we live in, rather than the need to solve an existing problem. It stems from observations of the world, a desire to organize knowledge, and an eagerness to predict how the world will behave. For example, questions about the natural world might include, are there animals with an odd number of legs? What chemicals efficiently store energy? What gases are on Jupiter? Questions about the made world might include, what is the impact of financial incentives on getting individuals to change their exercise habits? How can domestic conflicts be resolved before they become violent? Is there necessarily a trade-off between healthcare quality and costs? While most observers are happy to let individuals follow their curiosity, when they or their organizations seek public funds, valid questions include, how much curiosity-driven exploration is appropriate? A central criterion is whether answers are actionable; will research outcomes lead to changes that bring near-term economic or other benefits?

Basic research employs reductionist models: A second common feature of basic research is the reductionist model, which presumes that phenomena can be studied by changing one variable at a time. Basic

Stopping Cholera with Science, Satellites, and Saris

Rita Colwell, Distinguished University Professor, University of Maryland

http://www.umiacs.umd.edu/people/rcolwell

For centuries, cholera epidemics have sickened and sometimes killed people who did not understand the water-borne transmission of the *Vibrio cholerae* bacterium. While improved water filtration and treatment have lessened the problems, floods still carry raw sewage into the water supplies of developing nations, thereby still bringing devastating and deadly epidemics.

Fortunately, promising science, engineering, and design strategies are producing change. Bacteriologist and oceanographer Rita Colwell led a team that came to understand the physical, biological, and social conditions underlying cholera epidemics; this understanding enabled them to make a clever and effective intervention that dramatically reduced the severity of Bangladesh's cholera epidemics.

This remarkable story begins with a deep understanding of the scientific foundations of spring and late-summer plankton blooms that carry the cholera bacteria. The plankton include copepods, which are 1–2 mm long crustaceans that may each carry as many as 10,000 cholera bacteria. While boiling would effectively kill the bacteria, making a fire in a flooded area is not easy.

Colwell's team detected the location of floods, water surface temperatures, and plankton growth areas using NASA satellite-based remote sensing data. These data helped refine the theories of how cholera epidemics spread and guided the researchers to target areas for pilot-study interventions.[1]

Colwell and her team realized that filtering drinking water with eight layers of widely available sari cloth might remove the troubling copepods carrying the deadly bacteria. Colwell's team conducted a 16-month pilot study in 18 villages involving 2212 households. Residents were trained to place 4–8 layers of cloth over the mouths of water bottles. When water was poured through the cloth into the bottles, the layers of cloth acted as filters to trap sediments and the copepods, producing water that was clearly cleaner than the unfiltered water. But many questions remained, such as whether the copepod-trapping filters would stop enough of the much smaller free bacteria and whether the residents would reliably use their sari cloths in this new way.

After revising the training to improve compliance and illness data collection strategies, the team conducted a 19-month study in 65 villages and involving more than 130,000 people. The dramatic results comprised a 48% reduction in cholera cases for those who used the simple, cloth-based filtration process. This clear application of the ABC principle

(Applied and Basic Combined) validated scientific theories and produced life-saving health benefits. Researchers gained a deeper understanding, and practitioners learned many principles that could be applied in other public health contexts—a great example of the twin-win goal of expanding knowledge while bringing societal benefits. Dr. Colwell's career has included other research projects, but her life trajectory moved on to top leadership roles for the American Society for Microbiology and the American Association for the Advancement of Science, as well as for the University of Maryland Biotechnology Institute. Then, as Director of the National Science Foundation (1998–2004) she helped shape policies that expanded funding, especially to ensure that young researchers would have ample long-term funding to dig deep into hard problems. Dr. Colwell always wants to know how a fundamental research program will weave threads of discovery into potent new findings that will lead to solutions of meaningful problems. Her clarity of thought, calm confident style, and capacity for team building won her the trust of many colleagues and the 2006 US Medal of Science, as well as Congressional respect for her belief that the National Science Foundation should include "research at and across the frontier of science and engineering, and connections to its use in service of society.[2]

In the aftermath of the 2010 Deepwater Horizon failure that killed 11 people and caused broad environmental damage, British Petroleum called on Rita Colwell to lead their $500 million Gulf of Mexico Research Initiative (GoMRI).[3] Undaunted by the challenges of taking this funding from a controversial source, she ensured that the funding would be managed by an independent research community governed by its own research board. She astutely applied the US National Science Foundation's rigorous peer-review process to select project proposals from researchers in dozens of states and more than a hundred universities. The GoMRI Research Board selected research themes based on the physics, chemistry, and biology of how petroleum leaks dispersed and impacted the environment. They emphasized research on engineering and technology systems to improve detection, response, and remediation of damage. One of the bold components of the GoMRI research agenda was the inclusion of sociotechnical systems design research to improve environmental risk assessment, develop community response capabilities, and address public health issues. The requests for proposals appropriately required interdisciplinary research consortia containing participants from science, engineering, and design (in other words, it employed the SED principle).

Few researchers will have as much impact as Dr. Rita Colwell has had. However, I see her career as an inspirational model to those who understand how to form and lead teams that produce breakthrough research with profound societal benefits.

[1] Colwell, R. R., Huq, A., et al., Reduction of cholera in Bangladeshi villages by simple filtration, *Proceedings of the National Academy of Sciences* **100**, 3 (February 4, 2003), 1051–1055.

[2] Colwell, R. R., *Testimony before the House Appropriations Subcommittee on VA/HUD and Independent Agencies* (April 4, 2000) http://www.nsf.gov/about/congress/106/rc000404approp.jsp.

[3] Gulf of Mexico Research Initiative, *Investigating the Effect of Oil Spills on the Environment and Public Health* (2013) http://gulfresearchinitiative.org/.

researchers may be naturalists exploring forests, but basic research is often tied to laboratory situations where conditions can be controlled to limit variability and promote replicability. Basic researchers like the process of solving one problem at a time, in the belief that putting together independent results can explain larger interconnected phenomena. For example, a chemist can study the conductivity of electricity in a metal while controlling the room temperature, altitude, and magnetic field. The results from other chemists can then be combined to make formulas that have the fewest variables needed to predict what might happen in novel situations.

Basic research searches for universal principles: Proponents of basic research often claim that it leads to general theories and predictions. Tracking the movements of Mars was meant to lead to a general theory of planetary motion, and studying *Escherichia coli* is meant to produce knowledge that is true for many bacteria. Promoters of basic research believe that their work will result in broad understanding of multiple phenomena. Critics argue that a narrow focus on special cases chosen in controlled experiments may not generalize when the results are applied more widely.

Basic research relies on simplifications and idealizations: A fourth feature of basic research is that the use of simplifications or abstractions of complex phenomena is acceptable in order to facilitate research. Physicists study gravitational attraction between bodies by assuming that the mass of each body is concentrated in a single point; similarly, social network theorists assume all nodes in a graph have the same properties. These simplifications and the use of synthetic data with uniform or normal distributions, rather than real data with unusual distributions, make research easier and support application to other idealized problems. Basic researchers see these simplifications as clean, clear problems that yield elegant solutions.

Critics of basic research argue that simplifications and idealizations remove the interesting domain-specific aspects of a problem and thus render the work less applicable. Critics complain that basic researchers who fail to engage with real-world situations and with practitioners produce oversimplified and possibly unhelpful results. The problems addressed in basic research may miss key ingredients of real-world problems, thus making technology transfer more difficult. In addition, such difficulties are aggravated when basic researchers do not spend sufficient time building relationships with practitioners, making the gulf of communication between researchers and practitioners even more difficult to bridge.

An indication that science policy is changing can be seen in the rule change for medical clinical trials, announced by the US National Institutes of Health Director Francis S. Collins. The rule requires the inclusion of women participants in clinical trials so as to ensure that the basic research is applicable to women.[2] It seems startling that this consideration is only now being addressed to make controlled experiments more realistic.

1.4 Process Models for Research

Promoters of applied and basic research differ in more ways than just in the kinds of problems they like. They also differ in how they select problems, conduct their work, and then promote their solutions.

Basic researchers cherish the "linear model" in which basic research leads to applied research, then development, and finally production and operation (Fig. 1.1). The development stage can refine practices or software for broad usage, bring technologies to wide audiences, or lead to commercial products and services. The linear model gives precedence to basic research, seeing it as the forerunner of applied research.

The linear model was given strong support by Vannevar Bush, who, as President Roosevelt's science advisor and head of the Office of Scientific Research and Development, wrote an influential 1945 report *Science: The Endless Frontier*.[3] He described basic research as "pure research" and argued that "pure research is research without specific practical ends" and which often results in surprising outcomes. Bush wrote that "many of the most important discoveries have come as a result of experiments undertaken with quite different purposes in mind," although it is equally true that applied research can lead to surprising insights and new products. Bush aligned himself with those who saw pure or basic researchers as brilliant minds who spawned breakthrough ideas and spotted fresh patterns. Bush and others recognized that sometimes a basic research

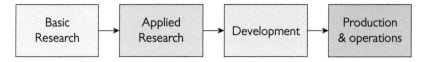

Figure 1.1 The old Linear Model: Simple but misleading model that rarely works.

effort might take decades to be appreciated and applied, but they speak confidently of the payoffs from such investments.

Writing for government policymakers, Bush argued that university researchers needed special protection from administrative interference, confidently promising "statistically it is certain that important and highly useful discoveries will result from some fraction of the work undertaken; but the results of any one particular investigation cannot be predicted with accuracy."

Bush also described applied research in a positive way, writing "applied research and development differs in several important respects from pure science. Since the objective can often be definitely mapped out beforehand, the work lends itself to organized effort. If successful, the results of applied research are of a definitely practical or commercial value." It is ironic that Bush saw little possibility that applied research could stimulate pure or basic research. The irony is striking since his book is filled with examples of how wartime needs, especially in medicine, produced remarkable basic research payoffs. Of course, the most compelling example from Bush's own experience is the Manhattan Project, in which the practical goal of building an atomic bomb invigorated basic research in physics, materials engineering, chemistry, and many other disciplines. Pascal Zachary, Bush's biographer, believes that Bush felt obliged to promote unfettered government support of basic research in order to pay back his colleagues, who had left their families and worked so hard in difficult conditions to achieve their dramatic applied goal.[4]

The irony is that Bush not only emphasized the flow from basic to applied research but also sternly warned that "applied research invariably drives out pure." This disturbing statement, so at odds with much of the historical evidence, seems even more troubling to contemporary readers.[5] A classic example of an applied problem leading to a basic research breakthrough is the story of Arno Penzias and Robert W. Wilson's work for Bell Labs in developing a very sensitive microwave receiver to capture signals reflected from earth-orbiting satellites. None of their efforts succeeded in eliminating the noisy background radiation which ultimately proved to be the remnants of the cosmic big bang. Their work led to the 1978 Nobel Prize in Physics, a result that reaffirms how working on applied engineering problems can trigger basic research advances.

Still, the linear model, which assumes that basic research precedes applied research, is widely accepted, especially by basic science researchers who want funding with few restrictions and no promises of productive outcomes. Of course, there are researchers striving to be the next Einstein, Curie, or Hawking, so some allowances are needed for bold innovators who show promise in developing fresh ideas. However, for the vast population of researchers, I advocate tying continued funding to encouraging early results and demonstrations of promising applications.

1.5 New Views of the Relationship between Basic and Applied Research

Critics of Bush's views, such as Venkatesh Narayanamurti, a former Bell Labs semiconductor research director, and his coauthors, cited the many cases of basic research progress that were stimulated by applied problems.[6] He and others suggest that the path to commercial success is not to promote technology transfer from universities to business but to get businesses to participate in setting research agendas based on the problems they face. The same strategy applies to working with government and international development partners to define problems and validate theories in living laboratories. Narayanamurti and his coauthors claim that this combined approach (which we can recognize as the ABC principle) "can open the door to game-changing discoveries and inventions and put the nation on the path to a more sustainable science and technology ecosystem." We will return to this powerful idea in Chapter 8 in discussing different forms of collaboration.

Innovation researcher Tom Allen claims that the "reverse linear model" often generates an appropriate solution to the problem as well as substantive advances in basic research (Fig. 1.2).[7] The reverse linear model, achieved by closely situating applied and basic researchers, was a central theme at Bell Labs, as described in Jon Gertner's bestseller, *The Idea Factory*.[8] In the early days, when Bell Labs was located in lower Manhattan, and then later, when new buildings were constructed in New Jersey, the architectural design encouraged encounters between applied and basic researchers. Even mathematically inclined basic researchers, such as Claude Shannon, worked closely with applied projects to steer their development of his influential theory of communication.

The argument for combining applied and basic research applies equally to research projects that serve the needs of civic organizations, especially in helping underserved communities or people with disabilities, and projects that address global priorities, especially in developing nations. Among the strong voices arguing to reframe research projects in the direction of the ABC principle is that of the Nobel Prize-winning biologist Peter Medawar, who wrote "one of the most damaging forms of snobbism in science is that which draws a class

CASE STUDY 1.2 GOOGLE'S HYBRID APPROACH TO RESEARCH

Google's reputation for rapid accurate search is just the beginning of what founders Sergey Brin and Larry Page dreamed of in the late 1990s. As a graduate of our Computer Science Department and son of the University of Maryland math professor Michael Brin, Sergey Brin was all about clever algorithms, but his ambition was raised when he and Larry Page set out to organize the world's information and make it accessible. Their two-person team, now surrounded by many collaborators, succeeded in astonishing ways by continuing to innovate with scalable services around the globe and in many languages.

But they created more than fast algorithms, efficient server farms, and rapid network access. They also found a way to make money by cleverly arranging for search terms to trigger placement of ads, creating a market for companies who bid up the price of desirable search terms around consumer items, travel destinations, or business referrals. Brin, Page, and CEO Eric Schmidt put their ample resources to work by developing ever broader applications or acquiring successful companies to lure users to a wide range of Google services. Maps, images, videos, and much more were made findable and sharable among users for free, all paid for by ever more carefully refined advertising strategies that worked remarkably well. The Google magic of free access depends on a successful business model combined with deep technical advances that supported generalized services for Google's engineers, such as MapReduce, the Google File System, and BigTable.

Google's formula for the rapid development of powerful services is a potent example of combining applied and basic research (the ABC principle), which was clearly described by their research leaders: Al Spector, Peter Norvig, and Slav Petrov.[1] They claim that the goal of research is "to bring significant, practical benefits to our users, and to do so rapidly, within a few years at most." Their approach is to have a team that "iteratively explores fundamental research ideas, develops and maintains the software, and helps operate the resulting Google services—all driven by real-world experience and concrete data." They explicitly align with Stokes's "use-inspired basic" and "pure applied" research, thereby rejecting the "pure basic" quadrant.

Spector, Norvig, and Petrov make minimal mention of basic research or science but seem to equate "research" with early stages of a novel idea, while "engineering" is associated with later development stages more tied to technology implementation, scaling up, and innovation dissemination. Design also gets minimal mention, but user interface design has been a vital part of Google's work. Spector confirmed that in recent years he has seen that "research and innovation in design and user interaction is exceedingly important." User experience research and design now account for an increasing fraction of their published work. In short, design is gaining ground, but explicitly including it as part of Google's philosophy and language might strengthen their work even further and ensure more integrated teams. Ironically, Google's greatest claim to visual design might be through its daily changing front page, which features clever interactive artwork tied to cultural, historical, or social themes.

The Spector, Norvig, and Petrov team make two more claims that support the ABC principle. They believe that Google's success is driven by focusing on delivery of services to real users, which frequently eliminates "most risk to technology transfer from research to engineering." They also make the bold claim that working on real data using in vivo research methods has a greater chance of producing better foundational, basic, or pure research that will also be well received by the academic community.

In summary, they make dual grand claims that, when their teams conduct experiments at scale, they generate "stronger research results that can have a wider academic and commercial impact" than when they conduct smaller experiments. This direct rejection of Vannevar Bush's belief that supporting basic research is the best way to produce applied research is a strong indicator of how much some business research organizations have changed. Critics complain that Google does relatively less publishing of its work than other companies, thereby failing to share its work and expose it to peer review; however, Google responds that in many cases they offer free open-source versions of their work and present their results in nonacademic forums to accelerate application while gaining meaningful feedback. Norvig points to the increased stream of peer-reviewed academic papers by Google authors.

Since Google's research management team is aware of the need for open-ended exploration of new ideas, their staff is encouraged to spend one day a week (20% of their time) on some personal project to explore novel directions. These curiosity-driven projects may mature into something that becomes part of Google's research directions.

Apple's termination of its Advanced Technology Group, which was devoted to research, and its shift to rapid development strategies is another indicator that companies are changing their directions. Similarly, ATT, Microsoft, IBM, and many other technology companies also show signs of shifting to the SED principle, which blends science, engineering, and design. Other indicators of change are the increased attention to design methods to drive research, and the inclusion of ethnographers and anthropologists as team members to make sure the users' voices are heard.

---

[1] Spector, A., Norvig, P., and Petrov, S., Google's hybrid approach to research, *Communications of the ACM* 55, 7 (July 2012), 34–37.

---

distinction between pure and applied science."[9] Medawar valued real problems as triggers for basic research.

Another often-cited book by the widely admired academic leader Donald Stokes is cleverly titled *Pascal's Quadrant: Basic Science and Technological Innovation*.[10] Stokes sees high impact from research that is motivated by both considerations for use and fundamental understanding. His favorite example of "use-inspired basic research" is Louis Pasteur's repeated success in working on

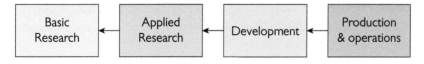

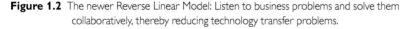

Figure 1.2 The newer Reverse Linear Model: Listen to business problems and solve them collaboratively, thereby reducing technology transfer problems.

genuine problems such as the spoilage of milk and failures of wine fermentation, to produce basic science breakthroughs about bacterial processes and vaccines. We continue to honor his contributions with the term "pasteurization" that describes the careful process of heating (not boiling) dairy or other food products to reduce the number of bacteria while preserving flavor and texture. Pasteur's basic research work overturned the prevailing belief in spontaneous generation, leading to applied advances in public health and medical care, such as Joseph Lister's development of antiseptics for surgery. In his later work, Pasteur addressed problematic animal diseases, developing the immunization methods that led to an array of modern vaccines.

Donald Stokes comments liberally about the influence of Vannevar Bush's linear model but then gently but firmly criticizes it "since it obscures as well as reveals." Stokes sees Bush as "too narrow" in assessing the inspirations for basic research and the "actual sources of technological innovation." Stokes reports on many research breakthroughs, repeatedly showing how applied problems have led to foundational advances. Narayanamurti and his coauthors reported that "Stokes's book excited many in the science policy and academic communities, who believed it would free us from the blinders of the linear model, [but] it did not go far enough, nor did his work result in sufficient change in how policymakers discuss and structure research ... We propose a more dynamic model in which radical innovation often arises only through the integration of science and technology."

Building on Stokes's thoughtful analysis and on encouragement from other analysts, I agree that a broader vision is needed to go beyond "use-inspired basic research." That phrase focuses on selecting problems, but I advocate a continuing collaboration between applied and basic researchers. I believe applied researchers can benefit from "theory-inspired applied research." Research that has solid theoretical foundations can often suggest practical solutions. In short, the ABC principle is more than about choosing problems: it is about a continuing dialog between those with strong practical experience and those with rich knowledge of theories. It's just possible that combining applied and basic research may lead to less effort and better solutions.

My first goal is to encourage research teams to raise their ambitions by combining applied with basic research throughout the project life cycle, so as to achieve breakthrough collaborations. The outcomes of such work should increase knowledge, accelerate technology innovation, drive theory refinement, and produce practical solutions.[11]

My second goal is to encourage research policymakers to embrace the ABC and SED principles. Since prevalent beliefs about the primacy of basic research guide many agencies, changes are necessary, for example, revising the US

Department of Defense's influential funding categories, which separate basic (category 6.1) from applied research (category 6.2).[12] A hopeful sign comes from the celebrated Defense Advanced Research Projects Agency (DARPA), which "works within an innovation ecosystem that includes academic, corporate and governmental partners . . . For decades, this vibrant, interlocking ecosystem of diverse collaborators has proven to be a nurturing environment for the intense creativity that DARPA is designed to cultivate."[13] Examples of their breakthroughs include the Internet, aircraft stealth technology, and driverless vehicles, which all combine elements of basic and applied research.

Former IBM chief scientist and government science advisor Lewis Branscomb supports the combined approach while condemning the "false dichotomy" between scientific creativity and utility. He argues that practical and theoretical work fit together well, claiming that mission-driven and curiosity-driven research invigorate each other.[14]

Sympathetic descriptions come from design researchers Linda Candy and Ernest Edmonds, who claim "there is a great deal to gain from looking at theory and practice as equal partners in the creative process." They advocate "practice-based research" in which there is a reflexive relationship between theory and practice. Theory can guide designers who develop novel products or services, and the realities of practice speed the evolution of theory refinement.[15]

Of course, some basic research will lead only to novel or refined theories, and some applied research will lead exclusively to engineering innovations or refined technology designs. However, I believe that the highest payoffs come when there is a healthy interaction of applied and basic research (Fig. 1.3). The ABC principle also suggests that applied and basic research are embedded in a rich context of large development projects and continuing efforts to refine production and operations.

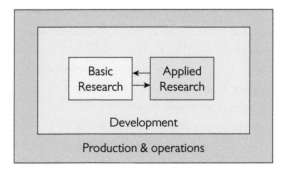

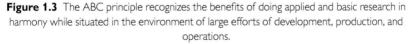

Figure 1.3 The ABC principle recognizes the benefits of doing applied and basic research in harmony while situated in the environment of large efforts of development, production, and operations.

1.6 How New Technologies Empower Researchers

The raised ambitions implied by the ABC principle are more easily realized today than in Vannevar Bush's day, in part because of the successful realization of Bush's "memex" vision. Paradoxically, his applied research vision triggered a half-century of applied and basic research that emerged as the World Wide Web. The 1945 memex was portrayed as a desk-sized microfilm device that enabled users to read texts and follow links to related references, thereby creating trails of associations that could be preserved for future users. The World Wide Web was designed to do even more than memex, since it supports far richer two-way communication and lively social media environments, offering a more potent source of rapidly updated resources, diverse commentaries, and historical archives. It is also engineered to support collaboration in grand projects, ranging from Wikipedia's multilingual encyclopedias to global citizen science projects in astronomy, medicine, biodiversity, and so forth. While Web science (see Case Study 10.1 in Section 10.4) emerged only after the design and engineering were well advanced, the results of Web science drive the redesign of Web-based tools and improve the engineering of the infrastructure.

The World Wide Web offers rapid access to scientific papers, government reports, and business websites, thereby enabling the discovery of related work and potential collaborators, such as academic researchers, government agency staffers, and commercial developers. Social media, such as email, blogs, videos, Facebook groups, Twitter posts, and wikis, enable rapid information dissemination. Social media also facilitate partnership formation and accelerate discovery processes in ways that are far more effective than earlier technologies. A majority of scientific paper readership comes from links embedded in emails, Web-based documents, and social media postings. Researchers are less likely than in the past to subscribe to a small number of printed journals, which they used to read conscientiously. They are more likely to be affiliated with research institutions that enable online access to digital libraries, which they read based on recommendations from colleagues. The growing movement to open publication helps those without access to costly publications. Crowdsourcing and citizen science projects are still-emerging ideas, which are further increasing the quality and quantity of research while increasing its impact.

Another benefit of these improving technologies is that civic organizations, commercial developers, and governments can more easily find academic research partners to help solve their problems or guide them to appropriate resources. The lower barriers to communication mean that practitioners and academic researchers can more easily form partnerships to conduct research with publishable and practical outcomes. Industry–university partnerships with government and professional society participation, such as the Advanced Manufacturing Partnership that successfully promoted the 2011 US National Robotics Initiative, can often be effective.[16] Of course, there are dangers and limitations to close collaboration between academics and civic, business, or government organizations, so careful design of such partnerships is necessary to preserve academic freedoms while addressing needs for personal privacy, intellectual property protection, and national security (Chapter 8).

Ideally, research teams with diverse skills work together to produce dual benefits: publishable research results and focused practical solutions that serve an existing need. By working together on genuine problems, basic researchers gain access to smart, motivated practitioners who offer new challenges that expand academic disciplines, provide big data resources to analyze, and enable access to natural test beds to evaluate results. Similarly, business developers gain access to savvy basic researchers whose complementary skills and energetic students could spawn potent mathematical models or mind-expanding totally unexpected solutions.

A key payoff of the ABC principle is that it lowers barriers to technology or innovation commercialization. When business developers suggest problems for basic researchers, there is a higher chance of producing rapidly implementable, high-payoff solutions for companies. Similarly, civic organizations and government agencies, especially those working with communities that are underserved, people with disabilities, or developing nations could gain access to student and faculty researchers to work on their problems as the basis for universal principles and publishable results.

However, the presence of the Web, social media, and visual communication tools is not sufficient to ensure that the ABC principle will be employed successfully.[17] Unfortunately, many basic researchers avoid business developers, who also have reasons to shun basic researchers. Fundamental problems remain, especially over the ownership of intellectual property, the need to publish, and sharing payoffs for successes. Healthy differences may also emerge over the pace of work and the priorities of theory versus practice; however, working through these differences may lead to improved outcomes.

The divergent needs of academic and business researchers are apparent in the 25-year history of the development of tree-structured visualizations.[18] My development of treemaps was motivated by a practical need to understand information stored in tree-structured data on computer hard drives. The solution led to a basic research contribution, an information visualization algorithm which I called treemaps (Fig. 1.4). The treemapping idea and algorithm were published openly in a leading scientific journal without patent protection.[19] Researchers at the Xerox Palo Alto Research Center (now simply called PARC) developed two competing proprietary ideas that were heavily patented, thereby suppressing application and research by others. The openness of treemaps led to many variations and improvements, as well as numerous empirical evaluations. My collaboration with companies took many hours of negotiations but resulted in the development of applications for financial markets, sales management, and manufacturing process control. The cascade of further basic algorithmic research on treemaps and extensive testing with increasingly diverse audiences laid the basis for widespread usage of the algorithm in hundreds of commercial and open-source implementations.

These and other case studies are the heart of this book. The ABC principle is meant to capture the shift in strategies that is happening in academic research, business management, and government policy. If individual researchers and organizational decision-makers can accelerate movement to the ABC principle,

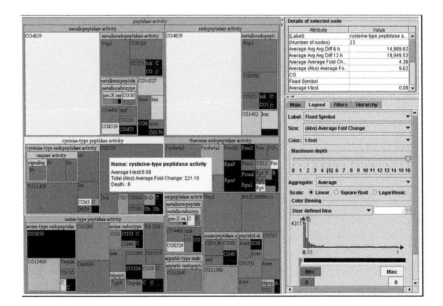

Figure 1.4 Treemap showing small portion of the gene ontology. The size of each gene's rectangle indicates the absolute value of the change in expression level, while the color indicates the significance of the difference, bright red being the most significant differences.

there can be remarkable payoffs for their organizations and national economies. Some funding agencies and foundations have come to recognize this path to high-impact research, but resistance remains from many basic researchers. While change is difficult for some, my goal is to accelerate this transformation in ways that benefit all parties.

The President's Council of Advisors on Science and Technology (PCAST) has regularly endorsed combining applied and basic research, but its November 2012 report on innovation was hijacked by those who are still devoted to Bush's dated linear model.[20] In the report, the authors complained about what they saw as a trend for business to shift "its investments toward applied R&D"; in contrast, I believe that business is wisely finding new ways to combine applied and basic research, such as Google's successful hybrid model of research.[21] Unfortunately, the 2012 PCAST report reaffirmed the old linear model with its unjustified claims that "basic research is the underlying platform on which applied research and engineering development are built" and that "basic research fuels the whole innovation ecosystem."

This book builds on Stokes's fresh thinking, taking in the fervent belief from research leaders Narayanamurti and Branscomb that the false dichotomy of applied and basic research needs to be replaced with a new unity of purpose, one which promotes the raised ambition of doing both.

1.7 Two Parents, Three Children

One way to convey the idea that research projects should combine a practical problem and an existing theory (in other words, employ the ABC principle) is what I call the pattern of "two parents, three children." I describe this pattern to my students as they are forming teams and deciding on their projects (see Case Study 11.1 on team projects in Chapter 11, Section 11.4). The idea is simple: projects should be designed to solve a practical problem for someone outside the classroom while framing the problem based on existing theories that will guide the work (Fig. 1.5). The goal is to create inspirational prototypes that survive beyond the semester.

The two parents are the practical problem and the existing theory, respectively. When the work is done, there should be three children: the solution (or at least partial solution) to the practical problem, refinement of the existing theory, and guidance for future researchers. This pattern of "two parents, three children" helps students organize their research teams and their written reports. Each team may assign 1–3 members to meet with the practitioner collaborator,

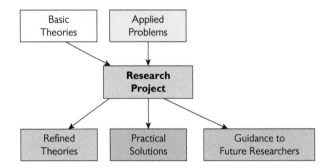

Figure 1.5 Two parents, three children: A pattern for organizing a research project.

who is the one providing the practical problem, while 1–3 members meet with knowledgeable experts in the existing theory.

Chapter 8 covers team strategies that can be used, and Chapter 9 explores research strategies that include prototyping, big data analytics, and ethnographically inspired case studies.

1.8 Skeptics' Corner

Traditional disciplinary researchers may point to their long history of success, questioning the need for novel approaches. Many junior and senior researchers remain devoted to a clear separation between applied and basic research because such projects are easier to manage and evaluate. Some basic researchers consider solving societal problems to be "not my job" and are devoted to their own curiosity-driven projects and abstract problems that are not tied to immediate applications. A recent report from 30 MIT faculty members states that declining basic research funding has led to an "innovation deficit" in 15 research areas.[22] However, most of the research areas cited in that report, such as cybersecurity, infectious diseases, and battery development, would benefit greatly from the close linking of applied and basic research, as called for by the ABC principle.

Similarly, many applied research advocates are devoted to working on practical local problems, with only modest effort directed to reading previous work or learning deep theories. They are often content to solve their problems, but they could have much greater impact if they published results in ways that others could easily draw on their solutions. I respect positions that stress basic OR applied research but hope to encourage both camps to try small steps in the direction of doing basic AND applied research.

There are also skeptical business research managers and policymakers, who find that the increased ambition required by the ABC and SED principles to be disruptive or even counterproductive.

In spite of these challenges, a growing number of research teams seek to combine applied and basic thinking. First attempts may prove daunting but, as interdisciplinary skills and teamwork practices are taught more widely, the chances for high-impact success should increase. Business research managers and government policymakers are pressed to measure payoffs rather than changes in practice to justify funding; however, I see such changes as a generally productive shift that clarifies goals and outcomes and thereby lays the foundation for better research and increased funding.

A common apprehension is that applied research steers students and faculty to business projects with short-term payoffs rather than to long-term, curiosity-driven problem-solving. This concern is certainly legitimate, but increased attention to made-world problems often provides feedback for researchers and triggers fresh ideas that produce novel basic research directions.

A further danger of close ties between academic and business researchers is that businesses are primarily driven to increase short-term profits and deliver value to stockholders. The frequently divergent goals of academic and business researchers remain a legitimate challenge to my encouragement to them to form closer relationships. Academic partners need to be clear about their pursuit of publishable research results and negotiate clear agreements with business partners so that joint goals can be attained. Similarly, too much emphasis on applied research can distort government research programs, so repeatedly making clear that using applied and basic combined (the ABC principle) means that both goals should be maintained.

Long-term projects such as going to the moon or understanding the human brain are best realized via short-term goals of developing improved technologies, small prototypes, and pilot projects to validate theories and develop operational experience. Each contribution can be seen as adding a small tile with clear shape and color to a larger mosaic that eventually produces a striking result. Then, scaling up from successful prototypes enables the larger long-term goals to be achieved.

1.9 Summary

The first guiding principle of this book is that, when research teams take on applied and basic research goals, they are more likely to produce strong applied and basic outcomes than when they focus on only applied or only basic research. Support for this idea is captured by the inside-the-Beltway quip that "think tanks need to become do tanks." The evidence grows that synergy, rather than a battle for primacy, is more often the winning strategy. The ABC principle and the five research life cycle strategies described in this book are a starting point for discussions and experimentation. I'm ready for constructive pushback, which could lead to still more potent alternatives that are more carefully tuned to diverse research environments.

My goal in promoting the ABC principle is more than improving research team productivity. I seek to provoke ambitious research projects that will more frequently cope with contemporary problems such as energy sustainability, healthcare delivery, community safety, and environmental protection. These and other complex challenges require foundational science theories, innovative technology breakthroughs, and compelling designs that together will produce prosocial change for billions of people. At the same time, these new directions will provoke paradigm-shifting basic research in science, engineering, and design. The rising tide of higher ambitions lifts all disciplines.

Building more bridges among academic, business, and government communities could bring the capabilities of academic researchers into close contact with business practitioners and agency staffers who often face meaningful societal problems. Academics are in touch with recent research and thrive on trying something entirely new. Business practitioners can be remarkably effective in turning pilot project prototypes into scalable successes that serve genuine social needs while ensuring economic viability. When academic researchers collaborate with practitioner partners, it means the choice of problems is informed by civic, business, and global priorities. It also means that theories can be validated through living laboratories and that technology and innovation transfer, sometimes called translation, is facilitated so that transformative solutions can be applied more rapidly and more successfully.

Of course, some problems, like healthcare delivery or energy sustainability, will require decades of work; but short-term intermediate milestones can bring measurable progress, redirect researchers to productive outcomes, and attract increased resources. These massive problems will also require teams of thousands of researchers who fundamentally change practices in vast research communities that impact trillion-dollar industries and national agendas. Innovations begin with an idea that might solve a problem; then, pilot testing begins and refinements are applied. Soon, large-scale prototypes are built, more useful measures are captured, and resources and support are gathered to implement a broad solution.

CHAPTER 2

Blending Science, Engineering, and Design

The SED Principle

It's the interaction between fundamental science and applied science,
and the interface between many disciplines that creates new ideas.

Herwig Kogelnik, Bell Labs laser scientist

2.1 Introduction

The inventors of the wheel were simultaneously applied and basic researchers, acting as scientists, engineers, and designers. He, she, or they brought together diverse knowledge and experiences. I like to believe that they were doing applied and basic research that required testing primitive physics theories, making crude mechanical engineering decisions, and applying rough product design principles. Maybe they had a grand celebration when they finally got a two-wheeled cart to function smoothly.

In the eighteenth century, the framers of the US Constitution argued strenuously, but in doing so they became an effective team by blending practical realities and competing theories of human behavior. The worldly farmer Thomas Jefferson, the clever statesman Benjamin Franklin, the visionary politician Samuel Adams, and a roomful of other remarkable characters struggled to engineer a practical, tripartite civic system. Their vigorous debates led to a successful strategy of checks and balances between executive, legislative, and judicial branches, producing design guidelines for political processes that have influenced many national political structures.

In this century, researchers are working on electric and driverless cars; two projects that require applied and basic research in science, engineering, and design. The ambitious and visionary Elon Musk leads the Tesla Motors effort to design, engineer, and build battery-powered electric cars that have race car performance, high consumer appeal, and a competitive price, while conducting basic research on new materials, battery chemistry, and consumer preferences. The trade-offs between a slower city car with a short range and a high-performance car with a long range present classic design and engineering choices, mediated by rapidly evolving applied and basic battery science. This is a clear application of the SED principle, which stresses the need to blend the methods of science, engineering, and design. In addition, Musk's team must also reshape public expectations, while catalyzing the construction of a reliable infrastructure with convenient recharging stations.

The driverless car teams at Google, Mercedes-Benz, and elsewhere face similar challenges of changing public expectations to accept a car without a steering wheel, while establishing legal precedents about liability for the inevitable accidents. The science and engineering have worked well in the million miles of prototype testing, but the realities of congested urban settings, stormy weather conditions, and road rage from surrounding human drivers indicate the rich set of design challenges that remain in scaling up to realistic usage conditions. Safe trips have to be the outcome more than 99.9% of the time. The potential benefits of increased mobility for people with disabilities and the aspiration to reduce accidents are attractions if scientists, engineers, and designers can achieve these goals.

Similarly, science, engineering, and design researchers are working to deliver high-quality healthcare for everyone. Improved medical science, more effective and safer drugs, and well-designed hospitals with well-trained staff members comprise a starting point, but the major advances will come if (1) social media technologies can be designed to encourage the behavior changes needed to promote smoking cessation, obesity reduction, and cancer prevention, and (2) business can be encouraged to reduce pollution from industrial processes and limit harmful contaminants in their products.

One model for change is to move from delivering healthcare for disease to promoting healthy lifestyles with diet and exercise to attain wellness—"wellth creation."[1] Basic research questions of motivation remain about how to get people to eat right, get exercise, and limit contact with contaminants. Applied research questions go into specifics of which populations respond best to financial, social, or personal rewards. No one discipline has all the answers, but the combination of disciplines could produce dramatic progress.

Other contemporary issues such as sustainable energy production, environmental protection, and community safety bring immense challenges that call for advanced applied and basic research. These challenges require large teams that can take an idea and design prototypes, work with stakeholders, collect measurable results, and refine engineering plans to support scaling up to respond to increased demand, and scaling out to accommodate diverse needs. While traditional science-oriented controlled experiments are still valuable, design-oriented case studies situated in living laboratories for trying out new ideas are gaining adherents. These strategies are what academic teams such as New York University's Center for Urban Science and Progress[2] or businesses such as IBM's Smarter Cities[3] are working on.

2.2 The Seed-Root-Flower Metaphor

The interdependent cycle of science, engineering, and design can be compared to a plant that thrives when its seeds receive sufficient water and nutrients to grow the strong roots and flowers that produce more seeds. The roots anchor the plant firmly in the ground and enable it to send up shoots whose role is to support the flower. In turn the flower exists to produce seeds, which are needed to produce the next generation of seeds that ensures the survival of the species.

The seed-root-flower metaphor describes three kinds of thinking, each with distinct ways of formulating problems. Seed thinking concentrates on the scientific core of the problem, abstracting away other parts of the plant. Root thinking establishes the sturdy anchor for the plant, delivering nutrients that enable the growth of stalks and energy-gathering leaves. Flower thinking produces colorful fragrant blossoms, which are attractive to pollinators and which eventually produce the next generation of seeds.

Scientists can see themselves as focusing on seed problems, whose solutions they see as the source of subsequent growth. Engineers may be attracted to root problems, which evoke durability in the face of droughts or floods while delivering a steady flow of nutrients. Engineers may also be happy with stalk and leaf concepts, which are tied to structural support and energy management solutions. Designers are likely to resonate with the flower imagery for their problems, since they think of their work as yielding social solutions based on colors, textures, shapes, and the delicate complexity of stamens and pistils. Designers may be attracted to the flower metaphor because it aligns with their belief that their contributions often lead the way to the next generation of seed problems.

The seed-root-flower metaphor captures the interdependence of these three disciplines, which is the heart of the principle. Metaphors can help change thinking and lead to new ways of thinking, but implementing the SED principle will take time as a new generation of students adjusts to the context of immense societal challenges, ambitious collaborative projects, and powerful technologies.

2.3 Lowering Barriers Between Disciplines

As research managers and policymakers lower the barriers between science, engineering, and design, they will change how researchers are trained, conduct their work, and gain recognition. Educational experiences that cover the scientific method, engineering prototyping, and design thinking will enable future researchers to choose whether they conduct controlled experiments, do field studies, or brainstorm with diverse stakeholders. Better still, future researchers will combine these strategies to gain multiple perspectives that enrich their work. The seed-root-flower metaphor provides a holistic view in which all three disciplines contribute to successful research outcomes.

I believe that we are past the point when students and young researchers have to make unnecessary choices that narrow their identities, limit their thinking, and undermine collaborations. Just as balanced diets are healthier, doesn't everyone benefit from two or three ways of seeing the world? Learning about a few disciplines seems a constructive balanced strategy compared to excessive specialization or unlimited diversity.

Marshall McLuhan predicted reduced specialization as the electronic global village became more of a reality.[4] That aspiration is still being realized, but the expansion of powerful Web-based, social media, and visual communication tools for teaching and research is making it easier for students and professionals to take on a more balance diet of research strategies. Clive Thompson characterizes the amplification powers of these new tools:

First, they allow for prodigious external memory: smartphones, hard drives, cameras, and sensors routinely record more information than any tool before them. We're shifting from a stance of rarely recording our ideas and the events of our lives to doing it habitually. Second, today's tools make it easier for us to find connections—between ideas, pictures, people, bits of news—that were previously invisible. Third, they encourage a superfluity of communication and publishing.[5]

CASE STUDY 2.1 FRAUNHOFER-GESELLSCHAFT: APPLIED RESEARCH IN PUBLIC SERVICE

Professor Hans-Jorg Bullinger, President of the Fraunhofer-Gesellschaft (2002–2012), promoted the tag line "We Invent the Future" and proudly asserted that "Fraunhofer is Europe's largest organization for applied research.[1] However, he acknowledges that "not everything is within our control. There are the inescapable laws of nature, not to mention the overwhelming element of chance.[2] The inspirational source of the Fraunhofer-Gesellschaft is Joseph von Fraunhofer (1787–1826), whose work on optics made him a successful entrepreneur, inventor, and scientist.

The Fraunhofer-Gesellschaft, now run by Professor Reimund Neugebauer, was founded in Germany in 1949 and has 67 institutes and research units that employ more than 23,000 staff, with a budget of over €2 billion per year. The members of the society claim that their "research efforts are geared entirely to people's needs: health, security, communication, energy and the environment."[3] This agenda has much in common with the ABC principle, since it focuses on use-inspired research projects drawn from industry partners who supply 70% of the budget and have a strong role in shaping research directions. Important success stories come from video- and audio-encoding equipment and algorithms, especially mp3, whose widespread use for music recording produces substantial income and which laid the foundation for video-encoding algorithms, triggering a continuing stream of basic research.

The Fraunhofer-Gesellschaft pursues research activities that "are application- and results-oriented," seeking to implement "innovative research findings in industrial and social applications,[4] such as health/nutrition/environment, safety/security, information/communication, transportation/mobility, and energy/living,[5] with focused projects such as wind power, solar energy, bioenergy, and energy-efficient living (see "List of Fraunhofer-Gesellschaft Applied Research Topics" in Case Study Box 1).[6] The blend of basic science and applied problems leads to a steady stream of approximately 8000 research publications per year at conferences and in journals. The Fraunhofer's Open Access Policy is a model for others to follow since it stresses "a duty to inform the general public" and make available "full-text versions of all papers and articles" with "the obvious exception of confidential information supplied by customers."[7]

Some topics are covered by multiple institutes; for example, the Institute of Experimental Software Engineering (IESE) at the University of Kaiserslautern in Germany is tied to the Fraunhofer Center for Experimental Software Engineering (CESE, http://www.fc-md.umd.edu/) at the University of Maryland. Professor Dieter Rombach built the 250-person IESE with precision and care, taking on ambitious projects such as, for example, in the areas of car and aerospace control systems construction and certification, energy management, health management, and e-government. The IESE also has international partnerships, such as the one, led by Dr. Karina Villela, with the Federal University of Brazil in Bahia to support emergency and crisis management by using mobile crowd sourcing information.

Professor Rombach has gained a global reputation for himself and his institute as a premier software and systems competence center. His global outreach, which raises impact, includes conference organizing, journal editing, and serving on advisory boards of research groups and companies. Professor Rombach received the 2009 German Federal Cross of Merit, which is awarded for outstanding political, cultural, economic, and intellectual achievements.

At Maryland's CESE, Professor Rance Cleaveland applies formal methods as well as inspections, code analysis, and testing to validate and verify automobile and medical systems. In addition to a strong publishing and grant record, Cleaveland was Cofounder and Chairman of the Board of the commercial company Reactive Systems.[8] The company works on aerospace, medical, and automotive applications. A typical supportive story about its Reactis testing tool is from the automobile manufacturer Nissan, who used Reactis to validate their powertrain design in traditional gas-powered and newer electric vehicles. Cleaveland's corporate spin-off offers the opportunity to take research a further step in commercialization but invites concerns about conflicts of interest when researchers may have to decide whether new clients work with the research group or the corporation.

The Maryland CESE builds on the reputation of University of Maryland Professors Victor Basili and Marvin Zelkowitz. For 25 years they conducted empirical studies of software engineering and applied them to improve NASA's capabilities while producing a highly cited stream of papers. Their Experience Factory concept "enables Organizational Learning and acknowledges the need for a separate support organization that works with the project organization in order to manage and learn from its own experience. The support organization helps the project organization observe itself, collect data about itself, build models and draw conclusions based on the data, package the experience for further reuse, and most importantly: to feed the experience back to the project organization."[9] Their devotion of the CESE to multidisciplinary research and empirical data collection from real-world teams is well aligned with the ABC and SED principles.

Fraunhofer's global perspective on research is ambitious in covering many topics across many countries. The society's management strategy ties provision of support funds to the project revenues raised from corporate or government sources. Thus, an institute that brings in substantial project revenues gets more funding for exploratory efforts as well, potentially enriching the outcomes for both basic and applied research.

Case Study Box 1 List of Fraunhofer-Gesellschaft Applied Research Topics

Materials and Components	Polymers
Metals	Composite materials
Ceramics	Renewable resources

continued

Wood processing
Nanomaterials
Surface and coating technologies
Intelligent materials
Testing of materials and structures
Materials simulation
Self-organisation

Electronics and Photonics
Semiconductor technologies
Microsystems technology
Power electronics
Polymer electronics
Magneto-electronics
Optical technologies
Optics and information
    technology
Laser
Sensor systems
Measuring techniques
Information and communication
Communication networks
Internet technologies
Computer architecture
Software
Artificial intelligence
Image evaluation and interpretation

Life Sciences and Biotechnology
Industrial biotechnology
Plant biotechnology
Stem cell technology
Gene therapy
Systems biology
Bionics

Health and Nutrition
Intensive care technologies
Pharmaceutical research
Implants and prostheses
Minimally invasive medicine
Nanomedicine
Medical imaging
Medical and information technology

Molecular diagnostics
Assistive technologies
Food technology

Communication and Knowledge
Digital infotainment
Ambient intelligence
Virtual and augmented reality
Virtual worlds
Human-computer cooperation
Business communication
Electronic services
Information and knowledge
    management

Mobility and Transport
Traffic management
Automobiles
Rail traffic
Ships
Aircraft
Space technologies

Energy and Resources
Oil and gas technologies
Mineral resource exploitation
Fossil energy
Nuclear power
Wind, water and geothermal energy
Bioenergy
Solar energy
Electricity transport
Energy storage
Fuel cells and hydrogen technology
Microenergy technology

Environment and Nature
Environmental monitoring
Environmental biotechnology
Water treatment
Waste treatment
Product life cycles
Air purification technologies
Agricultural engineering
Carbon capture and storage

continued

Building and Living
Building materials
Structural engineering
Sustainable building
Indoor climate

Lifestyle and Leisure
Sports technologies
Textiles
Cosmetics
Live entertainment technologies
Domestic appliances

Production and Enterprises
Casting and metal forming
Joining and production technologies
Process technologies

Digital production
Robotics
Logistics

Security and Safety
Information security
Weapons and military systems
Defence against hazardous materials
Forensic science
Access control and surveillance
Precautions against disasters
Disaster response
Plant safety

Source: http://www.fraunhofer.de/en/
publications/brochures.html.

---

[1] Fraunhofer-Gesellschaft, *About Fraunhofer* (Accessed July 27, 2015) http://www.fraunhofer.de/en/about-fraunhofer.html.

[2] Fraunhofer, *We Invent the Future* (Accessed July 27, 2015) http://www.fraunhofer.de/content/dam/zv/en/documents/Fraunhofer_We-invent-the-future_tcm63-52364.pdf.

[3] Fraunhofer-Gesellschaft, *About Fraunhofer* (Accessed July 27, 2015) http://www.fraunhofer.de/en/about-fraunhofer.html.

[4] Fraunhofer, *Mission Statement: Applied Research* (Accessed July 27, 2015) http://www.fraunhofer.de/en/about-fraunhofer/mission/research.html.

[5] Fraunhofer, *Research Topics* (Accessed July 28, 2015) http://www.fraunhofer.cn/en/research_topic.jsp.

[6] Fraunhofer, *Energy/Living* (Accessed July 28, 2015) http://www.fraunhofer.cn/en/research_topic_list.jsp?id=114.

[7] Fraunhofer, *The Fraunhofer-Gesellschaft's Open Access Policy* (2008) http://www.fraunhofer.de/content/dam/zv/en/Publications/Fraunhofer_open-access-policy.pdf.

[8] Reactive Systems, *Reactive Systems, Inc.* (Accessed July 27, 2015) http://www.reactive-systems.com.

[9] Basili, V., Lindvall, M., and Costa, P., *Implementing the Experience Factory Concepts as a Set of Experience Bases* (Accessed July 20, 2015) https://www.cs.umd.edu/~basili/publications/proceedings/P90.pdf.

These powers are especially potent for researchers, since they are in the business of collecting data, making connections, and communicating with collaborators and peers. However, the adoption of these powers differs across disciplines and individuals, in part because of uneven presentation to students.

Sociologists Lee Rainie and Barry Wellman write vividly about the liberating "triple revolution" brought by social media, Internet connectivity, and mobile devices.[6] They focus on changes that also have especially potent impacts on researchers who participate in team projects: (1) greater diversity in social network relationships, (2) amplified powers of communications and information gathering, and (3) increased "communications presence and pervasive awareness" of their networked relationships.

Curriculum changes could send a signal to science students that their courses will involve team projects using examples that encourage creative solutions to meaningful problems. Similarly, design students who get more exposure to science and engineering will have a more solid foundation that enables them to think more broadly. Exposing engineering students to the reductionist experimental strategies of science and open problem-solving strategies of design enriches their capacity to work across disciplines.

A bottom-up approach to changing the curricula will eventually produce changes, but top-down initiatives from academic leaders, business executives, and government agency policymakers could accelerate the transformation.

If educational experiences change, then we could imagine a more interdisciplinary research future that blends the diverse knowledge and methods of these three disciplines. Could such a blend produce bolder, better innovations and more potent theories? The blended discipline strategies encourage individuals, small teams, large groups, or massive organizations to weave together these three disciplines as they conduct applied and basic research. This lofty ambition, which also calls for academic and business partnerships, is now possible since Web-based, social media, visual communication, and other research tools enable teams to be more informed about recent research, to collaborate more easily, and to test their results more rapidly than ever before.

The goal of this book is to promote innovative research projects that blend the knowledge base, work processes, and evaluation methods of science, engineering, and design. Each discipline has a proud history of success, but the challenges of our time require novel combinations, broad thinking, and creative validation methods to achieve high-impact research results. My emphasis is on the use of teams, as I believe this strategy could lead to novel research methods that achieve the "twin-win" combination of applied and basic breakthroughs.

In the past century, the term "science" was more frequently mentioned in English language books than "design" or "engineering" until 1975, when "design" took the lead (based on data from the Google Ngram Viewer; see Fig. 2.1). Data from another source, *The New York Times*, which offers users the chance to do word-frequency searches on the database of its articles, show a similar pattern (Fig. 2.2). While these two sources do not constitute strong proof, they signal that the design flower is blooming.

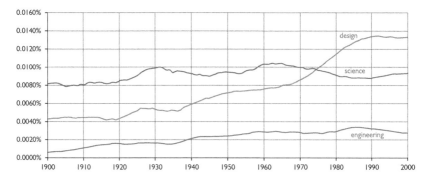

Figure 2.1 "Design" became the dominant term in 1975, as shown by data displayed in the Google Books Ngram Viewer (https://books.google.com/ngrams).

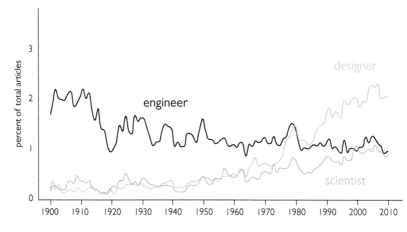

Figure 2.2 Use of the term "designer" in articles in *The New York Times* has increased since 1975. Created using http://chronicle.nytlabs.com.

Science has often been seen as the privileged source of research, while engineering and design were considered to be more for practitioners, who were expected to look up to scientists to lay out agendas. These older beliefs are changing as engineers and designers make stronger research claims by publishing results of their studies in peer-reviewed venues and proposing broadly applicable theories. Engineers and designers have the advantage of gaining rapid feedback from their prototypes so they can iterate repeatedly to solve real problems. Scientists who participate in these rapid development projects will speed theory development and have the opportunity to test their theories in a variety of contexts.

Another sign of changing attitudes is the reanalysis of historical accomplishments, as it now is more clearly seen how engineers and designers have often led the way with innovations that only later were confirmed and sometimes claimed by scientists. For example, Marconi's engineering success with transatlantic wireless transmission in 1901 defied scientific understanding for two decades till Oliver Heaviside identified the ionosphere, which refracts radio waves around the curved earth surface.

My goal is not to argue for superiority of one discipline over another but to promote a unification that combines the strengths of each discipline. I encourage a blended approach, which celebrates closer teamwork and increases respect for diversity. There is no need to compete for dominance when collaboration will be more productive for all.

Another path to blending disciplines will be to address the diverse ethical concerns and varying codes of ethics that will need to be revisited to accommodate the five research life cycle strategies described in Chapters 6–10.[7] Widely discussed ethical concerns include fairness in collaborations, honesty in reporting, and responsibility for failures. Any research that is sufficiently powerful to bring beneficial outcomes comes with the risk of unleashing unanticipated destructive forces. An inspirational source is the 85-year-old International Council for Science (ICSU), which promotes practices to benefit society. The IÇSU sees science as a

common human endeavor that transcends national boundaries and is to be shared by all people. Scientific progress results from global exchange of ideas, data, materials and understanding of the work of others.

On that basis, the Council focuses on three overlapping aspects of universality: freedom and responsibility in the conduct of science; access to scientific data and information; and, strengthening science in developing countries.[8]

Beyond fairness, honesty, and responsibility, researchers regularly deal with the rights for informed consent, privacy, data protection, and participant safety for experimental studies. These issues of research integrity have become the focus of major international conferences,[9] which produce summary statements covering key principles.[10] Some researchers have concerns about whether research topics such as nuclear physics, stem cells, eugenics, or surveillance are appropriate for their research. Professional engineers are certified and have legal obligations about the quality and methods for their work, but they also are committed to reporting improper behaviors and acting responsibly to their clients and colleagues. In addition, research engineers share the concerns of scientists about which topics are acceptable and how they conduct their work.[11] Design researchers often raise ethical issues about the impact on diverse stakeholders, so they actively seek to prevent unintended consequences such as misuse by malicious actors, destruction of the environment, or violation of human rights.[12]

2.4 New Research Questions

The past 400 years have been a great success for basic research in the natural sciences, and that work must continue. There are compelling established basic research questions that trigger widespread interest, such as, are there life forms on other planets in other solar systems? What happened at the big bang—the start of the universe? Will the study of supersymmetry or the Higgs boson lead to deeper understanding of matter? What is consciousness?

But there are equally compelling basic research questions such as, how do human memory and creativity work? How can human behavior be changed to reduce conflict, preserve the environment, and increase wellness? Can social, political, medical, and economic systems be revised to be more effective?

This book seeks to provoke a discussion of what that the new balance should be between studies of the natural world and those of the made world. Maybe public discussion can lead to ways to get the best of both. Another public discussion could clarify which are the most important short-term and long-term research questions. Is there sufficient evidence to help reset priorities among fusion research, climate change, energy storage, or mental health? Will public excitement shift the balance of support among Mars exploration, biodiversity preservation, behavioral economics, or conflict resolution? How much will public fear guide policymakers to invest in transportation safety, terror deterrence, cancer prevention, or environmental protection?

The positive side of all these discussions is that they can trigger the interest of young students in studying science, technology, engineering, or mathematics (STEM) and adding in art or design to make STEAM. Inspirational leaders and well-organized groups, amplified by social media, can also catalyze interest in learning about how to be innovative entrepreneurs who produce transformative solutions. Successful strategies will unleash the unbounded human creative resources to accelerate progress toward the dual goals of developing solutions and expanding foundational knowledge. In fact, seeking both at the same time is the central theme of this book.

An important voice for change is Brad Hesse, Chief of the Health Communications and Informatics Research Branch at the US National Cancer Institute. He explains the need for change by describing how "our extramural study sections . . . unabashedly favor reductionistic, curiosity-driven research over the broader, collaborative goal of refining our theories in the light of real-world problems in cancer care delivery. We've been trying to break out of that mold for a while, but the gravitational pull of old ways of thinking is strong."[13]

2.5 Moving Forward Step by Step

This new definition of research is intended to push researchers to take on focused, ambitious, yet realistic goals by scaling up from short-term milestones to long-term aspirations. Curing cancer is a great aspiration but not an immediately achievable goal. However, the milestone of raising breast cancer survival times by 30% within the next 4 years may be possible through increased public awareness, better screening, and improved treatments. Short-term milestones may also include scientific goals such as understanding genomic factors or building an effective social media community to promote cancer prevention.

Similarly, increasing high-school graduation rates among minority students in Maryland by 20% within 3 years could lead to specific interventions that have rapid impact. The long-term goal might include scaling out by raising educational performance nationally, through a deeper understanding of diverse student motivations and revised teacher training programs.

Some researchers may see small percentage improvements as a distraction from large basic breakthroughs that radically change outlooks. However, I argue that, if these researchers work on specific practical goals while developing a deep understanding of previous research and a broad theoretical outlook, then they are likely to achieve both the applied and the basic research outcomes. As theories get refined, and practical guidance accumulates, the processes of scaling up and scaling out are likely to become successful.

Solving practical problems which are placed in theoretical contexts produces well-defined applied and basic research contributions, which also influence large circles of practitioners and theoreticians. A practical solution presented as a theoretical advance has a synergistic impact, which comes from a clear explanation of why the practical solution works combined with case studies that validate the theoretical advance. When the "twin win" of a practical solution and the theoretical description can be broadly applied, the impact is still greater. Tim Berners-Lee was seeking to facilitate sharing of papers and data among physicists, but his invention of the World Wide Web

CASE STUDY 2.2
SHIRLEY ANN JACKSON
The New Polytechnic
Shirley Ann Jackson, President of Rensselaer
Polytechnic Institute
http://www.rpi.edu/president/

The president of Rensselaer Polytechnic Institute (RPI), Shirley Ann Jackson, is driven to fulfill the institute's 200-year old mission "to apply science to the common purposes of life." Her vision of the "New Polytechnic" calls for her faculty to "collaborate more effectively with businesses and governments to link the capabilities of advanced information technologies, communications, and networking—to the life sciences, and the physical, materials, environmental, social, cognitive, and computational sciences."[1]

She believes that "the New Polytechnic is predicated on the absolute necessity of educating our students in multi-disciplinary and collaborative thinking, and linking our researchers—in the arts, architecture, the humanities, the sciences, and the social sciences—as well as in engineering and the applied sciences . . . Engaged in by a broad spectrum of participants, guided by societal concerns and ethics, The New Polytechnic ultimately facilitates novel and effective approaches to global challenges."[2]

This vision fits well with the ABC and SED principles, although President Jackson's emphasis on science is natural for a remarkable person who became the first African-American woman to receive a PhD in physics from MIT in 1973 for her work on elementary particle theory. Her distinguished career in physics gained attention, leading President Bill Clinton to appoint her to be Chairman of the US Nuclear Regulatory Commission. In 1999, she became president of RPI, where she led the effort to raise the status of this small, privately held university by raising funds, hiring strong faculty, increasing education quality, and creating interdisciplinary units to push into emerging topics.

She understood that "the great universities of the 21st century will remain the physical crossroads where creative people interact across the disciplines and great ideas emerge from these connections. However, in this new digital era, the interconnections will be more global, the pace more rapid, the scale more complex, and the opportunities to change the world more immediate."[3]

President Jackson's action agenda was expanded in the *Rensselaer Plan 2024*, which seeks to celebrate the RPI's 200th anniversary by "addressing the Global Challenges that face the world of the 21st century—to change lives, to advance society, and, indeed, to change the world."[4] Her connections, from serving on boards of major companies and prominent advisory councils, including the US President's Council of Advisors for Science and Technology, make her especially aware of what it takes to produce meaningful change. Her strategy is to build interdisciplinary centers with strong leaders and ample resources to address contemporary issues; such centers include the Institute for Data Exploration and Applications (IDEA), the Experimental Media and Performing Arts Center (EMPAC), and the Center for Biotechnology and Interdisciplinary Studies (CBIS).[5]

The IDEA's director, Professor James Hendler, is addressing healthcare, business analytics, smart cities, cybersecurity, and other current problems for which big data is transformative. He is also active in promoting open data for government agencies.

Instead of describing design thinking, the EMPAC website celebrates its partnerships between artists and researchers to create novel perceptions and experiences. The CBIS was a bold departure for a traditional engineering school, since it shifted to the growing interdisciplinary topics around life sciences, physical sciences, informatics, and engineering, with projects in protein synthesis, regenerative medicine, and stem cell research. Tracking the impact of these centers is a challenge, but insights gained about what succeeds and what doesn't will be helpful to others who follow this path.

President Jackson is proud of these initiatives, which show that older institutions can be reformed and faculty can be energized to take on new agendas. The challenge will now be to show evidence of high-impact payoffs from The New Polytechnic philosophy.

[1] Jackson, S. A., Op-ed: The New Polytechnic: Preparing to lead in the digital economy, *U.S. News & World Report* (September 22, 2014) http://www.usnews.com/news/college-of-tomorrow/articles/2014/09/22/op-ed-the-new-polytechnic-preparing-to-lead-in-the-digital-economy.

[2] Jackson, S. A., *The New Polytechnic: Addressing Global Challenges, Transforming the World* (Accessed July 28, 2015) http://rpi.edu/president/speeches/ps040215-vassar.html.

[3] Jackson, S., Op-ed: The New Polytechnic: Preparing to lead in the digital economy, *U.S. News & World Report* (September 22, 2014) http://www.usnews.com/news/college-of-tomorrow/articles/2014/09/22/op-ed-the-new-polytechnic-preparing-to-lead-in-the-digital-economy.

[4] Rensselaer, *The Rensselaer Plan 2024* (Accessed July 28, 2015) http://www.rpi.edu/plan/.

[5] Rensselaer Polytechnic Institute (RPI), *Institute for Data Exploration and Applications* (2012) http://idea.rpi.edu/; EMPAC/Rensselaer Polytechnic Institute, *EMPAC: Curtis R. Priem Experimental Media and Performing Arts Center, Rensselaer Polytechnic Institute* (Accessed July 28, 2015) http://empac.rpi.edu/; Rensselaer Polytechnic Institute, Center for Biotechnology & Interdisciplinary Studies, *About the Center for Biotechnology & Interdisciplinary Studies (CBIS)* (Accessed July 28, 2015) http://biotech.rpi.edu/about.

has had broad and dramatic impacts while also accelerating theory development in network science, collaborative systems, organizational behavior, and much more.

Many research projects fail, but a more likely outcome is that they produce promising early results that take years or decades to refine, make practical, and disseminate widely. Ambitious research projects with bold goals could take thousands of people and several years to complete, but each component should be a focused effort based on scientific theories, engineering plans, and detailed designs. If the stages of a large project have clear milestones to assess success, refine theories, and build new collaborations, then the project has a better chance of success. At each stage, publishing results helps clarify the contribution, alerts colleagues to what has been accomplished, and can yield feedback to accelerate improvements.

The term "research" suggests working on new ideas with novel approaches that have the potential to disrupt the status quo. Research is the courageous conscious effort to improve existing ways of thinking, products, processes, and services. Research is the vehicle of change, fueled by curiosity and driven by the adventure of discovery. Research is a quest for innovation, an urge to improve, and a devotion to community; it requires an acceptance of responsibility, a toleration of failure, and a passion for exploration.

Research is not for everyone, nor should it be. There are many other satisfying and productive paths in life, in which people contribute to successful business and communities, spending time with friends and family. Many people proudly bake nutritious breads based on trusted recipes and are proud of the consistent quality of their products. Others deliver admirably competent medical care to patients, offer genuine empathy to families, or operate successful businesses in ways that are far from research. Research can be lonely and take years to produce results, while baking bread or delivering medical care can be a joyous social experience, with daily rewards from making people happy and healthy.

2.6 Skeptics' Corner

Many traditional researchers who are happy with disciplinary boundaries will rebel at the encouragement to blend disciplines. They are experts in their disciplines, work on well-established problems, use standard research methods, and publish in rigorously reviewed journals that have well-accepted criteria for contributions. They have a clear professional path to jobs and recognition. Such traditional thinkers are welcome to continue their work, but I hope to give them good reasons and compelling evidence to consider broadening their horizons, taking on higher-impact challenges, and working in teams.

Other researchers believe that blends of science, engineering, and design (the SED principle) are already possible for anyone who wants to pursue it. They believe that scientists gracefully become engineers or designers when they need to be or that designers pick up science or engineering methods when necessary. There are undoubtedly successful examples of such transitions, but making it more common by changing education and reward systems would certainly help increase the frequency of individual crossovers and teamwork.

Skeptics also point out that researchers, managers, and policymakers in the three disciplines have differing objective metrics of research team outcomes. Academic researchers, whether in science, engineering, or design, care about peer recognition, usually measured by citation counts for published papers, while industrial researchers in all three disciplines typically focus on innovation as measured by patents, copyrights, and comparative product sales figures. New media advocates suggest that alternative metrics such as provided by the World Wide Web and social media can yield more rapid and broader impact assessments than traditional metrics can. They see Web page visits, download counts, link statistics, and social media likes, retweets, or followers as effective early indicators of future impact across disciplines.

These objective measures are all useful but also all flawed for many reasons, so there is a continuing effort to find better objective metrics and develop fairer subjective social processes (Chapter 10). Each discipline also has well-refined and multiple subjective ways of assessing research contributions such as awards given by committees, endorsements from respected leaders, and press attention in prominent media outlets. In short, it will not be possible to rank contributions on a single scale; however, when researchers, managers, and policymakers are more explicit about their metrics and expectations, they are more likely to achieve them.

Since blending disciplines often requires teamwork, another challenge is to separate the dance from the dancers, or the team contributions from the individuals who made them. The objective and subjective metrics in the previous paragraph focus on measuring team contributions, but there is a parallel set of metrics for assessing individuals who make the contributions, based on lifetime citation counts, Nobel Prizes, honors conferred by colleagues, widespread industry application, or runaway product successes. Historically, recognition has gone mostly to individuals, even though they are embedded in a team, organization, or community. The charming legend of the lone researcher attracts journalists and filmmakers, but most research, innovations, and novel designs emerge from partnerships and teams that are embedded in a community. Of course, bold ideas and valuable innovations ultimately come from a single individual, but individuals are more likely to create them when working within a team, a well-organized network, and a supportive community. Therefore this book covers the strategies for nurturing individuals, managing teams, weaving networks, and cultivating communities.

Still, skeptics rightly argue that the differences across disciplines remain valuable sources of creative thinking, so they want to preserve disciplinary boundaries, rather than cross them. Finding the right blend of disciplinary focus and injection of new ideas from nearby disciplines may be a more acceptable balance.

2.7 Summary

The success of the natural science agenda over the past 400 years has produced a deep understanding of the world around us, enabling profound changes in health, transportation, communication, agriculture, and so forth. The science seed has reshaped the outlook that people have, increasing the level of control we have over our lives and raising our expectations for ourselves and our families. Deaths of mothers during childbirth or of children in their early years have become less frequent in many countries, changing the expectations for family size and altering the role of women. Nearly universal education has changed social structures and workplaces, even as automation has challenged the role of workers. Of course, diseases remain, conflicts arise, poverty is still widespread, and environmental degradation threatens our planet, making these persistent pernicious realities high priorities.

To address these disturbing realities requires a shift in thinking by researchers, managers, and policymakers so as to produce high-impact research. This shift begins with the foundational belief that embracing both applied and basic research goals at the same time is possible. I believe that, when research project leaders combine applied and basic research, they are more likely to produce synergistic and transformative results. This raised ambition, when facilitated by the Web, social media, and visual communication tools, enables researchers to readily deal with the complex problems of our time. These tools empower teams to form broad and dense networks that accelerate the pace of work by attracting more rapid feedback. To paraphrase an old commercial, "Feedback is the breakfast of champions."

The belief in combining applied and basic research goals has already had impacts on many educational and research programs. An interesting example is Virginia Tech's four-year-old program with the novel name "Scieneering," which combines education and research in science, engineering, and law.[14] This undergraduate program engages students in interdisciplinary research projects with mentors from diverse departments. Novel interdisciplinary programs, departments, centers, and colleges, all of which are devoted to blending science, engineering, and design, have also sprouted seeds-roots-flowers at dozens of other campuses such as Olin, University of Illinois, Northwestern, Stanford, and Arizona State University (several are described in chapters and Case Studies).

My hope is to lower the barriers between disciplines and encourage exchange of research methods so as to draw on the strengths of each discipline. The blended approach, which celebrates close teamwork and increases respect for diversity, seeks to link science, engineering, and design (the SED principle). I know it is a difficult message to promote, but there is no need to compete for dominance when collaboration will be more productive for all.

PART II

Science, Engineering, and Design

These three disciplines, science, engineering, and design, are as different as the seeds, roots, and flowers of a plant, but they are all vital parts of research. The personalities of scientists, engineers, and designers are often very different, but the growing awareness of the payoffs from working together can lead to blossoming collaborations.

As the introduction to Part I outlined, science is both the body of knowledge and the research methods for expanding that knowledge, such as observation and controlled experiments. Scientists seek to understand the world around them, while engineers build systems and services that never existed, based on stated requirements for efficiency, effectiveness, and safety. Designers gather requirements, question assumptions, and then seek open-ended possibilities through iterative social processes that include diverse stakeholders, so as to create novel, often unexpected, outcomes.

In the past science was often associated with research, while engineering and design were associated with practice. However, there are now a vast number of science practitioners and growing communities of engineering and design researchers (Chapters 3–5).

CHAPTER 3

What Science Contributes

Persistence in Understanding the World

Science is a thing of beauty in itself. Of surpassing beauty. And it is much more than its core structure of instruments, experiments, and explanations. It is a set of moral ideas: that nature is intrinsically knowable, that it can be probed, that causes can be singled out, that understandings can be gained if phenomena and their implications are explored in highly controlled ways.

W. Brian Arthur, *The Nature of Technology*

3.1 Introduction

Science is a glorious quest, requiring persistence in challenging existing beliefs so as to advance understanding of the natural world that surrounds us. Therefore, science is often controversial, undermining religious dogma or widely respected traditions. It forces people to confront their origin myths, sacred principles, or politically convenient philosophies. Science is often seen as a threat to religion or cultural traditions, forcing people to accept new and uncomfortable realities.

While the Copernican revolution is far enough back in history to avoid controversy, Darwin's theories of natural selection still generate passionate debates and stormy arguments over how to educate our children. Climate change science also produces angry battles that are often tied to business models but have equally potent religious and political undercurrents.

The New ABCs of Research. First Edition. Ben Shneiderman.
© Ben Shneiderman 2016. Published in 2016 by Oxford University Press.

Why does science have such power? How does it threaten firmly entrenched beliefs? Science, with all its failings, has potent authority that derives from its clarity based on adversarial discussions, elegant explanations that are refined over time, mathematical precision, and reproducibility. Science is powerful because of its astonishing capacity to generate accurate predictions about natural phenomena.

The *Merriam-Webster Dictionary* offers this compact definition of science: "knowledge about or study of the natural world based on facts learned through experiments and observation."[1] Wikipedia has this more process-oriented description: "a systematic enterprise that builds and organizes knowledge in the form of testable explanations and predictions about the universe."[2] These and other definitions emphasize a body of knowledge and a way of testing to enlarge the body of knowledge. The scope is usually tied to "the natural world" or "the universe," suggesting that the made world, social systems, or economics are outside traditional science. Most readers would agree that science includes physics, chemistry, and biology but might differ as to whether sociology, psychology, economics, computer science, and political science are part of traditional science.

These distinctions matter to educational administrators, science funders such as the US National Science Foundation (or similar organizations in other countries), and members of Congress or parliamentary bodies that set policy and control appropriations. They also matter to scientists, engineers, and designers, whose minds I hope to change about what goals they pursue and how they collaborate.

3.2 Scope of Science

Determining the scope of science is nontrivial, as perspectives continue to change over time. The Dewey Decimal Classification, first introduced in 1876, has separate top-level entries for social sciences, science, and technology, in keeping with traditional views of strong separations between these disciplines.[3] Science is further divided into a reasonable, but somewhat dated, set of specialties: mathematics, astronomy, physics, chemistry, earth sciences, paleontology, life sciences, plants, and zoological sciences. These reflect century-old conceptions that focus on the natural world but are still widely held understandings.

More contemporary definitions, which take a broader view than the ones described above, come from the names of the 31 sections of the US National

Academy of Sciences (NAS) and the 24 sections of the American Association for the Advancement of Science (AAAS; see Fig. 3.1).[4] While they agree on five discipline names (astronomy, physics, chemistry, anthropology and mathematics), they have differing terms for the remaining disciplines that are tied to applied mathematics, biology, medicine, geology, agriculture, and computing. The inclusion of anthropology is something of a surprise as in the Dewey Decimal Classification it was considered to be part of the social sciences.

National Academy of Sciences (31)	AAAS (24)
Astronomy	Astronomy
Physics	Physics
Chemistry	Chemistry
Anthropology	Anthropology
Mathematics	Mathematics
Applied Mathematical Sciences	Statistics
Evolutionary Biology	Biological Sciences
Cellular & Developmental Biology	
Biochemistry	
Biophysics & Computational Biology	
Cellular & Molecular Neuroscience	
Microbial Biology	
Plant Biology	
Animal, Nutritional & Applied Microbial Sciences	Agriculture, Food & Renewable Resources
Plant, Soil & Microbial Sciences	
Environmental Sciences & Ecology	
Human Environmental Sciences	
Medical Genetics, Hematology & Oncology	Medical Sciences
Medical Physiology & Metabolism	Dentistry & Oral Health Sciences
Immunology	Pharmaceutical Sciences
Systems Neuroscience	Neuroscience
Physiology & Pharmacology	
Genetics	
Geology	Geology and Geography
Geophysics	Atmospheric & Hydrospheric Sciences
Computer & Information Sciences	Information, Computing, & Communication
	Linguistics & Language Science
Engineering Sciences	Engineering
Applied Physical Sciences	Industrial Science & Technology
Psychological & Cognitive Sciences	Psychology
Social and Political Sciences	Social, Economic & Political Sciences
Economic Sciences	Societal Impacts of Science & Engineering
	Education
	General Interest in Science & Engineering
	History and Philosophy of Science

Figure 3.1 Section names in the US National Academy of Sciences and the American Association for the Advancement of Science (AAAS). Five section names are identical across both organizations (*top*), and three broad topics are included in the AAAS (*bottom*). The groupings, indicated by alternating colors, were created to show relationships across the two organizations, roughly focusing on biological sciences, agriculture, medicine, geology, computing, engineering, and social sciences.

Both the NAS and AAAS are admirable for their inclusion of engineering and social sciences within their scope. The AAAS takes on a few more disciplines by including education, general interest in science and engineering, and the history and philosophy of science. These latter topics assert the AAAS's aspiration to raise public awareness of science and for the study of science to be part of society.

Further insight to the scope of science as interpreted by these two national bodies comes from examining their publications. Since 1914 the NAS has published the highly respected and highly cited *Proceedings of the National Academy of Sciences* (*PNAS*), which includes peer-reviewed papers that span "the biological, physical, and social sciences."[5] The AAAS publishes the more widely read *Science*, with a mixture of refereed research results and commentary that is often reproduced in the popular press. The editors of *AAAS Science* regularly take on controversial topics that expand the scope of traditional sciences, with special issues on income inequality, parenting, and privacy. While publication in *PNAS* or *Science* may be the highest aspiration for many scientists, there are over 12,000 other scientific journals indexed in the Web of Science (formerly Web of Knowledge) produced by the Institute for Scientific Information (ISI).[6]

The Web of Science includes more than 54 million published papers and captures more than 760 million citations, revealing the patterns of influence of journals, key papers, leading researchers, and prominent institutions. Although ISI is a commercial enterprise, now run by Thomson Reuters, it is a highly respected and trusted source for information about science. Complaints about ISI's Web of Science center on its largely English collections, selection rules that may exclude nontraditional sources, and restricted access to some data.

Nevertheless, the Web of Science with its rich citation data can provide a useful view of science subfields, showing the relative sizes of the subfields via node size, and the existing collaborations across disciplines by the thickness of the links between the nodes (Fig. 3.2). This illuminating view of science, based on 7.2 million papers, shows 13 disciplines and 554 subdisciplines, whose surrounding circles show the relative size of each. Readers can see the closeness of "Math," "Physics," and "Computer Science" (on the left side), with nearby connections to chemistry and branches of engineering. In the middle are "Biology," "Infectious Diseases," "Medical Specialties," and "Health Professionals." Then "Brain Research" bridges to "Social Sciences" on the right. The small number of nodes in "Earth Sciences" shows its size compared to the larger set of nodes in "Biology" or "Chemistry."

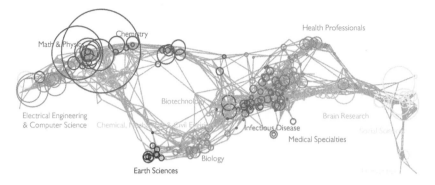

Figure 3.2 The "Map of Science" shows the size and relationship among 13 labeled disciplines and 554 subdisciplines, based on 7.2 million published papers. Image courtesy of Börner, K., Klavans, R., Patek, M., Zoss, A., Biberstine, J. R., Light, R., Larivière, V., and Boyack, K. W., Design and Update of a Classification System: The UCSD Map of Science. *PLoS ONE* **7**, 7 (2012), e39464. doi:10.1371/journal.pone.0039464 http://sci.cns.iu.edu/ucsdmap/.

3.3 When Understanding the World Supports Shaping the World

During the past four centuries, scientists have been hugely successful in understanding the physical worlds of planetary motions, biological systems, molecular structures, and much more. As the body of knowledge and range of research methods has been refined, human understanding of how the world functions has expanded dramatically leading to better predictions of eclipses, animal life cycles, and chemical reactions. During the same period, application-oriented scientists, as well as engineers, designers, farmers, medical workers, and others who believed in the ABC principle, generated huge practical payoffs that changed civilization with industrial, farming, medical, transportation, and other revolutions.

While scientists often claim that science comes first, then application, engineers and designers have demonstrated that often their work inspires and enables scientists. The case for the productive synergy of the SED principle seems strong: scientists who think abstractly can benefit by working with practically minded engineers and designers. Similarly, engineers could broaden their thinking by exploring theory-based opportunities for generalization and the more open brainstorming strategies of designers.

Scientists lean toward reductionist models and develop well-defined hypotheses, then apply variations of the scientific method to collect evidence in support of their hypotheses. They build on knowledge of fundamental principles, but these often are valuable in solving real-world problems while also leading to publishable basic research results.

Scientists tend to choose problems based on their previous work, guidance from mentors or colleagues, or current fashions, thereby keeping them in their zone of comfort and familiarity. Sometimes their choices lead to important contributions, but my claim is that scientists are more likely to make more valuable breakthroughs if they open themselves to interdisciplinary outsiders who bring meaningful real-world problems. Teamwork between a science-minded researcher and an informed, passionate domain expert could produce solutions that rapidly yield high impact. Sometimes, teams are further enriched by designers who are motivated by utility and elegance and who bring very different problem-solving strategies.

Louis Pasteur is often cited for his practical motivations in dealing with preventing failures in wine fermentation or limiting spread of diseases by vaccination. In addressing these practical goals, he developed the basic science of bacterial processes and the germ theory of disease. Donald Stokes has written about styles of science in his book *Pasteur's Quadrant: Basic Science and Technological Innovation* (see Fig. 3.3).[7] He developed a 2 × 2 framework based on two questions: (1) is the research a quest for fundamental understanding, and (2) is the research driven by considerations of use? His often-cited synthesis "use-inspired basic research" is what he sees as the most productive. Stokes's push to make science researchers more cognizant of practical applications is a big step in promoting high-impact research strategies.[8]

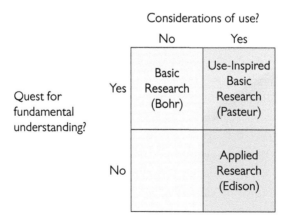

Figure 3.3 Stokes's two-questions structure styles of science (Stokes, *Pasteur's Quadrant*, 1997).

Stokes acknowledges that there can be value in doing only applied research in the style of Thomas Edison or only basic research in the style of Niels Bohr. Edison was not motivated by developing scientific theories or principles but by commercial product development using engineering and design strategies. He is often cited for founding the world's first industrial research center in Menlo Park, NJ, where he and his staff labored for hours to develop new products. Part of Edison's legend was that he worked around the clock, sometimes napping on the laboratory benches and also ignoring his family's needs, consumed by his passion to invent. His 1093 patents make him still the world's record holder and testify to his focus on applied research rather than basic science.[9] He wrote patents, not scientific papers. He engineered and designed products but did not develop theories or mathematical models.

In contrast, Niels Bohr was not motivated by commercial product development but sought to understand atomic structures as a fundamental principle of nature. His impact was not only the advancement of knowledge but the formation of a research community captivated by basic research insights.

3.4 Thomas Kuhn's Impact on Science

The scientific contributions of Galileo, Newton, Gauss, Leibniz, Lavoisier, Boyle, and many more are the foundational examples for Thomas Kuhn's world-famous 1962 book *The Structure of Scientific Revolutions*.[10] Kuhn's views, which were widely reprinted and translated, remain controversial but have had a dramatic influence in shaping views of the way science works. He sees stable periods of incremental contributions, called "normal science," which begin to reveal flaws in existing theories, followed by paradigm-shifting breakthroughs that yield new theories and fresh ways of doing research. Kuhn elevated the phrase "paradigm shift" to broad cultural visibility, while presenting science as the queen of disciplines. His book occasionally mentions engineers in a minor facilitating role and sometimes invokes designers in their role of preparing instruments for scientists and for the design of experiments. I suppose that fashioning instruments requires certain skills that are beyond science, and designing experiments depends on exploratory processes that require more than logic. Could scientists, who are willing to offer compliments for "an elegant experimental design," be convinced to value design thinking for its potential to contribute to breakthrough discoveries and innovations?

CASE STUDY 3.I A MULTICAMPUS CENTER IN PUBLIC SERVICE: THE UNIVERSITY OF CALIFORNIA'S CENTER FOR INFORMATION TECHNOLOGY RESEARCH IN THE INTEREST OF SOCIETY

Many academic researchers take pride in the basic and foundational nature of their work, giving it the virtuous label "pure research." Their devotion is to a challenging problem that is abstracted from reality and distilled into a clean formulation that invites precise solutions. Reductionist models, in which all variables can be controlled and experiments replicated in laboratory conditions, have produced value over the past 400 years, so the believers feel justified in sticking to their traditional ways of working.

However, there are fresh ways of thinking that are becoming attractive to academic scientists, engineers, and designers. These fresh approaches are more grounded in solving the problems in chaotic but realistic situations, often dealing with complex sociotechnical problems like sustainability, healthcare delivery, wellness, community safety, or educational environments.

Some academic research centers, like the University of California's Center for Information Technology Research in the Interest of Society (CITRIS), lay claim to these pressing social, environmental, and healthcare problems.[1] CITRIS's visionary leaders, including the founding director Ruzena Bajcsy, set out to invigorate collaborations among more than 300 faculty members at four campuses (Berkeley, Davis, Merced, and Santa Cruz) and work with 60+ corporations to develop real-world solutions that will boost economic productivity and solve vexing social problems in California and beyond, while producing foundational research results in academic journals. In short, they live out the ABC principle by combining applied and basic research.

Started in 2001 by Gov. Gray Davis in a time of financial surplus, more than $100 million was devoted to CITRIS's admirable agenda, which was recently distilled into four "thrust areas": energy, healthcare, intelligent infrastructure, and democracy. One mechanism for encouraging collaboration among faculty from the four campuses is CITRIS's seed grant program. Faculty from at least two of the four campuses can submit proposals for seed funding of $40K–$60K to conduct early stage research that will lead to larger proposals to companies or federal funding agencies such as the National Science Foundation. One of CITRIS's measures of success is how much outside funding its faculty attract for further research. In the last six years, investments of $6.2 million have led to nearly $40 million in outside funding. Another measure of success is how much individuals or corporate donors contribute, such as the $20 million given by Marvell Technology founder Sehat Saturdja, his brother Pantas Saturdja, and his wife Weili Dai for a nanofabrication lab and CITRIS headquarters on the UC Berkeley campus.

The link to California state government leadership has remained strong, as Deputy Director Camille Crittenden described, with Lieutenant Governor Gavin Newsome working with CITRIS faculty to develop the California Report Card. This website invites Californians to rate state government performance on key issues and suggest questions for future report cards. Newsom's book *Citizenville: How to Take the Town Square Digital and Reinvent*

Government promotes civic engagement, which fits right into the democracy thrust area. Development of the California Report Card is led by engineering professor Ken Goldberg, Faculty Director of the Data and Democracy Initiative.

The devotion to interdisciplinary collaborations leads to units such as the Center for Sustainable Energy and Power Systems (CenSEPS), based at UC Santa Cruz and devoted to innovative technologies for clean energy. Another project, called Motion Interfaces for Physical Therapy, a collaboration between UC Davis and UC Merced, addresses motion-capture and immersive 3D environments that could facilitate remote delivery of health-care. One of the much promoted success stories is the work of Berkeley's Steve Glaser and Merced's Roger Bales, who teamed up to create a wireless sensor array for measuring the Sierra Nevada snowpack in order to more reliably predict water resources. Their initial idea, part of CITRIS's Intelligent Water Infrastructures Initiative, led to a $2 million National Science Foundation grant.

While traditional researchers might call this applied research, the CITRIS faculty and students often think about their work as basic research in service to recognized societal challenges. The novelty of the problems and the fresh approaches give re-searchers the feeling that they are starting something new and therefore doing basic research. The drive to serve societal needs is a strong motivator for many of the researchers, who strive to see their work evolve from prototype to implementation. Some solutions may take years to mature, but the use-inspired agenda energizes them to produce implementable solutions. Often CITRIS researchers work with business or government partners, thereby lowering the barriers to technology transfer and commercialization.

When traditional researchers participate in such interdisciplinary societal challenges, they may face disapproval from colleagues, concern from tenure committees, and re-sistance from journal reviewers. By contrast engineers and designers have usually been more open to taking on real-world problems. The rocket engineer Theodore von Kármán (1881–1963) summarized the distinction neatly: "Scientists study the world as it is; engin-eers create the world that has never been."

Of course, there is room for the application of scientific, engineering, and design meth-ods (the SED principle) to real-world problems, so the scientists who wish to create what "has never been" may be excellent partners in research projects. Clarifying the reward structure for researchers will improve the likelihood that they will address real-world problems in an interdisciplinary team. Another motivation is that working on real-world problems is likely to steer researchers to produce more successful basic research (the ABC principle). The management challenge is to guide researchers to conduct their work and present it to colleagues, tenure committees, and journal reviewers in ways that gain acceptance.

Many state governments promote technology incubators and academic partnerships with industry, usually with the idea of promoting economic activity that creates jobs. While job creation metrics are difficult to trace to academic research, the payoffs of such part-nerships is touted by governors and state legislatures.

CITRIS's Crittenden is also proud of their technology incubator program, begun in 2013, which provides physical space and guidance to start-up companies. The incubator has hatched five companies already. These are in addition to the 36 start-up companies spun out from CITRIS researchers—about a quarter of all UC Berkeley start-ups over the past decade.

There is no single formula for forming collaborations, sharing intellectual property, or rewarding successes, but the widespread experimentation with management strategies could lead to more replicable results and widely accepted metrics. In fact, studying which management strategies have higher payoffs is yet another sociotechnical problem which could lead to high-impact research results.

Each interdisciplinary center seems to have their own strategy for addressing real-world problems, such as CITRIS's four steps:[2]

Learn: We are committed to meeting UC's educational mission and sparking the desire to learn among students and faculty alike.

Build: We offer unparalleled facilities to build prototypes and demonstration models for projects large and small.

Launch: Once a proof of concept has been tested and refined, it is ready to launch to the broader community of experts, agencies, or the interested public.

Connect: The final step is to connect these innovations with the sector or group that will benefit and promote its adoption or implementation.

This broad strategy is appealing, but faculty must take this loosely formulated process into management strategies that produce basic and applied results. Achieving high-impact research in a reliable and repeatable manner takes a carefully specified process, appropriate metrics to define success, and effective public outreach.

Skeptics rightly question the efficacy of such public service–oriented centers, but evidence is growing that if researchers use variations on the ABC and SED principles, they can solve real-world problems and produce better basic research. The emergence of units such as CITRIS suggest that there is a shift underway to apply academic skills to real-world problems, while at the same time producing more valuable foundational results.

---

[1] CITRIS, *CITRIS: The Center for Information Technology Research in the Interest of Society* (2015) http://citris-uc.org/.
[2] CITRIS, UC Merced, *Projects* (Accessed July 29, 2015) http://citris.ucmerced.edu/projects/infrastructure.

Critics of Kuhn point to his narrow Western view of science, which sees only limited contributions from Asian, Middle Eastern, or other cultures. His selective choice of individuals and topics honors those who worked within traditions that Kuhn understood, but older and newer approaches to understanding and shaping our world are gaining strength.

Thomas Kuhn's book and Vannevar Bush's *Science: The Endless Frontier*,[11] as well as works by other authors, gave science a key role in the mid-twentieth century. This is understandable in that scientific results, symbolized by the global reputation of Albert Einstein, captivated public attention and led to important outcomes. The physicists and other scientists who produced the atomic bomb became celebrated heroes as well as villains who had unleashed powerful technologies that unhinged geopolitical structures, disrupted military planning, and produced novel threats. After the war, nuclear advocates promised "electricity too cheap to meter," medical miracles, and transportation revolutions. However, the unresolved problems of nuclear waste, radioactive contamination, and medical disasters produced damaging side effects. The narrow focus on science problem-solving with insufficient consideration of broader impacts produced harmful outcomes that interdisciplinary design thinking might have anticipated.

Physicists also drew attention with their atom-smashing cyclotrons and synchrotrons, which produced basic results of particle physics with captivating neologisms: mesons, neutrinos, bosons, leptons, hadrons, and, even more compelling, quarks. The physicists used breathtaking and awe-inspiring language to describe their amazing breakthroughs as they probed the frontiers of knowledge to understand the fundamental principles of our universe. As the ideas and language became more esoteric, public fascination grew over the boldly conceived Large Hadron Collider, the incomprehensible and untestable superstring theory, and more recently the Higgs boson. Journalists, incited by breathless press releases and enthusiastic interviews with scientists, cheered these esoteric ideas and promoted the visionary descriptions of these audacious projects and grand visions of the big bang moment of creation of the universe.

Other work by "rocket scientists" also had profound public impacts, with the launching of the Soviet Sputnik in 1957, and Americans landing on the moon in 1969. While much of the work was engineering, the term "rocket science" became a cultural meme. Learning about science and being a scientist had cachet in an era when high-school science fairs drew almost as much attention as basketball games. NASA inspired public attention with admirable astronaut heroes who made historic trips to space, including moon landings. Planetary exploration and compelling celestial images inflated public interest and ensured continuing Congressional support.

NASA made space exploration exciting, thus encouraging science education; however, in recent decades the public fascination declined, as the Shuttle program had more modest aspirations, and the International Space Station produced questionable benefits. I was enthralled by the early space program and initially wanted to be an astronaut; however, as the decades passed, I wondered which of NASA's efforts were justified and whether the much-championed spin-offs were substantive. Certainly communications satellites, the Global Positioning System, earth resource data gathering, and climate change research had clear value, high impact, and broad application. NASA's science missions drive technology forward and pursue questions about planetary science, astrophysics, and many other topics, but how can their potential benefits be compared with the payoffs from research on healthcare, social participation, or community safety?

Scientists claim that "Surprising Discoveries" and "Long-Term Payoffs" come from basic research, but the same claims can be made for applied research. My concerns about the payoffs from basic science research were accelerated by John Horgan's troubling but mind-opening book *The End of Science: Facing Limits of Knowledge in the Twilight of the Scientific Age*.[12] Horgan's report about "the end of physics" and the limited possibilities of other science endeavors left me troubled but maybe wiser.

Horgan's interview with Thomas Kuhn included this tantalizing quote: "any scientific construct . . . has to be evaluated simply for its utility—for what you can do with it."[13] This powerful statement contains the essence of the paradigm shift I propose for science itself—combining the thirst for new knowledge with the pursuit of practical benefits.

The ABC and SED principles signal that it's time to end the normal science of science and to start pursuing a new paradigm of science. While traditional science deals with the natural world, the next paradigm for science could be to partner with those who study and create the made world, the world we build through engineering and which we shape with design.

I was raised in a culture that celebrated science, giving a lesser role to engineering and design. This may be understandable since the origins of the NAS go back to 1863, when it was founded as a nongovernmental body whose role was to provide informed scientific advice to government agencies. In contrast, the US National Academy of Engineering was only founded in 1964, finally giving recognition to engineering as having a distinct identity, a strong research component, and vital national role. The growing influence of the US National Academy of Engineering has done much to promote public appreciation of the role of engineering, as discussed in Chapter 4. How long will it take until there is a US National Academy of Design?

3.5 The Next Paradigm for Science

The next paradigm for science could be to focus attention on working on civic, business, and global priorities, which will broaden the scope of what scientists do and reshape public expectations for science. Overall, I see benefits to basic science research if scientists more regularly join teams devoted to solving contemporary problems (i.e., the ABC principle), just as physicists, space scientists, biologists, and others did in the past.

Auguste Comte coined the term "social physics" in the 1820s, suggesting there could be a scientific approach to social problems. That term and concept has been episodically used when physicists explored the application of their methods to social problems and has come back into fashion with Alex Pentland's book describing his work on social media and networks for communicating ideas.[14]

There is already movement to blend disciplines, as shown in the examples of institutions and individuals described in the sidebars across this book's chapters. There are other early indicators of support for these new directions. For example, Israel's highly respected Weizmann Institute of Science claims its work is driven by developing "Science for the Benefit of Humanity," a claim that strongly suggests use-inspired research, and their website lists world hunger, global warming, cancer and other diseases, and safety and security as research topics.[15] The New York–based Rockefeller Institute uses the Latin version, "scientia pro bono humani generis," to characterize its mission of "improving the understanding of life for the benefit of humanity."[16] It is difficult to assess which scientific research projects will produce the largest benefit for humanity, but it is a relevant question that every researcher should ask.

While benefit to humanity is a high aspiration, researchers who seek public funds need to ask themselves and explain to others how their scientific research project will produce the largest benefit to their nation. The US National Science Foundation has shifted away from using the terms "basic" and "applied." They require grant proposal authors to have succinct one-page summaries that include statements of both the "intellectual merit" and the "broader impact" of the proposed projects, with "intellectual merit" including "advance knowledge and understanding" by exploring "creative, original, or potentially transformative concepts."[17] Most grant writers can express their goals for advancing knowledge in a way that is responsive to the "Call for Proposals" and meant to impress their colleagues, who are potential reviewers. The goals, work plans, assessment methods, and qualifications of the team are part of the intellectual-merit justification.

The term "broader impact" includes advancing discovery while promoting "integration and transfer of knowledge" by "innovations in teaching and training" and "service to the scientific and engineering community."[18] While earlier encouragement to support K–12 learning and broaden participation from underrepresented groups has been reduced because of criticism, the goal of outreach and public understanding remains important.

Some researchers resent the pressure to consider "broader impact," arguing that it detracts from their main goal of advancing knowledge. Furthermore, cynics point out that proposal writers may describe ambitious "broader impacts," including outreach efforts, but then fail to address them adequately during the grant. Researchers are less devoted to outreach because they argue that hiring and tenure review committees see little value in it.[19]

The shift to "intellectual merit" and "broader impact" is a step past the traditional false dichotomy between basic and applied research, but clearer guidance about desired outcomes and reliable metrics would help researchers to direct their efforts and proposal reviewers to have a common understanding of what is expected.

Vannevar Bush proposed a "National Research Foundation," but the political exigencies of the late 1940s resulted in the agency title using "science." However, US National Science Foundation directors and the National Science Board have consistently included engineering in the scope of discussions and funding. The growing acceptance of engineering is likely tied to the recognition that public funding has to generate economic benefits by way of research results and training of practitioners.

Another key issue for US National Science Foundation policymakers has been the tension between respect for disciplinary focus, and the pursuit of interdisciplinary collaboration. These policymakers have long recognized that research projects that seek to achieve "high intellectual merit" and "broader impact" often benefit by taking an interdisciplinary approach. They rely on a definition from a National Academies report:[20]

Interdisciplinary research is a mode of research by teams or individuals that integrates information, data, techniques, tools, perspectives, concepts, and/or theories from two or more disciplines or bodies of specialized knowledge to advance fundamental understanding or to solve problems whose solutions are beyond the scope of a single discipline or area of research practice.

Achieving interdisciplinary success is difficult, as many teams fail to collaborate effectively. Successful collaborations are based on previous work together, shared clearly defined goals, and respect for each other's contributions. The US National Science Foundation has a deep commitment to interdisciplinary work (sometimes called "cross-cutting" to indicate the involvement of principal investigators from at least two of the eight divisions).

Interdisciplinary thinking could also help ensure that the contributions of research projects will be applied in positive ways. While it is difficult for researchers to control how their work is used by others, early reflection on potential negative outcomes could swing the pendulum toward positive outcomes.

3.6 Science Education

Science education has a long history with regular efforts to reinvent the curriculum to bring in new topics or teaching methods. The shift from memorization and lecture to active learning methods that often stress inquiry-based learning is a repeated theme for both lower school and university courses. Research and innovation centers for science teaching have been opened at many universities such as the Stevens Institute of Technology's Center for Innovation in Engineering and Science Education, whose mission statement is "to inspire, nurture and educate leaders for tomorrow's technology-centric environment while contributing to the solutions of the most challenging problems of our time."[21]

Other science teaching initiatives include the physics-focused research group at the University of Maryland's Physics Education Research Group or the National Association for Research in Science Teaching, whose goal is to improve "science teaching and learning through research."[22] The dozens of research journals and conferences on science teaching, such as those run by the National Science Teachers Association, indicate the strength of activity.[23] New directions in science education are to employ media such as well-produced televisions programs, World Wide Web sites, citizen science projects, and informal science learning programs at nature centers and museums. A recent addition was the White House Science Fair to raise prominence of science education.[24]

CASE STUDY 3.2 SCIENTIFIC COMPUTING AND IMAGING IN-STITUTE: THE UNIVERSITY OF UTAH'S INNOVATION ENGINE

Christopher Johnson, Director of the University of Utah's Scientific Computing and Imaging Institute

https://www.cs.utah.edu/~crj/

The goal of blending science, engineering, and design is shared by Chris Johnson, Director of the University of Utah's world-famous Scientific Computing and Imaging (SCI, playfully pronounced "ski") Institute.[1] During the past 20 years he creatively fashioned a thriving community of researchers whose visually compelling images, animations, and interactive tools are widely celebrated and imitated. Driven by healthcare, science, and engineering challenges from on-campus, national, and international collaborators, the 200+ researchers and staff produce practical solutions and publishable, often award-winning, scientific papers, plus colorful imagery that graces the covers of technical and popular magazines.

Their work has many foundational pillars that bridge science, engineering, and design. Team members may have been trained as scientists but work as engineering solution developers who manage large volumes of data or write efficient code. Software engineering skills are deemed important, and some team members are proficient in user interface or visual design. Other team members may be fluent in perceptual psychology theories that enable them to design effective color palettes that are meaningful to practitioners while highlighting the key features in an image or interactive environment.

Many of the SCI Institute researchers study medical problems such as Parkinson's disease, heartbeat irregularities, and neurological failures, as well as dozens of others. The collaboration strategy utilized by the researchers provides meaningful results for their medical partners, often directly benefiting patients via improved surgical procedures, better diagnostic tests, or pharmaceutical agents. In the future, SCI Institute work may reveal as yet unidentified medical processes in the brain, heart, or skeletal system, as well as novel structures in bacteria, viruses, and DNA.

In addition, collaboration often generates new computational or visualization strategies that are widely applicable. Effective strategies may be embedded in a software tool that gets refined through further testing and then distributed by way of a network of hundreds of collaborators across the United States and increasingly around the world. Sometimes the software tools trigger spin-off companies, which work to develop markets while tuning the products to a wider range of user needs. Since the SCI Institute leans toward large data analyses that push the limits of current hardware, some projects develop improved use of graphics processing units and refined chip designs that have become part of every microprocessor.

Internally, there are more than a dozen centers that have specialties, such as the Musculoskeletal Research Laboratories, the Utah Center for Neuroimage Analysis, or the Center for Integrative Biomedical Computing. Such internal divisions can be helpful for enabling independent thinking, seeking specialized funding, and building leadership skills. The opportunity to be a center director or a lab head sets aspirations for junior researchers or attracts stars from outside.

Chris Johnson stresses that one reason for his interdisciplinary success is the external administrative structure through which the SCI Institute fits into the University of Utah. Rather than reporting to a department chair or a college dean, as most institute directors must do, Johnson reports directly to the provost. This system provides Johnson with high-level visibility and avoids squabbles over resources; such squabbles are typical within units, especially in lean times, when research institute staff requests are typically given less attention than those from departmental tenured faculty. Furthermore, since the bulk of funding comes from outside sources such as the National Science Foundation, the National Institutes of Health, and corporations, Johnson manages his own budget, plus the commonly applied university overhead. Of course, he has to keep writing big proposals, wooing corporate partners, and pushing his team to write their own proposals.

Chris Johnson is a big guy with a self-confident big smile and playful style that is often a characteristic of creative leaders. His ample office has one large wall with books, a floor-to-ceiling whiteboard for brainstorming, and a floor-to-ceiling glass window looking out over the campus to the nearby snow-covered mountains. He works at an elevated desk with large computer display, while pedaling on a semirecumbent bicycle. His office also has a conference table for small meetings and cozy chairs for relaxed discussion, all surrounded by books, journals, sculptures, art work, and some games. In the hallways a ping-pong table, colorful furniture, and comfy lounge chairs around coffee tables encourage social play and shop talk. The five espresso machines in the lounge cater to diverse passions, fueling the intense work sessions to meet proposal or publication deadlines. The all-glass building also has natural light filtering through its four floors. These admirable comforts are due to the generous donation of Utah alum, John Warnock, who cofounded Adobe Inc. and served as its long-time CEO. He gets his name on the front of the building but leaves Johnson to manage what goes on inside.

Johnson's flair for personal expression is apparent in his Bauhaus-inspired home, which also has floor-to-ceiling glass windows overlooking a scenic valley. His home office has a big desktop computer and an exercise bicycle with a computer mounted on it. A large aquarium has a dozen colorful marine fish and corals, but the real treat is the custom-built greenhouse that stretches for more than 60 feet along the house's foundation on the hillside. Johnson's 300 orchids are a stunning manifestation of an interest triggered by a college botany course. He knowledgeably explains unusual species whose elaborate adaptations were selected to attract unique pollinators or nocturnal insects.

Many interdisciplinary institutes are founded on the basis of winning a major grant, but they often flounder because they cannot keep their funding stream going. Johnson points to examples at well-respected universities such as Harvard and Princeton, where promising institutes were eventually dissolved. He sees their origins in narrowly focused disciplinary units as a major cause for their failure. This narrow focus may happen because strong universities keep to traditional disciplinary boundaries, attracting mature leaders who expect to work on their own research agenda rather than bend to the needs of collaborators.

Some universities try to make their mark by emphasizing interdisciplinary niches that are not filled by traditional departments. Arizona State University's President Michael

Crow has chosen this bold approach, forming units around hot topics such as sustainability, educational technology, and human evolution and social change (see Case Study 7.1 in Section 7.4). He values the existing respected universities for what they do, while claiming to be creating the "new American university."[2]

[1] University of Utah, Scientific Computing and Imaging Institute, *SCI Home* (Accessed July 29, 2015) http://www.sci.utah.edu/; University of Utah, *Scientific Computing and Imaging Institute Centers* (Accessed July 29, 2015) http://www.sci.utah.edu/centers.html.

[2] Crow, M. M. and Dabars, W. B., *Designing the New American University*, Johns Hopkins University Press, Baltimore, MD (2015).

3.7 Science Roadmaps and Challenges

A popular way of imagining future directions in science has been through the use of roadmaps, as these kinds of strategy documents can be helpful for forming and building consensus among particle physicists, space scientists, astronomers, and biologists. Having a community-agreed document, possibly endorsed by major universities and professional societies, is very effective for gaining funding from government agencies and philanthropic foundations.[25] These documents are often written for more general audiences so that journalists and nonspecialist government policymakers can understand the goals. These roadmaps often have compelling images of particle accelerators, swirling galaxies, genomic double helixes, or colorful networks, and breathless prose about unique moments in history, the potential for revolutionary breakthroughs, and the capacity to probe deeply into hidden secrets of nature.[26]

This sample from NASA shows their well-polished style:

NASA leads the nation on a great journey of discovery, seeking new knowledge and understanding of our Sun, Earth, solar system, and the universe—out to its farthest reaches and back to its earliest moments of existence.[27]

And a more detailed description promises "remarkable discoveries to address three defining questions: Are we alone? How did we get here? How does the universe work? Seeking answers to these age-old questions are Enduring Quests of humankind."[28] Physicists, space scientists, and genomic researchers are doing important work, in part because they have united to present well-written roadmaps that excite the public and funding agencies.

Roadmaps are a global phenomenon across many areas of science, often focusing on infrastructure building such as chemistry laboratories, marine research ships, radio telescopes, and genome sequencing technologies.[29] Additional challenges are covered in Chapter 6.

3.8 Skeptics' Corner

Traditionalists may argue that the scope of science and disciplinary boundaries are sufficiently well defined. They believe that discipline-focused, curiosity-driven scientific observation and experimentation leads to important results whose value may not be appreciated until much later. They believe that scientific knowledge of all kinds benefit society, so they resist the pressure to address current societal or business challenges, which they believe produce only short-term payoffs. In short, traditionalists reject the ABC and SED principles, strongly defending their right to scientific freedom in choosing research topics.

They also argue for the "Long-Term Payoff" theme, which claims that basic research will invariably have value, even though this value may not become apparent until decades later. They offer compelling examples of how data collected by one person can lay the foundation for insights by another, such as the way Tycho Brahe's astronomical records led to Kepler's laws of planetary motion, and how contemporary genomic data collection will lay the foundation for future discoveries.

Another recurrent theme, the "Surprising Discovery," is that scientists who are given freedom to explore often make unexpected findings and astonishing innovations, such as Alexander Fleming's discovery of antibiotics or the chemist Donald Stookey's creation of superstrong glass when, because of a failed temperature controller, he inadvertently overheated a sample. However, it is an equally valid claim that basic research motivated by applied goals could generate even more "Surprising Discoveries."

These traditionalists who are skeptical about my raised expectations have legitimate concerns, so those who follow my advice would be wise to be cautious but deliberate in taking on ambitious goals in applied and basic research. However, I believe that working on realistic problems and collaborating with researchers from other disciplines, while maintaining a basic research outlook may produce even more "Long-Term Payoffs" and "Surprising Discoveries," thereby increasing the frequency of high-impact results.

3.9 Summary

Science remains a miraculous seed that sets down roots and sends up flowers. The seed contributions of scientists to understanding the natural world have produced a remarkable forest of inspiring impacts. But the future seeds of science will more regularly sprout into studies of the made world, so that scientists can play important roles in addressing twenty-first century problems. While physics, chemistry, biology and other established sciences will continue to be important, new components such as medical, social, environmental, and information sciences will gain strength. These changes will be resisted by some but embraced by others.

Tying research to civic, business, or global goals is another concern for scientists who believe that they should be free to follow their instincts about what seems important. Erik Fisher's study acknowledged the problem, but showed that this attitude could be changed[30]:

Most industrial researchers . . . indicated that the integration of societal concerns was not one of their core professional obligations, whereas by the end of the study, all agreed that it was . . . many scientists and policy makers believe that this sort of integration is not possible, or that if it were possible, it would be undesirable. Not only would it undermine the scientific process, some believe, it would "slow down research and development." In his view, the . . . project has demonstrated both that socio-technical integration is possible and that it has utility: "It aids scientific creativity and expands decision making." Making science more responsive to societal concerns and demands also enhances its public value.

The appreciation of engineering methods and design thinking as valuable partners may be the next paradigm shift for science itself. The idea that reductionist models and tightly controlled experiments should be complemented by large-scale interventions and case study projects with practical payoffs is still novel, but acceptance is growing.

I believe that these changes will expand the scope and enhance the power of science to make fundamental breakthroughs that have widespread impacts. At the same time, taking on societal challenges is likely to increase the attraction of science for many students and its acceptance by the general public. Policymakers, research managers, journal publishers, professional societies, and journalists will all have key roles in promoting the ABC and SED principles that shift science research toward serving societal needs.

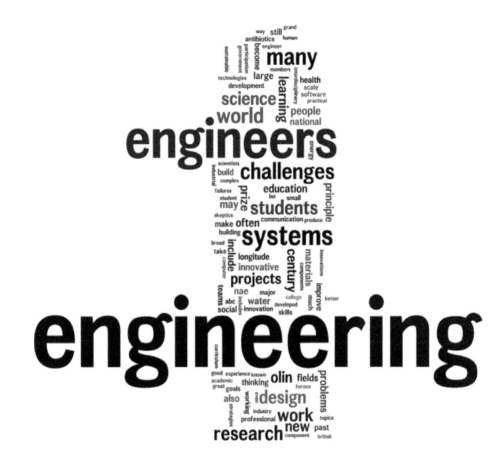

CHAPTER 4

What Engineering Contributes

Devotion to Innovative Technologies

Scientists study the world as it is; engineers create the world that has never been.

Theodore von Kármán

4.1 Introduction

Engineering is about aspirations, requiring bold visions and clear plans, driven by attention to detail, repeated measurement, and persistence in the face of set-backs. It requires experience, but each research project is a step into the un-known to build something that was never done before. Engineering successes come from an innovative spirit and an entrepreneurial style that can enlist the participation of others to create something valuable. Engineering research is risky, so anticipating and coping with failures requires mental planning to limit their damage and frequency, plus a resilient personality to pick up and keep working.[1] Science experiments may be risky too, but the scale of engineering projects (e.g., rocket launches, dam construction, or public health websites) is often massive; thus, failures in engineering projects may be more dramatic and more visible and may affect many more people than failures in scientific experiments would.

In the past, engineering was seen primarily as professional practice within companies or government agencies such as, for example, the US Army Corps of

The New ABCs of Research. First Edition. Ben Shneiderman.
© Ben Shneiderman 2016. Published in 2016 by Oxford University Press.

Engineers. However, in universities, industry, and government, a growing component of engineering research expects innovative outcomes to be described in published peer-reviewed journal or conference papers.

The roots of engineering go back thousands of years to the stone-age toolmakers and to the still-standing civil engineering masterworks such as the pyramids of Egypt, the Roman roads, or the Great Wall of China. Civilizations around the world also developed sophisticated techniques for building, as evidenced by the Mayan cities in Mexico, the palace at Knossos in Crete, and the ancient temples in Japan. By medieval and Renaissance times, remarkable constructions such as Notre Dame in Paris, the Blue Mosque in Istanbul, or Brunelleschi's dome in Florence put engineering skills to work in building these impressive structures.

Any engineering project as vast as these necessarily includes design decisions about aesthetics and function. However, the science of these engineering marvels is modest. Stonework, wood carving, or metallic components were based on design experience and rough rules of thumb known to master engineers. Trial and error produced many building failures till the engineers became more confident of their products.[2] The tradition of taking responsibility for their work is an admirable trait of many engineers, carried into contemporary practice by those who become licensed Professional Engineers.[3]

The goals in engineering research differ from the clear theories or single formulas often pursued by scientists. As Brian Arthur points out, engineering is about multiple components, complex assemblies, and integrated systems that function smoothly in normal and extreme conditions.[4] Engineers produce contemporary automobiles, which each year offer new features and greater safety, while keeping costs reasonable. Engineers produce astonishing aircraft whose safety record makes air travel the benign component of a trip. Some travelers may still worry about their flight because what happens is astonishing, but most travelers know that their taxi ride to the airport is the dangerous part. Engineers also push the limits of what is possible in graceful bridges, smoothly functioning canal locks, and reliable spacecraft that explore planets.[5]

Famed engineers include British heroes of the industrial revolution, such as Isambard Kingdom Brunel (1806–1859), whose innovations such as railways, ocean liners, bridges, and tunnels were visible manifestations of a changing world. Another legendary British engineer was Henry Bessemer (1813–1898), whose innovative steel-making process improved quality and reduced costs, but he is also remembered for his entrepreneurial persistence in turning his patent into a commercial success. There are many other celebrated heroes such as the French civil engineer Alexandre Gustave Eiffel (1832–1923), whose wrought-iron railway bridges and legendary Parisian tower made him world famous. American heroes include Thomas Edison (1847–1931), whose inventions still shape modern life, and Hyman Rickover (1900–1986), whose nuclear engineering for the Navy changed military and diplomatic practice.

The Queen Elizabeth Prize for Engineering, which only began in 2013, celebrates "engineers responsible for ground-breaking innovation that has been of global benefit to humanity."[6] The 2015 prize went to Robert Langer for the development of "polymers to control the delivery of large molecular weight drugs for treatment of diseases such as cancer and mental illness" and which are documented in his admirable list of 1000 patents and 1300 research papers, as well as for his documented track record of bringing treatments to market.

The list of influential personalities is long, but many engineers are not as well known as they should be, possibly because most advances involve diverse contributors, many stages, and integration with existing systems. For example, mechanical engineers have made fundamental innovations such levers, gears, pulleys, pumps, and plows. As Brian Arthur stresses, combinations of these innovations eventually had huge impacts on manufacturing, shipping, agriculture, and many other vital domains. The general public will more easily recognize the larger systems such as trains, ships, cars, water mills, or factories rather than appreciate each individual component.

Similarly, chemical and materials engineers started with natural materials and eventually synthesized new compounds or combined materials to make modern steel, plastics, fiberglass, and so on. In the past two centuries, electrical engineers emerged as key shapers of our civilization by combining electrical components into complex systems such as cameras, computers, or cars. In the past half-century, software engineers became heroes by building up modules, libraries, and toolkits to speed development of powerful systems—which are still flawed but always being improved.

Engineering has gained favor in educational institutions, as engineers have proven to be highly desired new hires for companies and governments. Engineering is a way of thinking, based on a devotion to making a better world and improving people's lives and driven by the desire to solve problems: "Engineering combines the fields of science and maths to solve real world problems that improve the world around us. . . . This ability to take a thought, or abstract idea, and translate it into reality is what separates an engineer from other fields of science and mathematics."[7]

While research-oriented engineers are more likely to publish papers about their work in ways that refine theories and promote generalized solutions, professional engineers are more focused on solving their given problem. To their credit, engineers often work in large teams because projects such as building airplanes, bridges, or software require diverse skills and thousands of coordinated workers. Engineers already follow the ABC principle and new research strategies but they could benefit by drawing more on theoretical foundations and publishing results more regularly to capture their generalizable insights.

Engineering has several major branches, typically, civil, mechanical, materials, and electrical, with many sub-branches:[8]

acoustical, naval, mining, agricultural corrosion, aerospace, automotive, computer, software, user interface, electronic, petroleum, systems, audio, software, architectural, biosystems, biomedical, geological, industrial, materials, and nuclear.

The US National Academy of Engineering (NAE) was founded only in 1964 but it has done much to raise the stature of engineers. The NAE taxonomy of engineering branches comes from their dozen section names:[9]

Aerospace Engineering
Bioengineering
Chemical Engineering
Civil Engineering
Computer Science & Engineering
Electric Power/Energy Systems Engineering
Electronics, Communication and Information Systems Engineering
Industrial, Manufacturing & Operational Systems Engineering
Materials Engineering
Mechanical Engineering
Earth Resources Engineering
Special Fields & Interdisciplinary Engineering

The 2000+ highly respected NAE members annually select 60–70 new members, continually redefining the scope of these branches. New topics such as "Earth Resources Engineering" and "Interdisciplinary Engineering" reveal the continuing evolution of engineering and endorse the growing value of interdisciplinarity. Although the organization's major event is devoted to recognizing new members, the NAE also gives three major engineering awards: The Draper

Prize, The Gordon Prize, and The Russ Prize.[10] These awards have honored developers of innovations such as the lithium ion battery, cellular phone networks, automating DNA sequencing, implantable cardiac pacemakers, and much more. These awards have yet to capture as much attention as the Nobel Prizes, which are focused on science, but often the innovations that Nobel Prizes are awarded for, such as the transistor, the integrated circuit, the laser, or magnetic resonance imaging, have major engineering components. Sometimes researchers find successful and imaginative synergies in blending the reductionist strategies of science with the systems thinking of engineering.

One of the sections of the NAE is "Computer Science & Engineering," which comprises the emerging fields of software engineering, usability engineering, and related areas such as information visualization and visual analytics, which are my areas of interest. These fields share a common interest in the human aspects of systems, with a warm linkage to design thinking. While these fields have had dramatic successes and shown broad influence, their acceptance is still mixed among traditional science and engineering groups. Usability engineering and its academic variant, human-computer interaction, represent the blend of science, engineering, and design (i.e., the SED principle) that is also necessary for sustainability, healthcare delivery, community safety, and other interdisciplinary fields that will become key research topics in the coming century.

4.2 Engineering Education

These lofty aspirations are what the next generation of engineering students is already learning at some forward-thinking universities that advocate variations on the ABC principle. An innovative example is Olin College, which was founded in 1997 at Needham, MA, thanks to a $500 million grant from the F. W. Olin Foundation. Olin College began with the radical idea that there would be no departments and no tenure. It's hard to overstate how large a change this is— read it again! Instead, the guiding academic philosophy was to create a college that "instills passion and ignites innovation by focusing engineering students on the needs of people in the real world. This broad perspective in the hands of creative and motivated students inspires technical mastery for a purpose. Olin 'engineer-innovators' envision and deliver products, services and systems that transform the way people live on this planet."

To carry out this philosophy, Olin College's founders focused on a tripartite curriculum to teach (1) "superb engineering," (2) entrepreneurship with attention to ethics and philanthropy, and (3) the arts, which are considered to include creativity, innovation, design, and communication. These guiding principles were instantiated with practical requirements, just like what good engineers would do if they were developing an educational program.

The Olin curriculum seems strongly influenced by the philosopher John Dewey, who emphasized experiential education by having students engage with authentic projects that taught the skills of reflection, collaboration, communication, and leadership, skills that apply across all of life's challenges.[11] Experiential education and later variants such as experiential learning and service learning stress the importance of defining problems, working with community stakeholders, and coping with failures.[12] While a traditional environmental learning project might be to understand the causes of pollution in a nearby stream, the experiential or service learning approach would be to collect data, identify responsible parties, and then take action so as to reduce pollution. Such an effort might take several years of student projects, but each student cohort would learn from the past and know that their work would be carried on in the future.

The Olin curriculum includes (1) experiences for students to work independently, as members of teams, and as leaders of teams; (2) opportunities for students to perform before an audience that includes experts in the field of the presentation or performance; (3) an international or intercultural immersion experience; (4) demonstrated significant creative artistic expression; (5) significant work experience in a corporate culture; and (6) the ability to apply basic business practices necessary to bring a product to the marketplace.

The Olin agenda ensures that students will have

- hands-on design projects in every year;
- authentic, ambitious capstone senior/advanced student projects;
- substantial constructive impacts on society; and
- skills that will enable them to communicate logically and persuasively in spoken, written, graphical, and visual forms.

The explicit goal is to produce a self-sufficient individual who is able to articulate and activate a vision and then bring it to fruition. It may be too early to determine the full impact or success of the Olin philosophy and practices, but they have gained widespread visibility and a high number of student applicants. Many Olin students will become industrial workers devoted to corporate goals, but their broad education may steer many students to become researchers who publish basic science research results as well as implement widely applicable applied research solutions.

The Olin College model is attractive to many students, especially women, who seek to have a meaningful impact on the world. Groups such as Engineers Without Borders,[13] whose goal is "to partner with disadvantaged communities to improve their quality of life through education and implementation of sustainable engineering projects," directly address the twenty-first-century challenges of the made world. Yet these forward-thinking groups draw only a small fraction of engineering students and faculty.

Similar, innovative engineering education programs are emerging at mainstream campuses such as the University of Illinois, where the Illinois Foundry for Innovation in Engineering Education (known as iFoundry), promotes student-led teams to take on realistic problems. The organizers seek a curriculum that "is driven more by student-centered autonomy, mastery, and purpose," and they want education to include "liberal arts, critical thinking, and design-based learning: building new courses, experiences, and opportunities for students to develop the broad learning and practices essential to good engineering work."[14] The iFoundry leadership uses the NAE Grand Challenges to shape their projects, workshop, and courses.

4.3 Engineering Roadmaps and Challenges

One of the NAE's efforts to raise public interest in engineering has been to select 14 "Grand Challenges in Engineering." When the NAE president Charles Vest presented them in 2008, he proudly claimed that "in the century just ended, engineering recorded its grandest accomplishments. The widespread development and distribution of electricity and clean water, automobiles and airplanes, radio and television, spacecraft and lasers, antibiotics and medical imaging, and computers and the Internet are just some of the highlights from a century in which engineering revolutionized and improved virtually every aspect of human life."

In selecting the 14 "Grand Challenges" for the next century (see Box 4.1), Vest said:

Through the engineering accomplishments of the past, the world has become smaller, more inclusive, and more connected. The challenges facing engineering today are not those of isolated locales, but of the planet as a whole and the entire planet's people. Meeting all those challenges must make the world not only a more technologically advanced and connected place, but also a more sustainable, safe, healthy, and joyous—in other words, better—place.[15]

CASE STUDY 4.1 BELL LABS: DESIGNED TO ENSURE APPLIED RESEARCH INSPIRED BASIC RESEARCH

Working in an environment of applied science, as one of Bell Labs researcher noted years later, "doesn't destroy a kernel of genius—it focuses the mind.[1] Of all the respected industrial research centers, Bell Labs stands out as the legendary home of high-impact research. From the early part of the twentieth century it attracted brilliant researchers who wanted to participate in a vigorous research culture with heroic leaders and productive teams whose contributions remain unmatched. Bell Labs was the home of the transistor, the laser, digital photography, and key computer programming tools such as the UNIX operating system and the C language. Seven of its researchers received Nobel Prizes for their work.

While this remarkable lab had inspirational leaders and motivated researchers, the take-away message of Bell Labs is that organizing creative individuals in fluid teams to solve applied problems is a successful strategy. Bell Labs was the research branch of the monopolistic American Telephone and Telegraph Company (AT&T) and its manufacturing arm, Western Electric Company. The immense resources and stable commitment to research were used wisely to solve applied problems in telecommunications, which required solutions to basic research questions in material science, physics, and mathematics. The managers of Bell Labs were early advocates of the ABC principle and consciously promoted fluid physical spaces that kept basic researchers close to product developers, even ordering circular lunch tables to encourage open discussions.

Started in 1922, the *Bell System Technical Journal* (*BSTJ*) published articles detailing engineering innovations and scientific breakthroughs. Even Claude Shannon's foundational paper *A Mathematical Theory of Communication*, which *Scientific American* called the "Magna Carta" of the information age, was published in the *BSTJ*. Shannon was a tinkerer, a musician, and a brilliant mathematician, who may be the best example of how working in an applied research lab can lead to profound, widely influential basic research. Shannon's paper may be the most cited scientific paper of all time.

Jon Gertner's history of Bell Labs, *The Idea Factory*, is filled with stories of how problems were solved, reputations were made, and failures were overcome.[2] He writes: "At the peak of its reputation in the late 1960s, Bell Labs employed about fifteen thousand people, including some twelve hundred PhDs. Its ranks included the world's most brilliant (and eccentric) men and women. In a time before Google, the Labs sufficed as the country's intellectual utopia. It was where the future, which is what we now happen to call the present, was conceived and designed.[3] He goes on to say that Bells Labs was a place "where the very point of new ideas was to make them into new things.[4] The legendary success of Bell Labs has been used to promote various theories of how research should be managed. For example, some argue that outstanding individuals are vital, while others see teamwork as the accelerator of research. Gertner writes: "In a math department that thrived on its collective intelligence . . . members of the staff were encouraged to work on papers together rather than alone . . . it had become a matter of some consideration at the Labs whether the key to invention was a matter of individual genius or collaboration.[5]

Another contentious issue is whether disciplinary strength or interdisciplinary collaboration brings greater success. Gertner's book celebrates many individuals but appears to recognize that interdisciplinary teamwork is necessary to deal with contemporary problems: "So many of the wartime and postwar breakthroughs—the Manhattan Project, radar, the transistor—were clearly group efforts, a compilation of the ideas and inventions of individuals bound together with common purposes and complementary talents. And the phone system, with its almost unfathomable complexity, was by definition a group effort . . . a vast amount of multidisciplinary expertise was needed to bring any given project to fruition.[6]

Walter Isaacson captured the spirit of blending basic and applied research in his book *The Innovators*: "The need to combine theorists and engineers was particuluarly true in a field that was becoming increasingly important at Bell Labs: solid-state phyics.[7] Throughout his book Isaacson celebrates the power of teamwork, and in the section on Bell Labs he stresses that "invention sprang from a combination of collaborative teamwork and indvidual brilliance.[8]

Sometimes the Bell Labs story is distorted for political purposes. Advocates of continuing government support for basic science research in the Vannevar Bush tradition refer to Bell Labs as one of the "great industrial centers of basic research" in a 2012 report.[9] The authors of the report threaten that "if U.S. willingness to support basic scientific research is undermined . . . the United States will in effect cede leadership to other countries.[10] While other sections of the report promote science and technology and even mention interdisciplinarity, the underlying message is still the wishful thinking of Vannevar Bush: "basic research fuels a whole innovation ecosystem, often in unpredictable ways.[11]

While science and technology policy researchers rarely emerge with a clear single message, the story of Bell Labs seems strong in supporting the SED principle of blending science, engineering, and design.

---

[1] Gertner, J., *The Idea Factory: Bell Labs and the Great Age of American Innovation*, Penguin Press, London (2012), p. 154.

[2] Ibid.

[3] Ibid., p. 1.

[4] Ibid., p. 3.

[5] Ibid., pp. 133–134.

[6] Ibid., p. 134.

[7] Isaacson, W., *The Innovators: How a Group of Hackers, Geniuses, and Geeks Created the Digital Revolution*, Simon & Schuster, New York, NY (2014).

[8] Ibid., p. 148.

[9] President's Council of Advisors on Science and Technology, *Transformation and Opportunity: The Future of the U.S. Research Enterprise*, Washington, DC (November 30, 2012), p. 5; available at http://www.whitehouse.gov/sites/default/files/microsites/ostp/pcast_future_research_enterprise_20121130.pdf.

[10] Ibid., p. 1.

[11] Ibid., p.42.

Box 4.1 Grand Challenges in Engineering from the National Academy of Engineering

Advance personalized learning: Instruction can be individualized based on learning styles, speeds, and interests to make learning more reliable.

Make solar energy economical: Solar energy provides less than 1% of the world's total energy, but it has the potential to provide much, much more.

Enhance virtual reality: True virtual reality creates the illusion of actually being in a difference space. It can be used for training, treatment, and communication.

Reverse-engineer the brain: The intersection of engineering and neuroscience promises great advances in health care, manufacturing, and communication.

Engineer better medicines: Engineers are developing new systems to use genetic information, sense small changes in the body, assess new drugs, and deliver vaccines.

Advance health informatics: Stronger health information systems not only improve everyday medical visits, but they are essential to counter pandemics and biological or chemical attacks.

Restore and improve urban infrastructure: Good design and advanced materials can improve transportation and energy, water, and waste systems, and also create more sustainable urban environments.

Secure cyberspace: It's more than preventing identity theft. Critical systems in banking, national security, and physical infrastructure may be at risk.

Provide access to clean water: The world's water supplies are facing new threats; affordable, advanced technologies could make a difference for millions of people around the world.

Provide energy from fusion: Human-engineered fusion has been demonstrated on a small scale. The challenge is to scale up the process to commercial proportions, in an efficient, economical, and environmentally benign way.

Manage the nitrogen cycle: Engineers can help restore balance to the nitrogen cycle with better fertilization technologies and by capturing and recycling waste.

Prevent nuclear terror: The need for technologies to prevent and respond to a nuclear attack is growing.

Develop carbon sequestration methods: Engineers are working on ways to capture and store excess carbon dioxide to prevent global warming.

Engineer the tools of scientific discovery: In the century ahead, engineers will continue to be partners with scientists in the great quest for understanding many unanswered questions of nature.

Source: National Academy of Engineering, *NAE Grand Challenges for Engineering* (2015) http://www.engineeringchallenges.org.

The NAE list of challenges is fascinating for what it emphasizes and what it leaves out. Medical informatics to improve treatment is featured but not wellness, good diet, exercises, and health equity. While many of the challenges involve large and complex social systems, the word "social" never appears in these descriptions. I hope future engineers will include social considerations in their solution strategies. Fortunately, "design" gets ample mention, a fact that suggests that engineers seek to work with designers to address the challenges.

Another compelling list of challenges comes from the newly reconstituted British Longitude Prize, which commemorates the 300th anniversary of the famed eighteenth-century challenge to enable sailing ships to know their longitude, so as to avoid dangerous coastal features. This applied problem engaged many Royal Society astronomers, but a practical solution was produced by country clockmaker John Harrison. After producing many prototypes, still on view in Greenwich, he developed a precise chronometer that kept precise time even on swaying ships in bad weather. The astronomers were reluctant to reward Harrison with the prize, but the British Parliament finally recognized his important contribution.

The current Longitude Prize began with six carefully selected topics: water, paralysis, flight, dementia, antibiotics, and food.[16] They are stated as questions: How can we

ensure everyone can have access to safe and clean water,
restore movement to those with paralysis,
fly without damaging the environment,
help people with dementia live independently for longer,
prevent the rise of resistance to antibiotics, and
ensure everyone has nutritious, sustainable food?

These six Longitude Prize topics clearly demonstrate the utility of the SED principle, since they all require some science, with strong engineering aspects to scale up to serve wide audiences, thereby necessitating application of design thinking. The design component involves product design and high levels of social design to motivate participation in schemes that will change behaviors. Solutions will involve the ABC principle, since a combination of foundational research plus business and professional society participation is needed, as well as actions by local and national governments.

Following current crowdsourcing strategies the selection of the Longitude Prize topic for a £10 million prize was done via an Internet-based vote, leading to selection of the antibiotics challenge. It is unlikely that any of the six practical problem-oriented challenges would be solved by a lone researcher or even a small team. In the case of the antibiotics challenge, a central task in preventing the rise of antibiotic resistance will be to form strong partnerships with food industry leaders, who are the major users of antibiotics for meat production. Then the challenge will be to identify changes that will promote animal health, ensure customer satisfaction, and preserve profits.

All six Longitude Prize challenges emphasize the shift from striving to understanding the natural world to producing made-world interventions on an international scale and which involve both industry and government partners. These interventions will require use of the ABC principle in order to develop and evaluate prototypes using the knowledge and methods of science, engineering, and design (the SED principle).

4.4 Skeptics' Corner

Many engineers like to build devices, tinker with prototypes, work with their hands, or make circuits that have measurable and reliable effects and are more commonly aligned with applied research and product development. As their skills will continue to be needed, skeptics of the lofty ambition of the ABC principle may resist the pressure to add basic research theories, to expand their horizons to include interdisciplinary agendas, and to become builders of sociotechnical systems. However, engineers have vital skills that could help solve the immense global problems of the twenty-first century.

The skeptics are uncomfortable with the expansion from technical requirements to include diverse human needs, personality differences, and varying social constraints. The growing need to accommodate users with differing abilities and disabilities is still novel, but these challenges often drive innovative solutions. Skeptics are not drawn to addressing the needs of poorer communities and less developed regions, preferring to work closer to home on more familiar problems.

Collaboration, in small and large teams, is necessary for larger projects. Professional engineers are familiar with working toward large common goals, set by companies and government agencies, but academic research engineers tend to prefer smaller personal projects. Some engineers deplore the competitive academic culture and choose to work in industry, where there is a greater sense of shared purpose.

4.5 Summary

Engineers have an instinct for innovation, a devotion to devices, and a passion for prototyping. The great successes of engineers in the past centuries shaped the modern world with railroads, bridges, dams, automobiles, airplanes, and much more. The urge to build is strong, with the production of ever larger buildings and ever smaller computer chips, but the new demands are shifting from physical devices to service systems such as user interfaces, biomedical processes, and social participation. Engineers often lead the way in working in large teams on common goals, so they may have lessons to teach scientists and designers.

Engineering research students and faculty are often devoted to team projects that serve broader goals, and increasingly they publish their methods, guidelines, and principles so others can build on their work. Engineers are motivated to build new technologies and promote their innovations, but their paths are more likely to include patents and products. They are ready to take on complex sociotechnical systems and deal with difficult problems such as monitoring medication efficacy, rebuilding earthquake damaged cities with cost-effective, yet strong buildings, or developing secure financial systems. They know that working on these challenging problems often leads to new foundational and practical breakthroughs.

Students and young engineers appear to be taking the lead in reforming their discipline, but action by senior engineers, business leaders, and policymakers could accelerate the transformation.

CHAPTER 5

What Design Contributes

Fresh Thinking to Serve Human Needs

The natural sciences are concerned with how things are. . . . Design, on the other hand, is concerned with how things ought to be, with devising artifacts to attain goals.

Herb Simon, *Sciences of the Artificial*

Design must become an innovative, highly creative, cross-disciplinary tool responsive to the true needs of men. It must be more research oriented, and we must stop defiling the earth itself with poorly designed objects and structures. . . . Design is the conscious and intuitive effort to impose meaningful order.

Victor Papanek, *Design for the Real World*

5.1 Introduction

Design thinking goes back to cave dwellers and toolmakers of 50,000 years ago who fashioned tools that were suited to a need. They evolved designs of knife blades and handles that served their need and also added decorations to enhance the user experience. Design thinking is needed to fashion physical objects such as pottery vases, clothing, or magazine covers, as well as intangibles such as Web pages, business services, or healthcare/wellness plans.

Design thinking begins with deep consideration of users, related stakeholders, and their multiple requirements. Lewis Mumford eloquently described the goal of serving human needs by asking "The real question before us lies here: do these instruments further life and enhance its values, or not?"[1] In addition, two further principles of design thinking are (1) to question the original statement of the problem and (2) to continuously refine the goal as more knowledge is gained. Scientists and engineers may also reconsider their assumptions and goals, but these principles are deeply ingrained in the reflective practices of designers.

Design researchers and practitioners often demonstrate playful open-minded approaches that emphasize team and social processes in ways that are very different from those used by science researchers and practitioners. They typically generate a range of possibilities in the form of sketches or prototypes (see Chapter 9) and then courageously trim the possibilities, conduct early evaluations, and consider trade-offs, while keeping an awareness of ethical implications.[2] The flowering results of design thinking often have entrancing colors, shapes, and symmetries, delighting the eye and the mind.

When pushing beyond the limits of current practices, design practitioners become design researchers, especially when they write papers and publicly describe their processes and products. Scientists may see designers as only practitioners, but the growth of design research has brought academic rigor, greater attention to theories, an increased focus on evaluation, and wider publication of results.[3] This rise of design as a research discipline has been especially strong in human-computer interaction research, where careful observation, elaborate interventions, and rigorous controlled experiments are widely used to develop theories and practical guidelines.

Academic design theorists Zimmerman, Forlizzi, and Evenson point out that designers bring (1) "a process for engaging massively under-constrained problems that were difficult for traditional engineering approaches to address . . . (2) a process of integrating ideas from art, design, science, and engineering, in an attempt to make aesthetically functional interfaces . . . and (3) empathy for users as a part of the process."[4] Design researchers and practitioners are proud of the distinctions between their open-ended explorations and what they see as the rigid limits of scientific methods. They resist efforts to "scientize" design.

The movement of design practitioners to become design researchers raises their acceptance among science and engineering researchers and will contribute to the increased use of design methods in those disciplines. The opportunities for science and engineering researchers are to more commonly adopt the design processes of early engagement with varied stakeholders, diverse forms of brainstorming, multiple early prototypes, and more widespread discussion.

Traditional design practitioners, such as metal smiths and potters, who worked in guild communities to cultivate studio-based apprenticeship learning, created elegant and widely used teapots, mugs, and serving bowls. While much of their work was production, they sometimes broke new ground through the use of advanced materials or novel shapes, colors, or textures. Designers such as William Morris made popular nineteenth-century textiles and wallpapers at reasonable prices as a way to allow popular appreciation of design. Multiple twentieth-century designers sought to popularize their work with stylish, low-priced consumer goods. Now attention focuses on cell phone designers, who join useful functions with a comfortable durable case and engaging visual animations to trigger reviewer enthusiasm and consumer satisfaction.

Wikipedia defines design as "the creation of a plan or convention for the construction of an object or a system," where attention is focused on function and fun.[5] Design should enable users to accomplish their tasks and enjoy their experience. This blend of functional requirements and aesthetic aspirations means that, in the best cases, designers assess their products by objective performance and subjective reactions. Satisfying these dual goals requires integrative thinking that attends to left-brain and right-brain desires—logical thinking and emotional responses. Scientists and engineers are encouraged to think logically about their work and use rational arguments to convince colleagues, but designers are expected to evoke passion about their products and elicit delight from their users.

What's striking about design thinking and design research is how broadly it is applied and how much impact it has on daily life. The Wikipedia definition includes, among other design disciplines, these fragrant flowers of design: architecture, communication design, engineering design, fashion design, game design, graphic design, information architecture, industrial design, instructional design, interaction design, interior design, landscape architecture, lighting design, military design methodology, product design, process design, service design, software design, sound design, transition design, urban design, visual design, and Web design.[6] Surprisingly, many of these are related to intangibles, experiences, and social or business services, testifying to the broad reach of design thinking. Even so, this list is incomplete, leaving out such topics as food, voting technology, healthcare systems, and the hundreds of other products and services in which design enriches life.

The broad scope of design thinking is impressive but it has its boundaries, although they may be blurry. Craftworkers and artisans may develop novel designs, but they are typically more devoted to consistent high-quality production of established designs than to innovative exploration. By contrast, fine artists are freed from the constraints of serving functional needs and thus have greater freedom to explore aesthetic and emotional impact. The blurry boundary is also a feature of the relationship to design science and engineering design, but encouraging these crossovers is very much the subject of this book.

Designers work with established and novel design processes, based on guidelines (Keep it Simple Stupid [KISS], strive for consistency) and principles (form follows function, accommodate diverse users). Often, they also follow Christopher Alexander's notions of a pattern language to guide design (rooms should have "light from two sides") and build on experience (golden ratio layouts are appealing, limit short-term memory load to 7 ± 2 chunks).[7] Design pattern languages have also become a regular feature in software engineering, Web design, and even community design.[8]

More than science and engineering, design has a variety of recognizable styles such Scandinavian, Art Nouveau, or Bauhaus, with competing schools of design seeking to promote their unique style. Individual designers (e.g., William Morris, Rennie Mackintosh, and Alvar Aalto) or design practices (developed by, e.g., Frank Lloyd Wright, Charles and Ray Eames) may develop their own style, color palettes, or iconography, which become identifiable to fellow professionals. Designer logos help broadcast their style and often raise the value or attraction of their products. This is maybe most noticeable in fashion, where names like Armani, Ralph Lauren, Coco Chanel, Gucci, or Diane von Furstenberg are world famous—certainly more famous than most scientists or engineers.

Admirably, designers often focus on more than just the look and feel of their products; they consider the user experience, which opens discussion to research on novice learning, expert usage, chances of errors, and user satisfaction by diverse users across age, gender, skill levels, and literacy abilities. Still broader research issues include emotional reactions such as pleasure, engagement, frustration, and rejection, international acceptance across different cultures, and efficacy for users with disabilities that include visual, auditory, motor, and cognitive limitations.

5.2 Design Processes

So design is about products and services, but it is also about the design process.[9] Most design schools teach systematic teamwork approaches to developing designs. They usually begin with requirements gathering, explicit identification of constraints, familiarization with previous work, and divergent thinking to generate many rough designs. Then professionals advocate discussion and reflection to trim the number of designs, refine each, and converge on a small number of candidates. When colleagues, users, clients, and stakeholder representatives participate, presentations provide further feedback. Then user studies with prototypes yield subjective impressions of aesthetic aspects and performance results on functional aspects. Final stages are commitment to a design followed by scaling up and scaling out, and then production, dissemination, and continuous feedback to refine designs.

Many versions of the design process have been described; for example, a leading user experience designer, Aaron Marcus, proposes a twelve-step approach:

- Plan project
- Analyze needs
- Gather requirements
- Design initial solution
- Evaluate design solutions (iterate with initial and revised design steps)
- Design revised solution
- Evaluate design concepts (iterative)
- Deploy product/service
- Evaluate product/service (iterative)
- Determine future requirements/enhancements
- Maintain and improve processes
- Assess project

By contrast, the International Standards Organization prescribes a stripped-down set of four components for a user-centered design project:[10]

- Requirements gathering: understanding and specifying the context of use
- Requirements specification: specifying the user and organizational requirements
- Design: producing designs and prototypes
- Evaluation: carrying out user-based assessment of the site

Reflecting the complex realities of design, the British Design Council developed an appealing two-phase design process called "The Double Diamond"; in each phase, divergent thinking is followed by convergent thinking, nicely captured with the terms "Discover," "Define," "Develop," and "Deliver" (Fig. 5.1).[11] The first phase of the process might be thought of as a requirements gathering to determine what the problem or goal is, while the second phase focuses on shaping the solution or product.

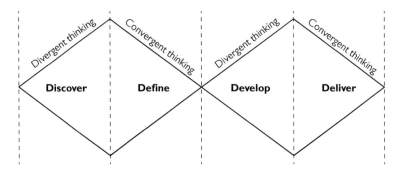

Figure 5.1 British Design Council design process called the double diamond (*A Study of the Design Process-The Double Diamond*, reproduced with permission from the Design Council), as shown by Onarheim and Friis-Olivarius (2013) (Onarheim, B. and Friis-Olivarius, M., Applying the neuroscience of creativity to creativity training, *Frontiers in Human Neuroscience* (October 16, 2013). doi: 10.3389/fnhum.2013.00656).

For larger projects there might be a triple diamond, in which a scaling-up phase has been added to turn the design solution into a delivered product or service that has reliable quality, low cost, and maintenance or repair services. Each phase of the double or triple diamond process typically represents increased time, effort, personnel, and costs.

Design processes are often highly social with studio-like discussions of designs among students and teachers to consider the strengths and weaknesses of initial or mature designs. In some design circles, the review and discussions sessions are called "charrettes," which is a nineteenth-century French term associated with the Parisian École des Beaux-Arts, but modern variations might be the design reviews for websites and the agile programming approaches to software development. Such design reviews give students a chance to present their early ideas and engage in open discussions and allow divergent thinking to flourish. Scientists and engineers often make presentations of their completed work, but they could gain much by taking up the spirited discussions of emerging ideas that are normal for designers.

A strong feature of most design projects is the need to address trade-offs, especially in situations in which diverse users may have opposing needs. Using smaller fonts will allow the inclusion of more text in a Web page or brochure but make it harder to read; designing a single standard model will simplify manufacturing, training, maintenance, and so on, but the standard model may not serve the needs of all users. Additional features empower users but require longer training and increased complexity that could lead to slower performance and increased errors. Decisions about trade-offs are part of the design process, which is accomplished by thoughtful comparisons leading to team consensus or alternatively by the bold decision of an experienced forceful leader.

While structured design processes may be attractive to some designers and especially many design educators who want to teach formal processes, a large number of design theorists resist the very idea of a structured design process. They feel that structured design processes risk bringing counterproductive rigidity to problem formulation and solution. They believe that the repeated experience of doing design is the path to design excellence and bold innovations.

The design community celebrates Donald Schön's 1983 book *The Reflective Practitioner: How Professionals Think in Action* for its illuminating discussion of creative problem-solving by experienced professionals.[12] Schön builds on Michael Polyani's notion of "tacit knowledge," which humans acquire through experience but cannot express in clear rules. For example, humans can recognize a familiar face in a crowd but cannot describe how they do it. Professionals, with thousands of hours of experience, can solve challenging, unique, and novel problems such as how to treat a patient with multiple symptoms, make a winning chess board move, or pitch a baseball to a skillful batter.

Schön described how professionals, even working in novel, complex, puzzling, or ambiguous situations, manage to reflect-in-action (be self-aware in the moment of decision) and reflect-on-action (consider their recent behaviors to learn lessons that improve future behavior). While Schön used examples from psychotherapy, medicine, urban planning, and even science, designers drew inspiration from Schön's architecture and other design examples. Designers appreciated Schön's characterization of the too-strong dependence on technical rationality in science and engineering and his sympathy for experienced professionals who apply design thinking to define problems, propose possible solutions, and make choices. Many designers seek alternatives to technical rationality and formal methods, preferring their almost-mystical capacity to apply experience and find innovative solutions. Schön voices the designer belief that "in real-world practice, problems do not present themselves to the practitioner as givens. They must be constructed from the materials of problematic situations which are puzzling, troubling, and uncertain."[13]

Schön's phrase of "reflection in action" and conceptualization of the professional's capacity to see solutions in the blink of an eye was applied by many writers and popularized in Malcolm Gladwell's bestseller *Blink: The Power of Thinking without Thinking*.[14] However, it takes a long training period for designers and other professional practitioners to make quick decisions and solutions in their areas of expertise.

5.3 Design Heroes

Design heroes such as Williams Morris, Charles and Ray Eames, Raymond Loewy, and Henry Dreyfuss shaped many of our life experiences with their work on furniture, trains, telephones, kitchen tools, and thousands of other products.[15] They were effective in amplifying their impact by their influential writings, broad community of followers, and prominent disciples. Contemporary designers continue to attract consumers and delight them with home furnishings, automobiles, or consumer electronics.

Several of the compelling stories in Walter Isaacson's engaging biography of Steve Jobs describe how he pushed for excellence even though no one would see it, such as for orderly layout of circuit boards and well-designed computer back panels.[16] Jobs also recognized the importance of personal responsibility by having the designers sign the inside plastic mold for the Macintosh, even though the case was sealed. The legend and legacy of Steve Jobs grows over time, showing that design heroes can become cultural icons. His early devotion to creating excellent user experiences encouraged him to concentrate on type fonts, user interfaces, color choices, and even the "Out-of-the-Box" experience customers undergo as they unpack their purchases, putting them to work for the first time.

The growth of user experience design, usability engineering, and the academic research community devoted to human-computer interaction research shows the power of crossovers that blend science, engineering, and design.

The astonishingly rapid and pervasive impact of the World Wide Web was due, in part, to user interface research to reduce learning times, speed performance, and reduce errors while improving user satisfaction. These scientific advances, engineering breakthroughs and design innovations enabled information resources such as Google search and Wikipedia, shopping sites such as Amazon and Walmart, customer-to-customer businesses such as eBay, and health information sites such as MedlinePlus and WebMD. In Web design, the annual Webby Awards have juried selections of winners in more than 100 categories, and a People's Voice award that invites the general public to select their favorites.[17] Tiffany Shlain's thoughtful and energetic promotion of the Webby Awards has focused public attention, educated a generation of designers, and motivated organizations to give high priority to Web design.

Similarly, the rapid success of mobile devices and their broad dissemination to more than six billion users certainly benefited from the rapid improvements and cost reductions from Moore's Law. However, equally important contributions came from the scientists, engineers, and designers who studied diverse users with controlled experiments and ethnographic methods. Mobile devices do much more than support communication, music listening, and digital photography; they have become the key platform for the transformative social media technologies that are rapidly reshaping our daily lives, family relationships, and business strategies.

The next major challenges for user experience designers is to make reliable websites, mobile devices, and smart phone apps that motivate users to carry out prosocial behaviors. There is a growing literature on persuasive design strategies for encouraging voting, civic participation, citizen science, and energy conservation.[18] Similarly, healthy behaviors such as smoking cessation, obesity reduction, exercise, or cancer prevention could be dramatically increased with scientific experimentation, engineering approaches to feedback mechanisms, and design strategies to entice users. At the same time, successful persuasive design strategies could be put to work by international cybercriminals, terrorists, or malicious actors of many kinds.

The maturation of design thinking is clear in the rapidly emerging field of behavioral economics.[19] Using the language of "choice architecture," proponents such as Richard Thaler and Cass Sunstein describe how simple changes such as putting high-calorie desserts on low shelves can encourage students to choose healthier foods placed at eye level in school cafeterias.[20] Their book, *Nudge*, gives potent examples of how design can guide important life decisions such as participation in retirement or organ donation plans. Their theory of choice architecture deals with deep issues such as opting in versus opting out, ordering of choices, and delaying the start of unappealing alternatives such as contributions to retirement plans. They describe strong effects with simple variations in the language used to present choices such as focusing on positive outcomes or linking new ideas of well-accepted ones. Their research and others has already had impact in government programs and corporate strategies, as well as in academic research, where studies of choice architectures have blossomed.[21]

The important process of linking healthcare with design research and practice has begun with human factors groups more regularly addressing medical instruments, personal health management, and hospital process coordination.[22] An innovative and important contribution is emerging from architects designing hospital rooms so as to promote patient comfort and recovery. Simple principles included single rooms with more space for visiting families, natural light from larger windows, and handrails to decrease falls. Additional improvements such as reorganized call buttons to reduce false alarms and consistent layouts to lessen staff errors not only made for happier patients and staff but reduced the need for pain medications by 30% and possibly shortened hospital stays.[23]

The integration of design thinking is progressing rapidly in the business world, especially in product design and information systems technology. Alan Hevner and his colleagues advocate strongly for "design science research" to develop theories and practical improvements to business processes and information systems artifacts.[24] They believe that behavioral science, a traditional source of theory in information systems, is devoted merely to understanding organizational systems, while design science gives a more solid foundation for building innovative and effective systems. Hevner calls for a blending of theory-focused methods, which are now pervasive among information systems researchers, with more applied design research and artifact building methods. His work initiated a growing movement in the information system area, which has led to a spirited discussion of design science research roadmaps and theories of innovation, creativity, and knowledge.[25]

The great hope for design comes through clearly in a manifesto for a design-led revolution, promoted by Autodesk. They envision "a movement to use design to reinvent how we work, create, and respond to our most pressing social, environmental, and economic challenges. Driven by designers and engineers, architects and entrepreneurs, educators and makers, this movement encourages the use of sustainable design practices everywhere to provide more for people, while taking less from the planet."[26]

While there is no Nobel Prize for design, there are world-famous awards for certain branches of design, for example, the Pritzker Prize for architecture, a prize which goes back to 1979, when it was first awarded to Philip Johnson. Other "starchitect" winners include I. M. Pei, Richard Meier, Norman Foster, Jean Nouvel, and Rem Koolhaas. In 2014, the Pritzker Prize went to Shigeru Ban for his innovative use of recycled-cardboard tubes to support low-cost construction for disaster victims as well as novel, sustainable permanent buildings.

Other recognitions include the National Design Award from the Smithsonian's Cooper Hewitt Museum, which "celebrates design as a vital humanistic tool in shaping the world."[27] Its 2015 Lifetime Achievement Award went to architect Michael Graves. In addition, the British Design Awards, the London Design

Awards, the Japanese Good Design Award, Australia's Good Design Award, the President's Design Award Singapore, and the Brazil Design Award demonstrate the international enthusiasm for design.[28]

5.4 Simon's *Sciences of the Artificial*

The growing role of design in shaping the made world has been noticed by many observers. Nobel Prize-winning economist Herb Simon wrote about this distinction in his 1969 book *The Sciences of the Artificial*: "The natural sciences are concerned with how things are. . . . Design, on the other hand, is concerned with how things ought to be, with devising artifacts to attain goals."[29] Simon broadly construes design as "the core of all professional training; it is the principal mark that distinguishes the professions from the sciences. Schools of engineering, as well as schools of architecture, business, education, law, and medicine, are all centrally concerned with the process of design."[30]

In constructing a curriculum for social design, Simon wants to ensure that students will think about the design of sociotechnical systems and organizations that evolve over time. However, Simon sees design as quite separate from science. He does encourage a scientific approach to studying design and comes close to arguing for design thinking to be included in science training and research methods. Building on Simon's proposals, I envision interdisciplinary partnerships of scientists, engineers, and designers in addressing contemporary global priorities. Effective responses to healthcare, sustainability, climate change, and other problems will require deep understanding of science, engineering, and design, plus multiple research methods that are drawn from these three and possibly other disciplines.

For example, the current aspiration to create a "Learning Health System" shows the challenges of blending science, engineering, and design.[31] The idea that massive electronic health records databases could be used to understand which medications, treatment plans, and hospitals produced the best outcomes has been emerging for more than a decade.[32] While the US National Science Foundation is promoting this innovative concept, its orientation toward science, even with its growing inclusion of engineering, still needs broadening to accommodate several branches of design. Will the National Science Foundation support social system design research to enable planners to initiate, refine, and expand a national "Learning Health System" which might take decades to build? Which National Science Foundation division would house the design science research needed to make successful "Learning Health Systems"?[33] With presidential support, and a growing community of devoted researchers and health-care industry leaders, the movement to realities of governance and evaluation methods will become critical.[34] Small versions of "Learning Health Systems" are already in place, so rigorous case studies describing efforts to scale up their designs will provide valuable guidance.

The Sciences of the Artificial was an important contribution that raised the prominence of design, but the ABC principle asks for more than equal respect for design. It promotes the combination of applied and basic research by using the methods of science, engineering, and design to achieve more ambitious goals. These goals could concurrently produce novel science contributions, high-quality engineering products, and socially appropriate design innovations that are aesthetically satisfying. This is asking for a lot from a single project, but teams with diverse backgrounds and complementary methods may be able to achieve such success stories.

5.5 Anticipation through Design Thinking

This idea of new forms or research that blend disciplines has been advanced before, notably by the remarkably visionary Buckminster Fuller, whose "comprehensive anticipatory design science" has much in common with the ABC principle.[35] Fuller's vision, sometimes wrapped in daunting language, was to break down specialist barriers, think comprehensively, anticipate the future, and design artifacts that promote positive human behaviors. His prolific writings, speeches, and innovations live on with the work of the Buckminster Fuller Institute, which promotes his ideas.

Fuller's early awareness of environmental dangers led him to focus on designing homes, lifestyles, and industries that would support a sustainable future. Most well-known is his lightweight elegant geodesic dome, yet he had greater hopes for his dymaxion home designs, which were meant to provide widely available, energy-efficient, comfortable housing. Fuller's global perspective led him to develop the World Peace Game (later the World Game), designed to give participants an understanding of the interconnectedness of all life on the planet that he called "Spaceship Earth."[36] His design-thinking strategy, called "synergetics," clearly stated that the "behavior of whole systems is unpredicted by the behavior of their parts taken separately."[37] This antireductionist world model is at odds with the traditional scientific methods of the past four centuries but wisely anticipates what is needed to deal with the challenges of the made world.

CASE STUDY 5.1 SEBASTIAN SEUNG

Role Model for Researcher Transformation

Sebastian Seung

http://blog.eyewire.org/play-eyewire-and-contribute-to-neuroscience-research-at-mit/

An inspiring example of redirection is the double transformation of Sebastian Seung, a brilliant teenager who soon earned a Harvard Ph.D. in theoretical physics, gained early tenure at MIT, and then achieved full professor status. His first shift was from physics to theoretical neuroscience, aligning his work with a contemporary hot topic that blended disciplines. His basic research on mathematical theories of brain functioning were widely followed, but Seung realized that to achieve his goal of understanding the human brain he needed to follow actual connections, down to the level of individual neurons. This kind of deep understanding of actual behavior, very much in the spirit of the ABC principle, could lead to solutions of dementia or other neurological pathologies.

His second shift took him from theoretical neuroscience to engineering and design, making him a poster child for the SED principle. Seung and two graduate students realized that scaling up high-resolution brain imaging by a factor of millions was necessary to collect the details of a human brain's connections. Scaling up required extensive efforts from his team to advance imaging technology and software engineering. Seung ignored the latent antipathy to applied research that brought complaints from "the more snobbish circles of theoretical neuroscience" who saw Seung's direction as "too blue-collar."[1]

He persisted in his massive engineering endeavor, then went down an innovative design path to create a competitive online game, EyeWire, that drew 165,000 people to help track the path of individual neurons.[2] Seung's embrace of design thinking for game design became an important success story in the citizen science movement. He made a sharp comment about the vast potential of these new research methods: "Think of what we could do if we could capture even a small fraction of the mental effort that goes into Angry Birds."[3]

Sebastian Seung's story is emblematic of the new spirit of research. He shifted to take on contemporary problems in neuroscience, went from basic to applied research, built a research team, and then embraced methods from science, engineering, and design. It's rare when one person, even a special person like Seung, can lead a team that takes on all these roles, but the payoffs have been enormous. Seung has a realistic long-term perspective on his efforts, described thus by the journalist who interviewed him: "Science progresses when its practitioners find answers—this is the way of glory—but also when they make something that future generations rely on, even if they take it for granted."[4]

---

[1] Cook, G., Sebastian Seung's quest to map the human brain, *New York Times Sunday Magazine* (January 11, 2015) http://www.nytimes.com/2015/01/11/magazine/sebastian-seungs-quest-to-map-the-human-brain.html.

[2] Eyewire, *About Eyewire, A Game to Map the Brain* (Accessed August 3, 2015) http://blog.eyewire.org/about/.

[3] Cook, G., Sebastian Seung's quest to map the human brain, *New York Times Sunday Magazine* (January 11, 2015)http://www.nytimes.com/2015/01/11/magazine/sebastian-seungs-quest-to-map-the-human-brain.html.

[4] Ibid.

Some see Fuller as an unrealistic visionary thinker whose extremely optimistic goals such as "make the world work for 100% of humanity, in the shortest possible time, through spontaneous cooperation, without ecological offense or the disadvantage of anyone" were not attainable.[38] Of course, setting ambitious goals can sometimes catalyze fresh ideas and bold actions that make progress in surprising ways. "Bucky" was one of my heroes and helped inspire my devotion to combining applied and basic research while blending science, engineering, and design.

Bucky had strong influence on those who followed him, such as Herb Simon and Nigel Cross. Cross became a persuasive and effective leader and in 1966 formed the Design Research Society, which in 1979 began to publish the journal *Design Studies*. He sought to make design more of a subject of scientific studies and to make design processes more research-like, but it is possible to argue that he also sought to make scientific methods more design-like.[39] His book on *Engineering Design Methods* describes systematic ways to carry out design research so as to collect user requirements, develop new designs, and evaluate design products.[40]

As a design science leader, John Gero also promoted scientific studies of design through his writings and by becoming Professor of Design Science at the University of Sydney. Gero was especially influential through organizing conferences and workshops, which led to edited collections of papers on design science. With inspiration from Fuller, Simon, Cross, and Gero, many others took design science more seriously, leading to clarifications of design science and design thinking.[41] Extreme efforts at theorizing sometimes yielded abstract mathematical formulations based on matrix theory and linear algebra, far removed from the design methods and design thinking but possibly laying the foundation for future formulations.

Computer scientist Gerhard Fischer at the University of Colorado Boulder developed theories of design for sociotechnical systems based on novel principles of metadesign and cultures of participation.[42] Metadesign is about designing systems that enable users to build other systems, thus amplifying the power of designers and speeding up the iteration process. Cultures of participation are communities with intense interaction, which stimulates new ideas, supports testing, provides feedback, and disseminates results. Fischer showed data on how a corporate discussion group could be improved with a simple change: when the number of comments made by each individual was made visible, it shortened response times for questions and increased participation.

Inspired by these efforts at scientific studies of design, Cynthia Atman at the University of Washington conducted detailed studies of designers at work. A key paper, published in Nigel Cross's journal *Design Studies* revealed that experienced designers spent substantial time in the early stages of defining the problem and proposing divergent ideas and then made steady progress in converging on a solution. By contrast, novice designers moved toward a solution quickly but then floundered and backtracked in revising their solution. The activities in her recommended design method included

- problem definition—identify need,
- gather information,
- generate ideas (brainstorm and list alternatives),
- modeling (describe how to build),
- feasibility analysis,
- evaluation (compare alternatives),
- decision (select one solution),
- communication (write or present to others), and
- implementation.[43]

A key feature in Atman's design method is the large number of steps required before a decision is made to commit to a solution, followed by the communication of the solution to gain commitments and feedback for refinement. Only then does implementation begin. This strategy is well aligned with building practices, in which architectural plans are completed and approved before construction begins; however, in some fields, such as software engineering, there is often a strong urge to write code before the design is complete. It may simply be that mature design fields develop stronger principles of "planful" activity, whereas emerging fields rely more on prototyping, testing, refinement, and revision.

Design processes and their relationship to science and engineering continue to produce lively discussions. Erik Stolterman points out that science research is tied strongly to rigorous methods, while design research emphasizes the quality of the outcome, no matter what methods were used.[44] The latter strategy reflects the more freewheeling, brainstorming, wild-idea-generation methods of design research. However, design excellence also depends on iterative refinement, rigorous testing with diverse users, and clarity about why a design succeeds. Design is a unique way of thinking that engages with stakeholders, reflects on ethics, and is devoted to human values.[45]

Design research and practice generate effective and possibly enjoyable products or services, as well as theories and principles. The most successful designs, such as the Apple iPhone or the Facebook social network, provoke discussions over the causes of their success, and practical guidelines that can be applied in related contexts.

5.6 Design Education

Design schools have flourished in recent years, probably because of the opportunities in business and the growing recognition that designers play powerful roles in shaping our world. Famed design-thinking firms such as IDEO are celebrated for their creative culture.[46] Another stimulus to students going into design is the growth of colleges and departments, whose websites and brochures make design exciting. SCAD (the Savannah College of Art and Design) trains students for a professional career, especially focusing on advanced technology skills, while "promoting a cooperative team spirit and a positive 'can-do' attitude."[47]

Even traditional schools with existing strengths, such as the Rhode Island School of Design (RISD) are "challenging assumptions" as they become leaders in digital media and interactive arts.[48] Their grander vision is to transform education nationally: "STEM to STEAM is a RISD-led initiative to add Art and Design to the national agenda of STEM (Science, Technology, Engineering, Math) education and research in America. STEM + Art = STEAM. The goal is to foster the true innovation that comes with combining the mind of a scientist or technologist with that of an artist or designer."[49]

The Stanford d.school (The Hasso Plattner Institute of Design) claims to be "a hub for innovators . . . to take on the world's messy problems together. . . . We focus on creating spectacularly transformative learning experiences." Their commitment to real-world problems has a broad reach: "Our deliberate mashup of industry, academia, and the big world beyond campus is a key to our continuing evolution." They promote not just collaboration but "radical collaboration" to "move quickly beyond obvious ideas."[50] The d.school's variation on the design process has five steps: empathize, define, ideate, prototype, and test. This human-centered process starts from a deep commitment to empathy so as to identify human needs, which are then distilled into an actionable clarification of the problem. The focused problem statement supports a prolific divergent thinking festival of wild ideas often presented as sketches or mock-ups. Then a calmer, more rational, convergent phase leads to a refined prototype that can be shown to stakeholders, tested with intended users, and further refined.[51]

OCAD University, formerly The Ontario College of Art and Design, calls itself "the university of the imagination."[52] Among its distinctions is its emphasis on inclusive design research, which "considers the full range of human diversity with respect to ability, language, culture, gender, age and other forms of human difference. . . . Designing inclusively results in better experiences for everyone."[53] A prime example of inclusivity benefiting everyone are the curb cuts for wheelchair users, as these also enable travelers with roller bags, parents with baby strollers, and delivery workers with pushcarts. A second example of inclusive design thinking is closed captioning for deaf users, as displaying audio content as text reduces noise in public spaces, facilitates language learning, creates string searches for content, and improves the reliability of automatic translation.

Design thinking can also be seen in the student-oriented inspirational community Design for America. Their vision is of "a world where people believe in their ability to innovate and tackle the most ill-structured challenges of our time. Our mission is to develop a pipeline of leaders of innovation and create impact through the implementation of . . . projects."[54] Founded by Northwestern University professor Liz Gerber, Design for America puts students to work on authentic challenges to cultivate a can-do attitude that she calls "innovation self-efficacy" and focuses on diverse student teams to "create fervently and act fearlessly."[55] This admirable educational effort engages students in design projects that address societal problems and could produce important impacts. However, better alignment with the ABC principle would come if she added a basic research component, which would ensure that students read related work and published their results as research outcomes for others to build on.

The graduates of design schools often become communication and graphic designers who produce brochures, advertisements, or Web pages for the vast global consumer culture. It is a highly competitive environment, so excellence in design is valued greatly. Some companies engage hundreds of people to design a single product, which could reach billions of users. Apple's iPhone is by now the classic example of how design excellence can help create the world's most valuable company. Steve Jobs comes across as a brilliant but arrogant designer who knew what he wanted and pushed on his team very hard to deliver highly polished designs.

Apple is among the most celebrated user experience design companies, but information communication and technology companies employ thousands of dedicated designers who promote a growing awareness in employees and management about the importance of design excellence. My own book, *Designing the User Interface: Strategies for Effective Human-Computer Interaction*, first published in 1986,[56] has been joined by many successful alternative books that present the diverse topics covered by the ACM SIGCHI (the Association for Computing Machinery Special Interest Group on Computer-Human Interaction).[57] The annual international CHI (computer-human interaction) conference draws 3000+ attendees, while hundreds of smaller conferences on specialized topics are held in countries around the world. Popular books such as Don Norman's *Design of Everyday Things* have brought user experience design issues to broad audiences, raising awareness of the central role of design processes and thinking in shaping our world.[58]

5.7 Design Roadmaps and Challenges

Designers are often in the position of responding to challenges and so formulating roadmaps and discussing challenges in a fresh theme. Still there are intriguing reports to read with visionary statements. For example, in 2007 Microsoft Research convened a >40-person group that prepared a bold vision of how design would impact human experiences. The editors of the resulting report wrote that "the design of computers is helping to create a new socio-digital landscape . . . [we] can make the world we live in one to celebrate rather than fear."[59] Their challenges included the need to cope with increased technology dependency with its shifting balance of control and still greater social connectivity that intensifies community while reducing the time for personal reflection. The report celebrates the potential to amplify human abilities but wonders about what happens when so many people become experts who create and innovate broadly.

My own efforts at defining a design research roadmap for human-computer interaction include these design-related aspirations:

- *Shift from user experience to community experience:* Fresh thinking could improve social media participation, game theoretic mechanisms, and motivational strategies. Successful examples such as Wikipedia or citizen science projects show what is possible, but the most common outcome is failure, raising the question of how could the frequency of successful outcomes be increased.

- *Refine theories of persuasion:* A periodic table of persuasion strategies would chart the microstructure of motivation for designers who create applications for individuals, friends and family, colleagues and neighbors, and citizens and markets.
- *Accelerate analytic clarity:* Well-integrated visual interfaces and statistical techniques could accelerate understanding that would lead to confident and bold decisions to improve individual, community, and planetary welfare.
- *Amplify empathy, compassion, and caring:* Compassionate and caring actions make life better and more satisfying for individuals, families, and communities.
- *Secure cyberspace:* Designing for usable privacy and security will help ensure that benefits are retained, intrusions minimized, and expectations of safety realized.
- *Encourage reflection, calmness, and mindfulness:* Reflection about life's challenges, the needs of less fortunate people, end-of-life decisions, and the digital afterlife, while difficult, could lead to comforting clarity.
- *Clarify responsibility and accountability:* Interfaces that clarify users' responsibility for their actions by making decisions and their outcomes visible, and sometimes public, could promote responsible user behavior. Similarly, algorithmic accountability would more openly expose the inner workings of algorithms, which are written by programmers, so that users could make better decisions about using the algorithm's results.

While many grand challenges in engineering (discussed in Chapter 4) have a strong design component, the design research community has yet to provide its set of design challenges that would have broad impact.

5.8 Skeptics' Corner

There is a dark side to design as well. Many designs fail to achieve their goals and can easily have unintended consequences. Design is difficult and unpredictable, making the trajectory of cost-effective implementation with broad dissemination far more complex than the elegant arc of science. Could the designers of automobiles have anticipated that their immense success would spawn traffic jams, urban sprawl, millions of accident deaths, and environmental destruction? Sociotechnical systems are notoriously volatile, so that even initial design successes can turn sour quickly.

Science skeptics of my encouragement to blend scientific discovery with design thinking have made clear that they believe their research is already challenging enough and that they do not want to get involved with design and implementation projects. Similarly, designers have spoken up for freedom in exploring new directions, which they feel will be constricted by the requirement to take scientific approaches that require digging deep into theory, measurement, and rigorous assessment. Some designers resist the expectation that they must write about their outcomes, insisting that the design speaks for itself. Both camps would rather keep to their traditions than have to respond to the raised expectations of blending disciplines, applying new research methods, and promoting their contributions in the marketplace of ideas.

5.9 Summary

Design thinking is tied to deeply understanding human needs, persistently reformulating the given problem, and continuously reconsidering the goals. Designers like to produce multiple divergent solutions, seek input from stakeholders, and engage in spirited teamwork critiques. At some point, design team leaders acknowledge the limits of time and resources, forcing them to converge on a potential solution. Enhancements and fresh ideas can be integrated as initial models get refined into more polished prototypes. Ultimately, the commitment to production gets made, but successful products can have a long life of continuous improvements.

Design methods for research and practice often lean to playfulness, openness to novelty, and sympathy for serendipity, while also keeping in mind the legitimate needs of users and the serious goals for clients. Designers are usually devoted to frequent engagement with all stakeholders (users, clients, colleagues, etc.), giving them a different perspective than scientists or engineers would. I hope design researchers will increasingly combine theory and practice, become more devoted to evaluation, and seek peer-reviewed publication that describes their processes and products.

Addressing the pressing sociotechnical design problems of the twenty-first century appears to require a blend of science, engineering, and design (the SED principle). Achieving the lofty ambitions of the ABC principle will take effort but could produce influential basic and applied research outcomes.

The first two parts of this book describe the guiding principles (the ABC and SED princples) and the component disciplines of science, engineering, and design, as part of a unified seed-root-flower metaphor. Of course, there is value in other disciplines such as mathematics, fine arts, humanities, and philosophy, but this book emphasizes science, engineering, and design. The third part of this book describes the five research life cycle strategies that could guide researchers to accomplish more ambitious goals.

PART III

Research Life Cycle Strategies

The five research life cycle strategies presented in the introduction are described in detail in the next five chapters. Taken together, they provide a classic case of the whole being larger than the sum of its parts: together, they create even more opportunities than when they are applied separately, as research leaders seek appropriate partners to define problems and then work with those partners to validate theories, using traditional research methods in fresh contexts. Academic, business, and government partnerships based on genuine problems, often smooth the way to successful technology transfer. These strategies emphasize the use of small research teams and larger collaborations, so that prototypes can be tested quickly to support scaling up (increased size) and scaling out (increased diversity). As solutions are found, these teams can reach out to their diverse audiences to promote the research results, while carefully measuring impact.

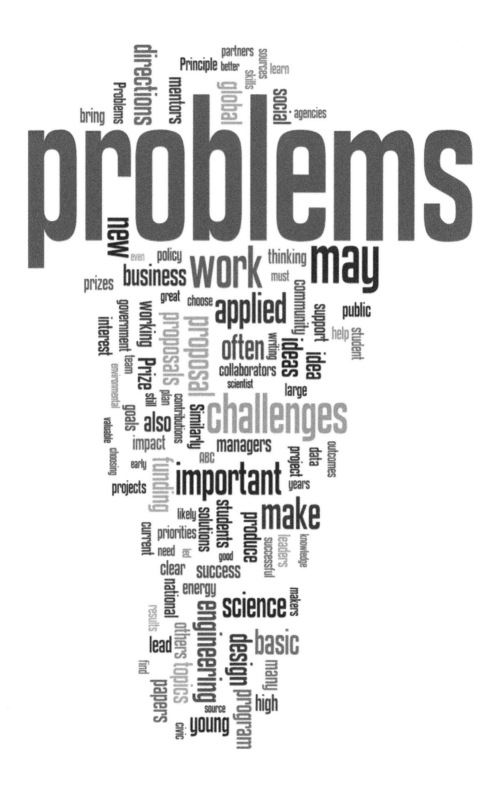

CHAPTER 6

Choose Actionable Problems that Address Civic, Business, and Global Priorities

The *choice of problem* is often the most important act of all in analytical work: the idea is to find *important* problems that can be *solved*. This requires a certain self-awareness on the part of the researcher.

Edward Tufte

6.1 Introduction

The problems of the twenty-first century present serious challenges for researchers, managers, politicians, and every person. Population growth, energy consumption, and environmental preservation are byproducts of successful growth, but the massive human influence on natural surroundings now presents profound challenges. Furthermore, the huge number of people on Planet Earth means that food production, healthcare delivery, and wellness become qualitatively more difficult problems. As urbanization rates increase, it raises new questions of community safety, adequate housing, and efficient transportation.

While all these problems have scientific components that build on knowledge of the natural world, engineering and design skills are major components of

The New ABCs of Research. First Edition. Ben Shneiderman.
© Ben Shneiderman 2016. Published in 2016 by Oxford University Press.

solutions. Resolving the global problems requires partnership with innovative engineers and creative designers of the made world. Science remains valuable, but blending science with engineering and design will produce higher payoffs in terms of basic research discoveries and applied research innovations.

Design thinking may help scientists reformulate their questions, encourage them to get out of their lab and talk to patients about their treatments, interview farmers about their use of water and energy, or visit developing nations to see their problems first-hand. Engineers and scientists could partner with designers to teach them how to better model, simulate, measure, and evaluate reward systems for energy reduction, motivational mechanisms for smoking cessation, or social proof plans for carbon offset programs.

Choosing Actionable Problems Triggers Great Research

Working on real problems with real data can lead to real solutions and enable theory validation in living laboratories.

6.2 Real Problems, Real Data, Real Solutions

Contributing to research by solving contemporary civic, business, and global priorities has an attractive dual-use or twin-win appeal for many researchers. Civic problems could be broadly defined to include neighborhood safety, campus environmental commitment, community soup kitchen development, or town hall organizing. Research skills can also help community leaders analyze policy alternatives, support consumer advocates, or help animal welfare groups. Increasingly popular "hackathons" bring programmers and others to work on civic problems; one example is the DataBay Innovation Challenge, which Maryland's governor launched to increase public engagement in restoring the Chesapeake Bay.[1] Hundreds of public hackathons or "data dives" tied to civic problems draw increasing numbers of enthusiastic researchers and practitioners who want to apply their skills to meaningful problems.

The growing movement toward "Open Data" for government, environmental data, medicine, and other fields but protection for individual privacy is a positive sign that researchers can make meaningful contributions to real problems. A related success story is the growth of citizen science projects that include amateur scientists working with professional scientists to collect large amounts

CASE STUDY 6.1 NATHAN EAGLE
An Individual as a Role Model for the
ABC Principle
Nathan Eagle, CEO of Jana
(http://alumni.media.mit.edu/~nathan/bio.html)

Skilled interdisciplinary thinking can sometimes solve practical problems and produce high-impact research results in a short time. Nathan Eagle has quickly gained a reputation for clever work at the intersection of engineering and sociotechnical systems. His recognition came while working in Africa, which few researchers see as the prime destination for career building. With his MIT Ph.D. in hand, he went to Kenya, taking a position in a district hospital in Kilifi, located outside Kenya's major port, Mombasa.

Eagle's story begins with a unsettling request from hospital nurses to donate blood for an emergency transfusion to victims of a road accident. Any needle pokes in HIV-prone African regions would raise concerns, but Eagle had a long history of fearing injections. He suppressed his anxieties and donated blood, but when blood donation requests recurred several more times he wanted to understand why the regional blood-bank system could not adequately serve local needs.

The apparent problem was that inventory listings of the blood supplies at the local blood bank was poor so, working with his University of Nairobi students, Eagle developed a text-messaging system that enabled local nurses in Kilifi to send messages requesting additional supplies to the regional blood bank in Mombasa. This technology fix was well received and celebrated as a successful intervention, but within a week nurses stopped sending text messages. The reason for the drop in participation was obvious; since nurses had to use their own phones, they wound up paying to request blood supplies when their local reserves dwindled.

Working with the regional phone company, Eagle arranged that text messages to the blood bank would not incur charges and, better than that, nurses who sent timely requests earned a small credit for their personal phone accounts. This small incentive for the nurses produced daily updates, while giving the phone companies good publicity and more devoted customers.

Eagle believed that small, phone-based incentives could trigger mass participation in civic, educational, and commercial projects in developing nations. His growing reputation and MIT connections produced start-up funding, which led to the formation of a new company, which was eventually named Jana (Sanskrit for "people"), with global aspirations.[1] Jana's business model is to "redirect the world's advertising dollars to airtime. Consumers in emerging markets spend ten percent of their daily wage on mobile airtime. If we can redirect half of the $200 billion currently spent on advertising in the developing world into the pockets of the consumers our clients are trying to reach, it would provide one billion people with the equivalent of a 5 percent raise."[2]

If international media buzz is an indicator, then Jana is on the road to success. Stories in *The Guardian, The New York Times*, CNN, *The Economist, WIRED*, and elsewhere trumpet Eagle's insight that social mechanisms can trigger vast participation in emerging markets by way of mobile devices. Eagle's blend of applied research in field study situations, and his emerging theory of social participation, support the belief that design interventions can catalyze prosocial activities to stimulate economies, improve health, and support education.

While it might be easy to see Eagle's effort as strictly commercial, his continuing stream of research papers show his commitment to basic research results which can be widely applied.[3] For example, the simple shift to micropayments for participation amplifies willingness to participate in socially beneficial efforts.

In addition to his role with Jana, he bridges to academic research within Harvard's School of Public Health by participating in an innovative interdisciplinary group called Engineering Social Systems, which seeks to promote global health and improved education by using mobile technologies. Their website promotes "big data for social good" by collecting a "wealth of information that promises to provide insights about the complex behavior of human societies."[4]

Eagle writes:

Ultimately, my research agenda is focused on generating actionable insights about complex social systems that can improve the lives of the billions of people who generate this data and the societies in which they live.[5]

Nathan Eagle's story of commercial success, academic contributions, and research results is admirable. He is a role model for other young researchers and also an inspiration for interdisciplinary teams, but skeptics will want to see if his impact produces durable changes and continuing research results.

---

[1] Jana, *Jana* (2015) http://www.jana.com.
[2] BBJ Focus: 13 Cool Startups to Watch, *Boston Business Journal* (July 26, 2013) http://www.bizjournals.com/boston/print-edition/2013/07/26/bbj-focus-13-cool-startups-to-watch.html?page=all.
[3] Harvard School of Public Health, Engineering Social Systems, *Publications* (Accessed August 5, 2015) http://www.hsph.harvard.edu//ess/publications.html.
[4] Harvard School of Public Health, Engineering Social Systems, *Big Data for Social Good* (Accessed August 5, 2015) http://www.hsph.harvard.edu/ess/bigdata.html.
[5] Harvard T. H. Chan School of Public Health, *Nathan Eagle* (2015) http://www.hsph.harvard.edu/nathan-eagle/.

---

of data about bird migrations, invasive plants, mushrooms, and much more.[2] Although the term citizen science has caught on, a great deal of the research is about how to engineer massive data collections and design interfaces to validate submissions. The research goals lean toward ensuring high-quality data and designing social structures to encourage, recognize, and reward contributors in ways that catalyze a durable supportive community.

A long-term success story comes from computer scientist Alan Borning and his University of Washington team, who developed the UrbanSim Project, which offers innovative collaborative simulation tools for city planners. Urban-Sim enables mayors, city councils, agency heads, and citizen groups to better understand the implications of their decisions on land use, the economy, transportation, and the environment, while the dozens of research papers generated by the project make important advances in science, engineering, and design.[3]

Business problems are a second attractive source of research problems, with the additional benefit that student internship or faculty consulting opportunities could become part of the package.[4] Students often have part-time or summer jobs that could provide the stimulus for a research project. A team of my students developed a promising prototype for a large marketing company to visualize customer walking patterns within a shopping center, thereby pushing the students to develop advanced algorithms to distill video data into actionable geospatial movement patterns.

Global priorities are a third source for research projects. Sometimes summer study abroad programs can bring young researchers in contact with international opportunities through study program contacts and nongovernmental organizations. Groups such as Engineers Without Borders seek to engage researchers to work on global priorities.[5] Nathan Eagle's clever use of mobile devices to ensure timely blood-bank resupply in Kenya produced a generalizable strategy that led to basic research publications and a start-up company (see Case Study 6.1 in Section 6.2).

Civic, business, and global partners can be helpful mentors, sources of financial support, and reviewers of work as it progresses. Each can also present problems and limitations that require careful negotiations to resolve. Civic problems may bring entanglements with local politics and strong egos that may need encouragement to make changes from traditional approaches. Business problems can lead to intellectual property discussions, conflicts of interest, or a lack of support for research publication orientation. Similarly, working on global problems requires learning about other cultures and can entail legal obstacles or other barriers to collaboration.

Dealing with these real-world problems may improve the research products and raise their impact. Having interested collaborators is a great stimulus for producing high quality, since someone cares about the research results and might put them to work promptly to improve products or services. Of course, dealing with real-world problems may produce resistance from academic colleagues, so researchers first need to find a compelling combination of theoretical foundations and practical projects and then consult with mentors. Each research team will have to find its own way to apply this book's ABC principle, which states that a combined strategy produces higher-impact results in applied and basic domains. Similarly, each research team will have to decide how to blend the methods of science, engineering, and design (the SED principle) to make progress.

6.3 A Theory of Problem Selection: Students and Young Researchers

There is a large body of research on how scientists, engineers, and designers solve problems, but much less attention to how they choose problems. However, choosing good problems can be the most important part of a research project, since it lays the foundation for all that follows. Thinking that others must have studied this topic, I did a Google search on "theory of problem selection," but found only one paper dealing with how the US Senate sets its agenda.[6] Some classic books such as Medawar's *Advice to a Young Scientist* steer novice researchers to work on "important problems" so as to have high impact:

It can be said with complete confidence that any scientist at any age who wants to make important discoveries must study important problems. Dull or piffling problems yield dull or piffling answers. It is not enough that the problem should be interesting: almost any problem is interesting if it is studied in sufficient detail. . . . the problem should be such that it *matters* what the answer is—whether to science generally or to mankind.[7]

Medawar does not characterize important problems, nor does he include engineers and designers, but his devotion to focus on important problems is still valuable. By contrast, systems biologist Uri Alon describes problems along the two axes of feasibility (easy to hard) and knowledge gain (small to large), suggesting that the easy problems that produce large knowledge gains are the ones to choose.[8] This is obvious advice, but knowing in advance which problems will be easy and produce large knowledge gains is itself an annoyingly difficult problem. Alon reassuringly encourages young researchers to listen to their "inner voice" and strengthen it by talking to "caring mentors."

Another classic source is Beveridge's *Art of Scientific Investigation*, which offers this advice about making contributions and aligning work with skills:

The student with any real talent for research usually has no difficulty in finding a suitable problem . . . It is best for the research student to start with a problem in which there is a good chance of . . . accomplishing something, and, of course, which is not beyond . . . [the student's] technical capabilities.[9]

Beveridge hints at the ABC principle by suggesting that applied research can trigger deep thoughts that lead to basic science contributions. His wording anticipates what later became Stokes's phrase: "use-inspired basic research."

The continuing shift to combining applied and basic research is prevalent in Thompson's contemporary "Advice to a Young Researcher," in which Thompson broadens his audience to include engineers and designers.[10] Thompson has practical suggestions about finding institutions with funding and equipment, as well as collaborators and mentors who will guide a young researcher's work. This is in the great tradition of apprenticeship, which for centuries has been a common engineering and design training method in which students learn from mentors by working on existing problems that are presented to them.

Traditionally, young researchers develop ideas of what is important by reading current research publications and announcements of conferences or journal special issues. But now young researchers have access to broader sources of inspiration, such as popular science, engineering, and design magazines, or general press articles that highlight promising research directions. These broader sources are more likely to be tied to national initiatives, which are often described in research roadmaps such as US, European, Asian, and so on, initiatives on cybersecurity, desalinization, visualization, renewable energy, and healthcare. These public discussions around national initiatives can give young researchers references to key researcher centers and potential civic, business, or global partners.

As Beveridge notes, working on a problem for three or more years requires intense enthusiasm to generate the necessary persistence, even in the face of setbacks. The ABC principle may help young researchers by bringing them in contact with sympathetic collaborators who are their civic, business, or global partners. Feedback from these collaborators and initial applied research successes can help build the passion, perseverance, and resources necessary to validate their results while producing theoretical generalizations.

There are legitimate dangers that applied projects produce longer delays, coordination is time-consuming, and debates about differing agendas delay progress. Teamwork is difficult, but the payoffs can be high (Chapter 8). Civic, business, and global partners can also help bolster commitments during the inevitable troughs when papers are rejected or competing researchers make important advances. Like so much of research, success depends on a healthy blend of personal reflection and social interaction.

6.4 A Theory of Problem Selection: Senior Researchers and Policymakers

Senior researchers also face challenges in choosing problems for their future work, especially if the funding priorities are changing and new topics are emerging. The temptation and encouragement to keep working on the same problems that previously provided success is great, but most researchers change topics every few years, pursuing the low-hanging fruit, then moving on to other topics, often in nearby areas.

Sometimes topics will revive as new demands or technologies arise, such as in database systems, where the commercial success of relational database systems led to reduced research interest until new problems such as temporal or network databases restored interest. New technologies such as map/reduce algorithms, graph databases, and text analytics invigorated research in managing and exploiting big data resources. Senior researchers may be skeptical about these ideas, seeing them as renamed and hyped versions of old ideas. However, following fashionable topics is very appealing to many researchers since widespread interest in "hot" topics can bring funding and lead to high impact.

Business research managers and university administrators face similar challenges in choosing which directions to support, while keeping in mind national and global priorities. As one of IBM's research leaders told me, "I've never seen a bad proposal from my staff. My job is to separate out the very good from the excellent proposals." But the definition of excellence has many dimensions, such as the intrinsic interest in an established general problem or need for new research tools that emerge from science, engineering, or design. IBM Research has an admirable track record in developing patent portfolios that provide substantial licensing income.

Business research managers must also achieve reasonable financial payoffs within the proposed schedule and budget. Successful managers are aware of the competitive landscape so they know which directions could yield advantages as opposed to working on problems where others are far ahead. University administrators must choose from faculty proposals for new institutes and research programs, with an eye to how they fit existing strengths while supporting future directions, as well as their potential for attracting outside funding, alumni donors, and international attention.

The selection of research problems is an issue for politicians and government policymakers who seek to set national agendas that will have high impacts on prestige while stimulating economic development and job creation. They gather input from active researchers but must also consider the political realities of which agendas will appeal to powerful Congressional and business leaders. Such policymakers may have other goals as well, such as promoting their own futures, and backing the wishes of national leaders.

As an example of national priorities, current US interest in understanding the human brain has many attractions, applications, and directions, but the US BRAIN (Brain Research through Advancing Innovative Neurotechnologies) Initiative focused on using neurotechnology tools to map the brain.[11] This initiative has a creative blend of science, engineering, and design (the SED principle) that is well crafted to appeal to broad constituencies and produce high impact. Similarly, the European initiative on brain research set ambitious goals that provoked productive controversy within the scientific community.

6.5 Forming the Research Plan

Once a research team chooses its initial research directions, reading previous work may reveal that others researchers have already solved the most prominent problems or, more happily, that solutions seem possible. Research journals were the traditional source, but conference papers, Web resources, and social media are increasingly important. Modern sources such as blogs, lab project pages, open publications, Wikipedia, Facebook, and Twitter provide rapidly accessible resources that are up to date. More importantly, they enable researchers to post questions, send email, and seek collaborations across a broader community that can bring applied and basic research challenges.

Another early step will be to ensure that the necessary resources or technologies are easily available and that colleagues, collaborators, and mentors are supportive of combining applied and basic research (the ABC principle). If these hurdles are overcome, researchers can push forward, but they will need to establish a constructive relationship with their administrators and collaborators. As young researchers begin to produce meaningful results that constitute valuable contributions, they will face other challenges in presenting, promoting, and disseminating their work.[12]

While reading background papers is important, most guides encourage jumping in to take the first steps on a problem. Actually doing research with available equipment and knowledge helps clarify the problem, triggering fresh thinking that leads to multiple solution strategies. Such agile early explorations may lead to visits with peers and mentors to gauge their support, elicit guidance, and build a network of those with shared interests. Clear definitions of the problem, existing solutions, and working backward from the goal helps solidify the research plan.

Giving a presentation to a group often produces dramatic payoffs, but even more important is writing the research narrative. The process of communicating by speaking, sketching, and writing guides thinking, shapes plans, and often produces solutions.[13] Some researchers may be more verbal, visual, or textual, but trying the less familiar modes can produce fresher thinking and clearer presentations.[14]

I expect students working with me to make a 1-page proposal that begins with a clear title, describes the problem, cites a few previous works, outlines their solution, and gives a short schedule. When appropriate, I ask my students to find an outside mentor who cares about the solution of the problem and send a copy to them to engage with them on refining the proposal. Finally, I expect there to be a balance between applied and basic research, invoking the two parents and three children pattern (see Chapter 2).

A now-famous list of questions about new research proposals was formulated by DARPA director George Heilmeier, and is still widely used under the names "Heilmeier's catechism" or "Heilmeier's criteria":[15]

1. What is the problem, why is it hard?
2. How is it solved today?
3. What is your new technical idea; why can you succeed now?
4. What is the impact if successful; who cares?
5. What are your midterm and final "exams" to measure progress and success?
6. What are the risks?
7. How long will it take?
8. What will it cost?

The clear specific questions are helpful in formulating a plan and thinking ahead to risks and measures of success. One management strategy for project managers whose planning is complete is to write a letter looking back on the project and explaining why it failed. This exercise helps highlight the dangers so as to address them early.

Many books and websites suggest strategies for research innovation and discovery.[16] Computer scientist Nick Feamster's blog post describes research patterns for finding and solving problems, including considering related problems, making analogies, considering nature, and working backward from the goal.[17] He also supports staying relaxed and letting "your subconscious work," following the great traditions of Henri Poincaré's country outings or Friedrich Kekulé's famed dream of a snake biting its tail—the dream which gave him the idea of benzene's ring structure.

Finding a compelling problem that has applied and basic components and invokes passionate commitment are vital starting points, but still more is needed. The next step is to read funding program descriptions to clarify what research policy leaders believe are important problems. Submitting a proposal and winning an award helps confirm the value of a research proposal and provides funding to support it. The US National Science Foundation and other funding agencies solicit proposals through hundreds of well-crafted program announcements.[18] Similarly the UK Engineering and Physical Sciences Research Council, the European Research Council, the Japan Society for the Promotion of Science, the Australian Research Council, the Canadian National Science and Engineering Council, the Brazilian CNPq, and other agencies have long lists of topics with detailed descriptions.[19]

Understanding how these government agencies, corporate funders, and private foundations operate requires time and energy. Government agencies typically fund only 5%–15% of the proposals they receive, usually by way of anonymous peer-review panels. Corporate funders and private foundations operate more on a personal basis, so building a relationship with technical partners and program managers can increase the chances of gaining funding. The inevitable proposal rejection is hard to take, but read the reviews carefully, revise the proposal, clarify methods and goals, and try again. Reviewers may have misunderstood the work plan, but don't blame them. Instead, consider how to improve the writing to make a clearer and more compelling proposal. Persistence is an important attribute for research success.

6.6 Rejection and Redirection

Most research projects start with enthusiasm and grand hopes. Most research projects also struggle with failures such as rejected papers and grant proposals.

Competitive conferences have acceptance rates of 15%–20%, a fact which means that 80%–85% of papers are rejected. Many reviewers provide feedback that is valuable and constructive, but they can be just plain nasty and unreasonably dismissive. It is tempting for reviewers to show off their devotion to rigor by being harshly critical, especially when hiding behind the barrier of anonymous reviewing and speaking through the narrow channel of a written report.

As a graduate student, I developed a novel flowcharting technique that my fellow student Isaac Nassi helped polish into a full paper. We called it structured flowcharting, to align with the then novel idea of structured programming and submitted our precious idea to a leading refereed publication.[20] In just a few weeks, we received a rejection from the editor, who attached the harshest review I have ever seen: "the best thing the authors could do is collect all copies of this technical report and burn them, before anybody reads them. My opinion is that it shows the inexperience and ignorance of the authors."[21] The reviewer referred to our idea as "ridiculous" and "silly," which registered strongly in our graduate student minds. Disheartened, but encouraged by supportive comments from others, we submitted the paper to an unrefereed but widely read newsletter for programmers. Its publication brought strong positive reactions, which led to the widespread adoption of our idea among practitioners, and hundreds of academic papers refining it, as well as textbooks teaching students how to use it. Dozens of commercial software tools, related patents, and an international standard secured our place in programming practices for at least three decades.[22] The takeaway lesson is, don't be discouraged by a single rejection. Bold new ideas are often resisted by those too immersed in their own perceptions to accept new directions. However, learning from constructive review comments and other feedback often leads to improved papers which can be resubmitted elsewhere. Sometimes research papers need to be presented to the right audiences to gain recognition.

Similarly, research funding proposals encounter resistance from the typically more senior members of review panels. Once again, the takeaway message is to stick with your idea, learn from the constructive feedback, and revise your proposal. The larger message is to avoid bitter attacks on what seem to be incompetent reviewers who failed to grasp your wisdom but to ask yourself, why did I fail to make my idea clear, and how could I revise my presentation to improve future outcomes?

Some research projects and proposals are more promising than others. Most researchers choose initial directions that don't bear fruit. The common experience is that midcourse corrections based on early findings are necessary—that is the nature of exploratory work that pushes past frontiers and probes unknown territories. Taking risks is part of doing research, so constructive feedback, sometimes painful, should be valued. Physicist Freeman Dyson recounts a memorable meeting with the Nobel Prize–winning physicist Enrico Fermi: "Fermi politely but ruthlessly demolished a program of research that my students and I had been pursuing for several years . . . I am eternally grateful to him for destroying our illusions and telling us the bitter truth."[23]

Researchers often redirect their work, adopting new research methods, selecting more appropriate applications, and revising proposed theories. Some researchers make even more dramatic shifts in their directions, for example, the theoretical physicist Sebastian Seung, who moved to mathematical neuroscience, then to neurophysiology in his pursuit of brain research. Next, he took on engineering challenges and finally became a game designer to elicit citizen scientist assistance in mapping neural pathways (see Chapter 5, Case Study 5.1).

Senior researchers often ask themselves if it is time to change their research direction, even though they have been successful in one topic for 3–5 years. Realizing that your skills and interests have harvested the low-hanging fruit is not easy, especially as recognition grows and the number of invitations to speak about your work increases. Senior researchers who shift to new challenges often develop the freshness and enthusiasm of young researchers, while bringing broad experience to a new problem, experience which enables them to make important contributions.

Government policymakers face difficult decisions in choosing research directions and defining which topics to support. Most agencies explore new ideas by convening workshops of researchers on a growing topic; the resulting report often becomes the basis for a funded program. Calls for proposals may elicit a small or large number of submissions, and the number of submissions is a good measure of current interest. Program managers describe "proposal pressure" as their guide to expanding an initial program, but weak proposal pressure or disappointing outcomes are likely to lead to program termination or at least restructuring.

Since many granting agencies have only 10%–15% acceptance rates, I estimate that more effort is spent on proposal writing than on carrying out the research. This is a painful reality for researchers but actually seems like a wise strategy for granting agencies. Proposal writing triggers new ideas, launches collaborations, and supports fresh research topics, so even those who fail to gain funding may go on to carry out their planned work or refine their ideas based on reviewer comments. The peer-review process is certainly flawed but seems very effective in promoting innovative thinking, active discussions, and providing program managers with a better understanding of research community directions.

6.7 Lists of Top Problems

Researchers aspiring to have high impact may take on problems proposed by leading individuals, professional societies, or think-tank organizations. The 14 US NAE engineering challenges, listed in Chapter 4, contains compelling problems such as how to prevent nuclear terror, advance health informatics, and make solar energy economical.[24]

The British Longitude Prize 2014 laid out six challenges covering dementia, sustainable food, restoring movement for those with paralysis, ensuring clean water, enabling environmentally sustainable flight, and reducing antibiotic resistance.[25] These are broad sociotechnical problems for which interdisciplinary applied and basic research thinking is needed.

Another list of top problems comes from the United Nations, whose eight Millennium Development Goals have clear metrics of progress and can be applied at a national level:[26]

- eradicate extreme poverty and hunger;
- achieve universal primary education;
- promote gender equality and empower women;
- reduce child mortality;
- improve maternal health;
- combat HIV/AIDS, malaria, and other diseases;
- ensure environmental sustainability; and
- form a global partnership for development.

The Millennium Development Goals were laid out in 2000 with a 2015 horizon. A revised set of 17 Sustainable Development Goals were put forth in 2015, setting goals for the year 2030.[27]

6.8 Challenges and Prizes

Another source of high-impact problems is a challenge or prize with financial rewards, clear review processes, and a prestigious awards committee. These public challenges usually have a deadline and public announcement of winners.

A classic example is the British Longitude Prize set by the British Parliament in 1714 (discussed in Chapter 4, Section 4.3) for whoever could enable ships at sea to determine their longitude. Triggered by the disastrous sinking of many British Navy ships, which ran aground on the rocky coast by the Isles of Scilly, the applied goal was to give navigators an accurate determination of their position.

Astronomers believed that accurate measurements of star, sun, and moon positions would solve the problem, while watchmakers argued that precise chronometers were the route to safety. The powerful astronomers influenced the award commission to regularly raise the bar to prevent watchmakers from claiming the prize. After 40 years of working to make an accurate chronometer that would function on turbulent oceans under changing weather conditions, the nonacademic country watchmaker John Harrison was honored with Parliamentary recognition in 1773. Visitors to Greenwich, UK, can still see the progression of ever more precise and compact chronometers that Harrison built. Those who can't make this trip can still enjoy the wonderfully told story in Dava Sobel's book *Longitude: The True Story of a Lone Genius Who Solved the Greatest Scientific Problem of His Time*.[28]

The takeaway message is that monetary prizes and national recognition can trigger intense efforts in science, engineering, and design, with such efforts often leading to applied research successes and to basic research advances. It's also a great story about how the traditional academic leaders could not accept the innovation coming from a practically minded and determined outsider.

As described in Chapter 4, the current revival of the British Longitude Prize could again trigger efforts to solve a key problem of global importance.[29] By arranging public input to select one of six problems, the organizers generated widespread interest, while educating the public about key problems with science, engineering, and design challenges.

Well-designed prizes and challenges have clear attractive goals with financial awards that bring broad recognition. A popular organizer of prize competitions is the X Prize, which calls itself "an innovation engine," delivering "radical breakthroughs" in energy and environment, exploration, global development, learning, and life sciences.[30] The mission of the X Prize Foundation is "to bring about radical breakthroughs for the benefits of humanity, thereby inspiring the formation of new industries and the revitalization of markets."[31] An early success story was the Ansari X Prize, which was inspired by the Orteig Prize, won by Lindbergh when he flew nonstop from New York to Paris in 1927. The Ansari X Prize awarded $10 million in 2004 to a private company for launching a spaceflight taking 3 people to 100 km above the earth. Following the fascination with spaceflight, the current Google Lunar challenges offers more than $30 million for sending a robot to the moon.

More earthly pursuits were triggered by the Gulf oil spill, which led to the $1 million Wendy Schmidt Oil Cleanup X Prize, which was won by a company for tripling the rate of oil recovery. Other environmental prizes address solar power, improving batteries, and providing clean water in developing nations, while life sciences prizes cover health sensing, low-cost genome sequencing, and studies of rare diseases. Many prize challenges are determined by the preferences of donors, resulting in criticism about their sometimes far-fetched topics whose benefits are less clear or may take decades to complete. I agree that some prizes seem exotic, but maybe their imagination is ahead of mine and maybe the publicity value generates unexpected positive outcomes.

A business-oriented short-term approach to prizes is led by the for-profit InnoCentive, which invites companies to post problems for public solution.[32] Some challenges are narrowly focused, such as the request for a method for measuring the thickness of thin polymeric films, while others, such as increasing social and community acceptance of renewable energy, have a broad scope. Both of these challenges were open for a 30-day period and offered prizes that were under $15,000. More than 1600 challenges have been posted since 2001, with more than $40 million awarded to some of the 300,000+ registered members. The reports on successful challenges make for convincing reading and show that crowdsourced innovation can work.

Maybe most interesting is the distilled wisdom of InnoCentive's managers, captured in white papers that describe how to write compelling challenges. Clear problem statements with measurable outcomes are best when accompanied by descriptions of which solutions have already been tried. InnoCentive's guidance to problem writers stresses the importance of using generic rather than highly technical language. Their point is that business practitioners have often tried known solutions but that many problems are likely to be solved by an outsider. Therefore, enabling these outsiders to understand the problem and apply novel approaches often leads to successful submissions that solve business or government problems while producing immediate financial awards and the opportunity to publish results.

6.9 Skeptics' Corner

Mentors may guide young researchers to old problems, and the challenges found in professional society lists may prove to be safe, consensus ideas. Big breakthroughs may not be on anyone's list. Similarly, while prizes offered by wealthy philanthropists may draw attention, they are likely to lean toward broad publicity rather than the most potent advances to science, engineering, and design. There is also a danger that wealthy philanthropists have their own political or social agenda, which may not be what researchers expect. Similarly, while business-sponsored challenges may attract practical problem solvers, the balance between applied and basic research may shift to the applied side, which is closely tied to business needs.

In spite of these concerns, knowing what is being discussed among senior researchers, business leaders, philanthropists, and government policymakers is valuable in shaping a research proposal. The trick may be to address the major problems of our times yet still find a fresh approach that advances theory and produces practical solutions.

Any theory of problem selection is necessarily incomplete, since existing funding programs, community-driven challenges, and anticipated breakthroughs will miss out on some of the bold ideas and "Surprising Discoveries" that emerge from fresh thinking. It's always possible that innovative researchers who have an unorthodox idea may defy expectations and produce important contributions. There is a long history of such ideas, including Marconi's belief in transatlantic wireless telegraphy, and Barry Marshall's belief that peptic ulcers were caused by the bacterium *Helicobacter pylori*. Marconi was right, but the scientific explanation had to wait for the discovery of the ionosphere. Barry Marshall infected himself to prove his point and won the 2005 Nobel Prize in medicine. On the other hand, I am regularly approached by people who believe they will change the world with what seem to me to be unrealistic ideas or reinventions of old ideas. Maybe I'm unreasonable, but remember that not every bold idea is a good one.

6.10 Summary

Students have many places to turn to for advice about choosing their research directions, but they will do well to read widely, reflect on their skills, discuss ideas with peers, and seek advice from mentors. Research is a social process, so learn to communicate and to listen. The presence of web-based social media has increased the number of possible sources of inspiration, the capacity to learn about current topics rapidly, and the number of communities of fellow researchers who may comment constructively on which proposed research directions could produce high-impact results. Furthermore, these social media tools enable young and senior researchers to engage with civic, business, and global partners to learn about current problems and find collaborators. Challenge problems from professional societies, wealthy entrepreneurs, and corporate or government sources are Web accessible.

Casting a wide net is only the first step. Researcher teams who are aware of their capabilities, available resources, and potential practical and theoretical outcomes are likely to converge faster and make better choices than those who are not. Those who start writing their research narrative, make presentations to peers and mentors, and then seek feedback from social media or other contacts will have the chance to gauge reactions and refine their plans. Investing a week or a month in a research direction by reading related work, followed by further rounds of discussion, will either begin to build confidence or lead to a reassessment that triggers a new direction. Answering Heilmeier's criteria can help clarify a plan by focusing on the success measures, risks, and payoffs. Similarly, considering how a research plan includes applied and basic components (the ABC principle) and blends science, engineering and design (the SED principle) could lead to more productive outcomes.

I require graduate students that I work with to write a 1-page proposal starting with the title of the paper they hope to write when they are done. I estimate that half of my students execute their plan fairly closely to the proposal, but some struggle and revise repeatedly. A memorable case was the student who took a full year to converge on a doctoral dissertation direction, but his work turned out to be highly successful and he is now a full professor.

Each researcher and team has to ultimately choose a problem that they will work on energetically and passionately for months or years. Those who develop a stable internal gyroscope to steer their research are likely to reach their goals. Then they can choose yet another destination because, for most researchers, the research journey itself brings joy.

Policymakers in business and government must make difficult choices that affect thousands of researchers involving billions of dollars. They formulate research program descriptions, which are meant to inspire broadly, yet focus narrowly, so project proposals can be evaluated fairly according to clear criteria. The program managers are in the unenviable position of having to say no to most proposals, but they also derive satisfaction by sharing the successes of the many proposals that they do fund. Future funding programs could more directly manifest support for the ABC and SED principles.

CHAPTER 7

Apply Observation, Intervention, and Controlled Experiments

It is difficult if not impossible to make much progress in the application without theory; conversely it is difficult to understand the theory without knowledge of the technique.

Denis Diderot, *Encyclopedie*

7.1 Introduction

The steadily refined research methods of science, engineering, and design (described in Chapters 3–5) have generated streams of successes for centuries. However, the novel challenges and complexity of twenty-first century problems might be better addressed by mixing these research methods. Learning to use multiple tools, rather than the same hammer, liberates teams and enables them to produce higher-impact research.

Just as telescopes, microscopes, or magnetic resonance imaging (commonly known as MRI) devices support solutions to different problems, using innovative research methods facilitates the exploration of new domains. Careful observations in the form of ethnographic, field, or case studies can be helpful in early stages to form hypotheses which then can be tested with interventions with small prototypes or pilot studies.

The New ABCs of Research. First Edition. Ben Shneiderman.
© Ben Shneiderman 2016. Published in 2016 by Oxford University Press.

> ### Using Multiple Research Methods Advances Research
> Observation, intervention, and controlled experiments all support rigorous analyses that lead to refined theories and improved solutions.

These prototypes and pilot studies will continue to be evaluated as they are scaled up (large-scale chemical plants or numerous Google search users retrieving from large indexes) and scaled out (using diverse raw materials or searches being done in multiple languages by diverse users with diverse queries). The challenges of scale will refine the science, engineering, and design to create successful solutions that serve business and personal needs while coping with failures, accidents, and attacks (see Chapter 9). Ethnographic, field, or case studies again become valuable to validate, refine, and understand causal factors for statistical results. In addition, the growing power of big data analyses that support advanced modeling and simulation offer fresh possibilities.

7.2 Evolution of Research Methods

While physics and chemistry are often studied using reductionist strategies in controlled laboratory experiments, environmental and made-world research often require deep contextual understanding, sensitivity for diverse behavior patterns, and an awareness of rapidly changing systems. The additional challenges of environmental and made-world research are the volatility of personal, group, and organizational dynamics, as assumptions are constantly fluctuating. The richness of ecological systems and human society means that often small variations of independent variables can have huge effects on dependent variables. In environmental research, small changes in temperature, time of day, or location can have profound impacts on the outcomes. In social systems, the phrasing of interview questions, the interviewer's gender, or the choice of metrics can all change responses to surveys. Successful theories will address contextual differences in ways that enable clear descriptions, causal explanations, reliable predictions, and practical guidelines.

The emergence of game theory, behavioral economics, persuasion theory, human-computer interaction, and other disciplines signals the eagerness of research communities to create theories and test solutions to the problems of the made world. However, strategies that work to engage smokers to stop smoking will need to be adapted in order to be used to encourage citizens to vote. Similarly, design strategies used to obtain individual, one-time charitable donations for disaster response will need modification in order to be used to get large corporations to commit substantial continuing effort to trimming their energy consumption.

Another challenge is to duplicate the remarkable safety record in civil aviation for healthcare systems, in which practitioners fear malpractice suits and thus are reluctant to report near misses and mistakes. Some healthcare providers have created a culture that emphasizes patient safety, so change is possible if bold thinking, novel practices, appropriate theories, and innovative research methods can be developed and applied. Investing in healthcare delivery as a major applied and basic research topic would do much to improve care and reduce costs.

A further opportunity for fresh research can be found in developing valid metrics for made-world behaviors. Mass, density, velocity, and acceleration are key metrics in the natural world, while trust, empathy, responsibility, and privacy could be the key metrics for the made world. For computing technology, variants of Moore's Law have tracked the increasing gigabytes, megahertz, and teraflops of machine performance, but made-world behaviors might be measured in "giga-contribs," "mega-collabs," and "tera-thank-you's."

Scientists, engineers, and designers have continuously refined their methods to include thousands of variations along the spectrum from careful observation to interventions to controlled experimentation (see Fig. 7.1).

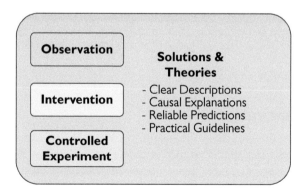

Figure 7.1 The spectrum of research methods ranges from observations, to interventions, to controlled experiments, with many variations along the way. The outcomes manifest in solutions and theories have four components: clear descriptions, causal explanations, reliable predictions, and practical guidelines.

Researchers typically seek to produce working solutions that demonstrate universal principles and to identify foundational theories with broad applicability. These outcomes have at least four components:

- *Clear descriptions:* precise terminology whose broad acceptance accelerates productive discussions within and beyond the research community; fruitful descriptions will often come with well-organized taxonomies, such as Aristotle's characterization of animals, or the Medical Subject Headings that facilitate current research.
- *Causal explanations:* pinpointing the causes of outcomes is often a big step forward; in the precise language of the scientific method, the goal is to find out how independent variables produce changes in dependent variables, whether over microseconds or over centuries.
- *Reliable predictions:* given a set of starting conditions, dependable, and where possible quantitative, statements about what the resulting conditions will be in a minute, day, or year are a key step in practical application; familiar predictions are weather forecasts, economic trends, or medical prognoses.
- *Practical guidelines:* guidance for those who must make decisions about starting a diet, building a boat, designing a commercial website, or launching a smoking-cessation campaign; guidelines, pattern languages, or simple lists of "do's" and "don'ts" capture valuable engineering or design wisdom at an early stage before issues are addressed in detail, to clarify their range of applicability and verify their validity.

What follows is my selective historical review of these research methods, chosen to highlight the evolution of methods and point the way to constructive syntheses.

7.3 Observation

All three disciplines, that is, science, engineering, and design, begin with the observation of the natural or the made world. However, effective seeing, focusing, and interpreting of the natural and made worlds requires planning, mindfulness, and intention. We start with Aristotle (384–322 BCE), who deserves admiration for his prolific writings across diverse topics. His rational processes drove him to elevate and record his observations as universal principles. For example, his observations of land and sea animals were distilled to produce meaningful distinctions such as vertebrates versus invertebrates. His taxonomies were imperfect, but they were intended to organize thinking about the world so as to provide guidance for later observers. Similarly, his descriptions of earth, air, water, and fire laid the foundations for our views of solids, gases, and liquids, categories that even today organize physics and chemistry.

On the other hand, Aristotle gets scorn for mistaken assumptions which could easily have been tested with more careful observation, such as his mistaken claim that, while men had 32 teeth, women only had 28. Such mistakes and his less-than-rigorous methods remind us that incomplete observations and quick leaps to universal principles are perilous. However, Aristotle's impact remained potent for more than 2000 years and he deserves admiration for his pursuit of foundational theories and universal principles, which are still core values of science, engineering, and design.

More rigor enters when communities of researchers carefully choose what to observe, develop shared models of how to record observations, and agree on how to derive accurate universal principles. Leonardo da Vinci (1452–1517) advanced science, engineering, and design through his remarkable capacity to make precise observations and record them in revealing, informative, and often beautiful drawings. He closely studied natural phenomena, such as the turbulence of water flowing around different shaped objects, or the shadows cast by the sun shining on the earth and the moon. Leonardo's engaging drawings presented his findings in ways that were not only understandable but widely appreciated both as art and as effective visual design.

In a risky but bold effort, he participated in approximately 30 dissections of cadavers, making repeated careful observations and precise drawings of the arteries connecting the heart and lungs or of the fetus's location in a woman's womb. Leonardo's skill in drawing was to be more selective than a photograph, so as to focus attention on physical details that produced understandable descriptions and even suggested causal explanations. But Leonardo was more than an accurate scientific observer; he was also an engineering innovator and product designer who turned his insights into practical water pumps, military fortifications, and mechanical devices, as well as some not-quite-practical designs for submarines, flying machines, parachutes, and much more.

Choosing what to observe so as to reveal important principles was Francis Bacon's (1561–1626) theme. Beyond advocating careful observation, he emphasized active tests of the natural world: to intervene and then observe what happens. For example, Bacon's method would be to rub amber with different materials to see which produced static electricity, or to burn materials and then study their ashes. Bacon's active methods were a giant step forward, because they emphasized interventions to push the limits of what an observer could learn about the natural world.

Much of science and engineering became closely tied to improved measurement, but Charles Darwin (1809–1882) made startling progress with careful observations and qualitative comparisons. Darwin's fame is deserved if only for his careful data collecting methods and skilled drawings used to record his findings. Darwin is justly celebrated for his bold theory of evolution, often summarized as "survival of the fittest," which explains the emergence of new species and their accommodation to ecological niches in response to natural selection.

Careful observation continues to be the source of science, engineering, and design progress. Observers of hospital procedures may notice frequent errors which could be addressed by more structured workflows and checklists.[1] Anthropologist observers may study cooking practices in elegant restaurants, social space in crowded public transports, and team coordination in sports, hospitals, or businesses. Increasingly, amateur observers are being recruited for vast citizen science projects that collect bird sightings, galaxy classifications, or museum object tags.

Designers are trained to carefully observe users of existing designs in natural settings, such as advertising executives using laptops in urban cafes, or farmers using cell phones in developing nations. They may observe elderly users of pill bottles, police officers on patrol, or children at playgrounds. Some design researchers capture large collections of images, such as rock-concert posters from the 1970s, ceramic teapots, or Swiss chalets; they then organize these images into coffee-table books, whose tables of contents provides a useful taxonomy for the next generation of designers who seek to follow universal principles and practical guidelines. Other design researchers make abstractions from individual cases into meaningful pattern languages and actionable guidelines.

7.4 Intervention

From ancient times, those who responded to public needs were asked to change the world by, for example, building Roman aqueducts, Turkish mosques, or English railroads. These engineers, designers, architects, and builders learned many lessons from their interventions, sometimes writing inspirational treatises

CASE STUDY 7.1 MICHAEL M. CROW

Launching Large-Scale Interdisciplinary Academic Units

Michael M. Crow, President of Arizona State University

https://president.asu.edu/about/michaelcrow

As Columbia University's executive vice provost, Michael M. Crow served as chief strategist and lead investor for Columbia's research enterprise and technology transfer operations. Then Crow joined a long history of pioneers who followed Horace Greeley's century-old encouragement to "Go West, young man!" He became the sixteenth president of Arizona State University (ASU) in 2002, bringing the perspective of a science and technology policy scholar with him as he formulated his plans to transform the institution into the foundational prototype for the "New American University."[1]

Crow's background in science and technology policy informed his approach to interdisciplinary research, teaching, and service.[2] He acknowledges the importance of core disciplinary departments but otherwise seeks to overcome the fixation on discipline-based research agendas.[3] Crow launched novel large-scale interdisciplinary academic units such as the Biodesign Institute and Global Institute of Sustainability, establishing the first-of-its-kind School of Sustainability, whose mission is to "create innovative modes of scholarship by bringing together people from multiple disciplines, leaders, and stakeholders to develop practical solutions to the most pressing sustainability challenges."[4]

Other transdisciplinary entities include the School of Life Sciences; the School of Human Evolution and Social Change; the School of Earth and Space Exploration; the School of Family and Social Dynamics; and the Center for Science and the Imagination. The College of Health Solutions, for example, includes innovative units such as the School for the Science of Healthcare Delivery, which seeks "safe, cost-effective, patient-centered health care systems" by focusing on "health economics, new technologies/biomedical informatics, health promotion/population health, care models/interprofessionalism, health policy, practice efficiency/quality improvement, and built environment."[5] The ASU Polytechnic campus offers students an experiential approach to engineering education and complements the research-oriented Ira A. Fulton Schools of Engineering. Hundreds of transdisciplinary research institutes and centers augment the new colleges and schools.

To advance his vision for research that benefits the public good, Crow brought the Consortium for Science, Policy & Outcomes (http://cspo.org) from Columbia University to ASU.[6] CSPO seeks to guide the contributions of science and technology toward useful outcomes and recently launched the *Journal of Responsible Innovation* to provide a forum for research and discussion of ethics, technology assessment, governance, and sociotechnical integration.

Another globally influential venture is a partnership to publish the science policy quarterly *Issues in Science and Technology* with the National Academies.[7]

Crow envisions a teaching and research enterprise aligned with strategic national goals as well as local and regional impact (see Case Study Box 2). His commitment to diversity is manifest in the unprecedented increase in the number of low-income and first-generation students, including ethnically and racially diverse students. ASU dramatically expanded its student population from 55,491 in 2002 to 83,301 in 2014, while increasing minority enrollment to 34% and more than tripling their research budget.[8] The New American University model[9] has also demonstrated its success, as attested by rankings that moved ASU into the top 100 universities in the world.

Case Study Box 2 Arizona State University's Design Aspirations

Leverage Our Place: ASU embraces its cultural, socioeconomic and physical setting.

Transform Society: ASU catalyzes social change by being connected to social needs.

Value Entrepreneurship: ASU uses its knowledge and encourages innovation.

Conduct Use-Inspired Research: ASU research has purpose and impact.

Enable Student Success: ASU is committed to the success of each unique student.

Fuse Intellectual Disciplines: ASU creates knowledge by transcending academic disciplines.

Be Socially Embedded: ASU connects with communities through mutually beneficial partnerships.

Engage Globally: ASU engages with people and issues locally, nationally and internationally.

Source: Arizona State University, *A New American University* (Accessed August 6, 2015) http://www.asu.edu/pb/documents/A%20New%20American%20University.pdf.

---

[1] Arizona State University, *New American University* (Accessed August 6, 2015) http://newamericanuniversity.asu.edu/.

[2] Crow, M. M. and Bozeman, B., *Limited by Design: R&D Laboratories in the U. S. National Innovation System*, Columbia University Press, New York, NY (1998).

[3] Crow, M. M. and Dabars, W. B., Interdisciplinarity as a design problem: Toward mutual intelligibility among academic disciplines in the American research university, in M. R. O'Rourke, S. J. Crowley, S. D. Eigenbrode, and J. D. Wulfhorst (Editors), *Enhancing Communication and Collaboration in Interdisciplinary Research*, Sage Publications, Los Angeles, CA (2013), pp. 294–322.

[4] Arizona State University, School of Sustainability: Integrated Solutions to Social, Economic and Environmental Challenges (Accessed August 6, 2015) https://schoolofsustainability.asu.edu/.

[5] Arizona State University, *School for the Science of Health Care Delivery* (Accessed August 6, 2015) https://chs.asu.edu/shcd.

[6] Consortium for Science, Policy & Outcomes, *The Consortium for Science, Policy & Outcomes* (2015) http://cspo.org/.

[7] University of Texas at Dallas, *Issues in Science and Technology* (2015) http://issues.org/.

[8] Crow, M. M. and Dabars, W. B., A new model for the American research university, *Issues in Science and Technology* 31, 3 (Spring 2015), 55–62.

[9] Crow, M. M. and Dabars, W. B., *Designing the New American University*, Johns Hopkins University Press, Baltimore, MD (2015).

that left durable impressions on their colleagues. These treatises had impact because of their impressive drawings of structures, their universal principles, and the practical guidelines they provided, guidelines that we would now call "best practices."

Marcus Vitruvius Pollio (~65 BCE–15 CE) composed *De architectura* to describe his theories of engineering and design; his approach can be summarized by the Latin terms "firmitas, utilitas, venustas," which translate roughly to the three virtues of solidity, utility, and beauty. These virtues, which might be called universal principles, have influenced architects, engineers, and designers for many centuries and remain durable aspirations. It's easy to see how these ancient virtues may have inspired the International Standards Organization to focus on three virtues of interface usability for interactive systems: effectiveness, efficiency, and satisfaction.[2]

The courage to commit substantial resources to making a building is an admirable trait of engineers, designers, architects, and builders. But even more important is their responsibility for the safety of their work. In the past, architects or builders were sometimes punished if their buildings collapsed, causing injuries. In other cases, the reputations of engineers and designers were often closely tied to the success of their constructions, forcing them to explore alternate designs to see which features produced improvements to effectiveness, efficiency, and satisfaction. In present times, engineers and designers often work in large teams on complex systems and so individual responsibility is lessened, a circumstance which can lead to the creation of flawed products. Similarly, many software engineers and designers, such as developers of electronic health records systems, typically include "hold harmless" clauses in their contracts and thus may have reduced motivation for providing continuous product improvements.

Research interventions are often tied to explorations of what we now call the design space, a repeated form of hypothesis testing to develop universal principles that guide future engineers and designers toward improved constructions and more reliable success stories. Sometimes these universal principles of engineering and design are quantitative and have predictive power; at other times, they are "rules of thumb," organized sets of best practices, or lists of "do's" and "don'ts."

Complex systems designers, such as Fred Brooks, who led the development of IBM's Operating System/360, describe their explorations using the language of architecture, design, and engineering more than the language of science.[3] Brooks describes the familiar design process of requirements gathering, conceptual design, and prototype building. Similarly, UC Berkeley Professor David Patterson talks about his 30-year history of developing advanced computing systems through rapid prototyping, open interdisciplinary discussions, teamwork, and multiple approaches to impact assessment.[4] These same strategies of building prototypes that evolve rapidly to usable products emerge in the hybrid research approach described by Google's managers (see Chapter 1, Case Study 1.2).

Research in social sciences is often devoted to understanding and developing metrics to at least compare two contexts. While many traditionalists resist activist philosophies, the movement is toward interventions that seek to change organizations, political processes, or adoption of new technologies. The traditionalists argue that understanding must precede intervention; others claim that, as social psychologist Kurt Lewin (1890–1947) said, "If you want truly to understand something, try to change it." The presence of the World Wide Web, social media, and tracking technologies have changed the possibilities, making it far easier than before to measure base line metrics and then intervene and measure changes at scale with millions of users.

7.5 Controlled Experimentation

Galileo Galilei (1564–1642) took mindful observation and thoughtful intervention a step further. He developed the idea that researchers should state testable hypotheses in advance of their observations and interventions. The classic but possibly apocryphal story tells of his taking small and large metal balls to the Tower of Pisa to prove that they fell at the same speed. Another story covers Galileo's proof that the time for a pendulum to swing was dependent on the cord length, not the bob weight, room temperature, or height above the ground. His actions were guided by a desire to test the validity of a lucidly stated hypothesis.

Equally important were Galileo's efforts to measure time, distance, or other quantities to derive universal principles that produced reliable quantitative predictions in a broad range of situations. His measure of time was said to be the beating of his heart, but accurate clocks, thermometers, and scales were becoming available, laying the foundation for Lord Kelvin's (1824–1907) famous statement, "When you can measure what you are speaking about, and express it in numbers, you know something about it."[5] Galileo combined scientific thinking with engineering innovation, especially as he fabricated instruments for his work, such as by grinding lenses to make his telescope, with which he made his shocking observations of the movement of Jupiter's moons.

By the start of the twentieth century, research methods had matured, and clear expectations of how to run controlled experiments were propagating through science, medicine, engineering, and related disciplines. A key figure was statistician Ronald A. Fisher (1890–1962), who developed experimental agricultural studies in which he altered independent variables such as water, fertilizer, and seed types and then measured outcomes such as yield, quality, or insect resistance (the dependent variables). This careful statement of hypotheses and experimental design led him to develop the standard statistical methods used for t-tests, analysis of variance (ANOVA), maximum likelihood, and statistical sampling. Fisher's methods helped control for bias and variance in experiments ranging from laboratory studies to agricultural tests, where weather or terrain variations could obscure the key experimental variables. The widely used F-statistic is named after Fisher, whose methods were widely adopted for psychological research on human motor, perceptual, and cognitive tasks, as well as for comparisons of samples from interview, survey, and observational data.

As medical randomized controlled trials soared in popularity, Fisher's methods were applied and adapted to fit these critical experimental studies. But even as refined statistical methods, including nonparametric variations spread, new ones were proposed. With more than 170,000 medical clinical trials being run each year worldwide,[6] lively debates emerged about bias, controls, and appropriate statistical methods.[7] Controlled experiments are standard expectations in most fields of science, engineering, and design, but new strategies are emerging.

In summary, the progress made in research methods includes expansion (1) from using observation alone to including intervention tied to hypothesis testing and (2) from using only qualitative measures to including quantitative measures that support prediction. Two further central shifts are (3) from single observations to repeated observations that support generalization into universal principles and (4) from personal observation to independently reproduced observations that support the validation of claims about the relationships between independent and dependent variables.

Finally, most researchers believe that the physics and chemistry of the natural world are best studied by using a reductionist approach under controlled laboratory conditions. This method enables researchers to control the changing conditions of complex real-world situations, so as to measure impacts of changes on one or a few variables at a time. Controlled experiments remain a powerful method, but environmental and made-world researchers often have to invent new research methods that recognize the subtleties of context, the nuanced effect of small changes, and the increased validity of working in real systems. Well-designed interventions could lead to an increased understanding of environmental system dynamics and the social systems patterns of human behavior, motivations, and willingness to participate.

7.6 Revisiting Observation, Intervention, and Controlled Experiments

My selective history of research methods is meant to lay the foundation for understanding contemporary innovations to research methods, as such innovations are often designed to accommodate the challenges of twenty-first century made-world problems. In the same way that a helix spirals around and yet upward, researchers return to old methods but with increased capabilities.

Observation can still produce breakthrough discoveries through studying the natural and made worlds with a trained eye to spot unnoticed phenomena. However, most contemporary observers are aided by an array of infrared, ultraviolet, x-ray, and radio telescopes, powerful microscopes, and assorted medical devices for MRIs, sonograms, and virtual colonoscopies. Their observations can be recorded by still and video cameras and, even better, their abilities are boosted through downloading billions of images and videos that are then amplified by potent computer vision tools that allow the detection of faces, sunsets, or cloud-free satellite images. In short, old-fashioned observation is being replaced by super tools that support the discovery of colliding stars in distant galaxies, of the nighttime hunting strategies of wolf packs, or of the evolving dynamics of political protests.

These and other big data opportunities are quickly changing the way research is conducted. The White House press release about its big data initiative described two challenges: "Developing scalable algorithms for processing imperfect data in distributed data stores" and "Creating effective human-computer interaction tools for facilitating rapidly customizable visual reasoning for diverse missions."[8]

The White House devotion to information visualization and visual analytics would have brought a smile to John W. Tukey (1915–2000), a famed statistician who made significant contributions, especially with his bold book on *Exploratory Data Analysis*.[9] He advocated the return to observational methods, but this time with the observations being made about visual patterns in data. Tukey proposed data telescopes and microscopes to view the distribution, trends, clusters, gaps, and outliers in data using visual methods rather than purely statistical methods.

Tukey's commitment to visualization was clear: "As yet I know of no person or group that is taking nearly adequate advantage of the graphical potentialities of the computer . . . In exploration they are going to be the data analyst's greatest single resource."[10] Tukey's request for careful observation of data so as to spot the clusters, gaps, outliers, relationships, and other patterns in the vast data forests is very much in the style of Darwin's careful observation of the natural world (for more on visualization, see Chapter 9, Section 9.5).

The work of me and my colleagues in identifying six types of Twitter discussions was influenced by both Tukey and Darwin. We felt like twentieth-century botanists in some newly discovered territory, trying to make sense of the abundant flora and fauna around them. Instead of tangled vines and predators-prey networks, we studied the social network patterns of Twitter discussions as viewed in NodeXL maps.[11] Our claim to seeing six types of discussions was based on scanning 10,000+ such maps, which we believed were generated by six types of Twitter usage. Our made-world observations and proposed taxonomy will need to be validated or challenged by others, just as hypotheses about the natural world have been refined for centuries.

Intervention is also producing surprises and new opportunities. Modest interventions in the natural and made worlds can now be carried out at a grand scale that is sometimes disturbing, while at the same time yielding fresh insights. Each time government agencies announce dietary recommendations, tighten smoking restrictions, or change highway speed limits, they are conducting an intervention that is now more than ever measurable: specifically, they are testing whether and how residents reduce intake of sugary sodas, give up cigarettes, and drive more safely.

Similarly, changes to tax laws, air quality goals, or educational practices have massive effects that researchers can now study because of the vast array of data collection sensors, online data sources, and open social media discussions. Never before in history has so much of what we do been online, and never before have we had such powerful "macroscopes" to measure what is happening, form hypotheses, and revise policies.[12]

Contemporary versions of intervention use terms such as field studies, case studies,[13] long-term case studies,[14] design research, design studies,[15] research in action,[16] and research in practice.[17] The common theme is to build something and study its behavior in realistic environments rather than under controlled laboratory conditions. Short-term controlled experiments in laboratory conditions were fine for studying *E. coli* bacteria, chemical reactions, and human motor or perceptual skills but, when dealing with more complex human creativity, motivation, and group behavior, it is hard to accept that a 3-hour or 3-day study represents what happens in other settings.

Case studies that last for weeks or months are well suited to studying the learning and use of our interactive information visualization tools. Not only did it take domain-expert users weeks to master these tools, but it took repeated training and collaboration with them to have them change their problem-solving strategies. Working closely with medical researchers, financial specialists, or transportation analysts built our confidence that the case studies from their thinking-aloud commentaries were giving us excellent feedback about needed improvements, as well as a deeper understanding of how their thought processes and language usage were changing. We were rewarded not only by their compliments and enthusiasm but by the capacity to find new patterns in their data that led to published research results.

Even if we could arrange for month-long studies, the number of domain-expert professionals is often too small to form a large enough sample for statistical testing. The use of university undergraduates as a proxy for their behavior is a poor substitute. The problem of needing participants with special skills is apparent in studies of experienced astronauts and in special cases such as predicting presidential decisions in crisis situations. Case studies of previous decisions in similar crises by the current or previous presidents are imperfect but can provide valuable guidance. Increasing the rigor of case studies by developing best practices would ensure accurate recording and reduce interpretation bias.

Critics of case studies complain about the reduced chances for generalizability and replicability. Their concerns are legitimate; but the alternative of controlled laboratory studies has reduced validity and relevance in realistic environments.

Controlled experiments also contribute to advances in science, engineering, and design. This strategy supports the ABC principle by providing evidence for combined applied and basic research projects; for example, human perceptual studies refine theories and lead to improved air-traffic control systems.[18] Controlled experiments are also used by physicists studying semiconductor materials in laboratory conditions, for example, when measuring changes in resistance in response to changes in temperature, impurities, or magnetic fields. These physical-world controlled experiments now seem easy to arrange compared to the complexities of environmental studies and the massive medical randomized controlled trials with tens of thousands of participants. However, new natural-world research strategies such as massive citizen science data collection strategies, the collection of satellite remote sensing data, and the widespread use of sensors for continuous monitoring provide semicontrolled experimental evidence to support hypotheses about complex environmental systems. Similarly, PatientsLikeMe and other medical data collection projects, such as Apple's Health ResearchKit,[19] provide a powerful novel approach to large-scale experiments in natural settings.

Other forms of semicontrolled experiments, such as the 200 daily A/B studies run by Microsoft and hundreds of other technology companies, involve tens of millions of users, who get slightly different user interface designs, consumer product offers, or social incentives based on varying forms of persuasion.[20] While critics worry about the lack of careful selection and the way in which participants are assigned to treatment A or B, the randomized assignment of millions of users and the replicability of the results builds trust in billion-dollar business decisions that come from the likes of Amazon, Netflix, Google, eBay, Yahoo, and LinkedIn. Large numbers of participants in realistic settings may provide more valid data than small numbers of participants in laboratory-controlled experiments.

While consumers seem to accept being unwilling participants in such commercial experiments, they have objected strongly when their emotional reactions were manipulated. For example, Facebook researchers tested the theory of emotional contagion, which suggests that, if users see more positive postings by their friends, they will respond with a more positive tone in their own postings; conversely, if users see more negative postings, they will respond with more negative postings. In short, their moods would be shaped by what they saw.[21] The National Academies journal editors were attacked for publishing this study, since the 689,003 participants were not asked for their informed consent. The editors responded with careful wording that the experiment was within the Facebook terms of use, even though the experimenters may have crossed some ethical boundaries. The change in moods was small, but the effect was statistically significant, giving the first large-scale evidence for the emotional contagion theory. Critics felt that it was unethical for Facebook to make its users sad, even though there was no apparent business reason for it to do so. The manipulation of mood was more troubling than Facebook's earlier study of 61 million users in which voter turnout was shown to increase if Facebook users were shown up to six photos of their friends who had already voted.[22]

The World Wide Web, social media, and tracking technologies have done more than make these new approaches to controlled experiments possible;

they have opened doors to studying made-world phenomena in productive ways that support new theories and vast practical applications. The capacity to go beyond understanding and to intervene to produce desirable outcomes is a powerful opportunity for researchers. But this powerful opportunity can be used by malicious actors such as criminals, political dictators, and terrorists; thus, decision-makers must also act to limit dangers. Buckminster Fuller's call for "comprehensive anticipatory design science" was meant to support the prevention of future problems. Difficult ethical challenges will be raised in the coming decades by the presence of these powerful opportunities to intervene at scale.

7.7 Skeptics' Corner

Research methods courses are often taught within disciplines, so it is rare for scientists to learn about the research methods of designers, and vice versa. Scientists may disparage the observational strategies preferred by designers, while designers may be reluctant to pursue the rigorous controlled experiments preferred by scientists. But even respected scientists find much to complain about in controlled experiments, such as John Ioannidis's famous paper "Why most published research findings are false."[23]

Engineers typically focus on device performance, so some are resistant to engaging in usability studies or customer interviews. A painful example for me is the Software Engineering Institute's reluctance to include user interface design in its agenda.

Scientists and engineers could make more extensive use of the studio methods or critiquing sessions that are typical in design work. I hope designers might more regularly question the biases that are naturally part of subjective reviews, interviews, and ethnographic observations. Of course, skeptics may have good reasons for sticking to their well-practiced methods, but let's at least have a respectful dialog about which research methods to apply for different situations.

Finally, remember that in many cases objective controlled experimentation that applies statistical hypothesis testing to quantitative data can be happily combined with ethnographic observations of human activity with qualitative data collection. Mixed and multiple methods are gaining appreciation, since different research strategies can provide complementary results the offer important insights for applied and basic researchers.

7.8 Summary

The spectrum of research methods ranges from observations, to interventions, to controlled experiments, with many variations along the way. Researchers seek working solutions and foundational theories so that they can make clear descriptions, causal explanations, reliable predictions, and practical guidelines. In choosing a research method, project teams will also consider the role of existing theories in guiding their work and sharpen the hypotheses they are testing with lucid statements about the independent and dependent variables involved.

Researchers typically structure their work by developing hypotheses and then testing them through observation, intervention, and controlled experiments that produce quantitative or qualitative data. Agreement on whether they believe reductionist models or contextual influences will simplify their choice of a laboratory or field/case study. The large-scale data collection from citizen science projects, environmental sensors, and online A/B studies are fresh methods of semicontrolled experimentation that provide appealing alternatives to laboratory-controlled experiments.

The opportunity to test environmental and made-world interventions at massive scale grows with the increasing availability of big data resources from sensors, commercial applications, government data, and open social media discussions. Rigorous guidelines for semicontrolled experiments would accelerate the adoption of such methods and obtain respect for large-scale quantitative studies (see the discussion of big data in Chapter 9, Section 9.3). Rigorous guidelines would also be helpful for promoting the adoption of replicated case study research using qualitative methods such as interviews and ethnographic observations.

Conference program committees and journal editorial boards all seek rigor and quality, but editors-in-chief and conference chairs who guide tradition-bound reviewers to be more sympathetic to new research methods could open up unexpected research possibilities. Similarly, funding agencies and proposal review panels who give new research methods a chance could accelerate development in new fields.

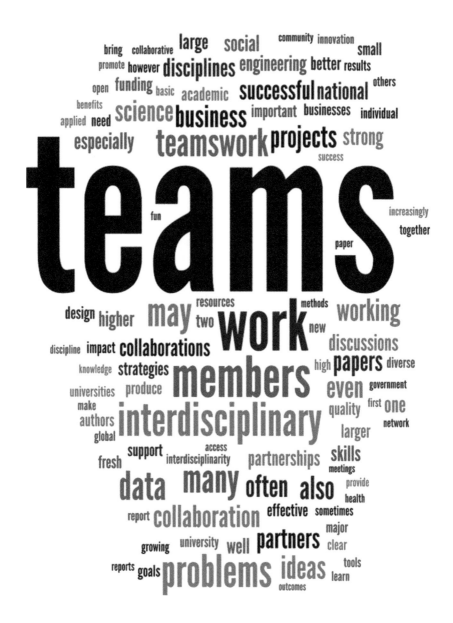

CHAPTER 8

Form Teams with Diverse Individuals and Organizations

One truth about the digital age is that the desire to communicate, connect, collaborate, and form community tends to create killer apps.

Walter Isaacson, *The Innovators*

Three helping one another will do as much as six working singly.

Spanish proverb

8.1 Introduction

Team research is the source of some of the great breakthroughs of all time, such as the 1947 invention of the transistor. It took the complementary skills of an applied researcher, Walter Brattain, a basic researcher in quantum theory, John Bardeen, and the solid-state physicist William Shockley. Walter Isaacson deftly tells the story of their teamwork, including Shockley's combative style, but Isaacson's focus is on the team's diverse skills:

By its nature, the transistor required a team that threw together theorists who had an intuitive feel for quantum phenomena with material scientists who were adroit at baking impurities into batches of silicon, along with dexterous experimentalists, industrial chemists, manufacturing specialists, and ingenious thinkers.[1]

The New ABCs of Research. First Edition. Ben Shneiderman.
© Ben Shneiderman 2016. Published in 2016 by Oxford University Press.

Their engineering invention and later their understanding of the transistor effect won the 1956 Nobel Prize in Physics, demonstrating again the tight integration of applied and basic research (the ABC principle) and the need for science, engineering, and design (the SED principle). The central claim of this chapter is that team research leads to higher quality outcomes and higher impact, compared to individual research.

> **Team Research Leads to Higher Quality and Higher Impact, Compared to Individual Research**
>
> Teams often produce higher quality research than an individual can because they bring complementary knowledge, skills, and attitudes, take on more ambitious projects, apply diverse research methods, and have larger networks.

This chapter lays out the arguments for team research and describes some successful strategies. Then it covers teams that bridge university, business, and government, as well as teams that explicitly seek to be interdisciplinary. The evidence for the high impact of well-managed research teams is strong, although special skills are necessary to manage large teams. We are all familiar with small teams,[2] but larger teams with thousands of researchers and nonresearchers are being put to work to deal with substantial applied and basic research problems.[3]

The journalistic myths of the lone researcher, such as the solitary scientist and the inspired designer, are hard to overcome, but balanced teams, collaborative communities, and nurturing networks are often the sources of high-impact results.

8.2 The Story of Team Research

Spotting emerging high-impact teams is difficult, but a few stand out, such as Leysia Palen's team and its creative work on analyzing social media data in the wake of disasters. At the University of Colorado Boulder, she leads an interdisciplinary team of devoted graduate students who bring together data-handling skills, text analytics algorithms, sociobehavioral observational experience, and organizational theories. This familiar strategy of a senior researcher leading graduate students enables Palen to advance her research agenda, and her team members to learn skills while gaining prominence by working with a respected leader on an important problem. Their mixed-methods analysis of Twitter discussions following the Haitian earthquake produced fascinating foundational research about social network evolution and applied results that continue to influence coordination strategies for disaster response teams.[4]

Edward Fox of Virginia Tech has promoted theory-driven system building as a founder of the digital libraries research area. The skills he acquired enabled him to quickly form an effective team to develop the Crisis, Tragedy, and Recovery Network (CTRNet), in response to the tragic 2007 shootings at his campus. His goal was to collect and index all information about similar events as a resource to guide future researchers and practitioners. The CTRNet community designed a database system and web-based user interfaces to enable users to find information about previous incidents. Their projects typically create teams with several senior researchers, partners at other universities, and student workers.[5]

Larger teams can be found in the 700+ teams documented in a database of "collaboratories," a term coined in 1993 by Bill Wulf to describe collaborative laboratories. These collaboratories, often involving hundreds of distributed participants, include teams that collect astronomical observations, curate shared genetic databases, or design physics infrastructures to be shared by many users.[6] Judy and Gary Olson and their team members study the efficacy of these collaboratories, especially for remote teams, and provide advice with their online questionnaire.[7]

Collaboratories are often ambitious project teams with hundreds of participants whose web-powered coordination strategies became possible only two decades ago. Teams of hundreds of scientists routinely coordinate their efforts and share expensive equipment such as telescopes, supercomputers, or gene sequence databases. Similar global teams of engineers and designers work on large open-source software projects, such as the widely used Linux operating system, to make sure they run across a dozen hardware platforms with small-, wall-, and mall-sized displays. Linux is an applied research project with remarkable bottom-up participation that has triggered basic research in computer operating systems, collaborative social strategies, and much more.

A more top-down approach to team formation can be seen in the US National Institutes of Health, which has made especially strong commitments to several problem-oriented interdisciplinary multiuniversity centers, such as the Transdisciplinary Tobacco Research Use Centers to study public health issues of tobacco use and cessation strategies. While it took longer than expected for this interdisciplinary center to start producing results, ultimately they produced more papers with higher impact than smaller individual grants which got the same amount of aggregate funding.[8] Large teams and multiteam systems are at the heart of world-famous international projects such as the particle physics research in Geneva at CERN (the European Center for Nuclear Research), the International Space Station, or the Antarctic Field Stations. Managing these massive long-duration teams deserves additional research to determine how to increase their efficacy and value.

Still larger are the growing number of nonconventional teams of tens of thousands of environmental researchers, amateur astronomers, and nature enthusiasts who participate in citizen science projects.[9] Often with only modest funding, these networked collaborations depend on social media and mobile devices to collect Amazon River plant photos, classify galaxies, or report bird migration sightings.[10] Early citizen science projects in astronomy, genomics, and biodiversity developed techniques to overcome the resistance that researchers had to using amateur-supplied data, as well as to motivate vast numbers of amateurs to learn about data quality, so they could file regular reports with increasingly high validity.[11]

The twenty-first century's problems present researchers with daunting challenges of scale, complexity, and urgency as well as grand opportunities to make substantial impacts. Human aspirations have soared into space, expanded excellence of medical care, multiplied the capacity to communicate, and much more. Even as the world's population has grown past 7 billion, the quality of life and life expectancy has improved for most people. However, sober pessimists point to the degradation of the environment, the exhaustion of natural resources, and asymmetric threats from terrorists and cybercriminals, all of which threaten to lead to the collapse of civilization.[12] Enthusiastic optimists point to progress and hopeful indicators, believing that human creativity will produce innovative science, engineering, and design outcomes fast enough to continue raising the quality of life.[13]

The need to produce scalable innovations such as renewable energy sources, economically viable desalination plants, and improved safety in transportation has dramatically expanded the research community and its organization around teams. Similarly, the pressure to solve substantial problems has stimulated organization into small and large teams, which has accelerated the production of research publications. Other high expectations include rapidly improving both the design of consumer goods such as personal phones, cars, and food and the quality of services such as education, healthcare, and banking. Team efficacy and productivity have risen, in part because of better communication tools such as the World Wide Web, collaboration software, data-sharing tools, and social media. In addition to having improved tools, researchers recognize that improved organization and collaboration strategies amplify their capacities in powerful ways. The dramatic and continuing growth of teams makes it more possible to adhere to the ABC and SED principles.

8.3 Why Teams in Research?

In spite of the expediency of individual work, researchers have moved strongly and clearly in favor of teamwork, because it often has even stronger advantages. Joshua Shenk's book on the *Powers of Two* promotes the ideal of two-person teams, with extensive examples going back to the bicycle shop–owning brothers Orville and Wylbur Wright, who developed airplanes, and Marie and Pierre Curie, whose work on radioactivity won them a Nobel Prize in Physics.[14] Later examples include James Watson and Francis Crick, whose teamwork led to the understanding of the structure of DNA. Computer innovations by Steve Jobs and Steve Wozniak led to Apple's early successes, with Job's relentless pursuit of design excellence pressuring Wozniak to deliver remarkable engineering feats. Bill Gates and Paul Allen's partnership in launching Microsoft showed similar brilliance, collaboration, and conflict. The simple model is that one person is the visionary and the other the executor of plans; the dreamer and the doer or the theorist and the practitioner. Some two-person teams bring complementary skills or opposing personalities that trigger the right level of tension and even confrontation. One colleague reports about his collaboration, "I'm not generally upbeat and enthusiastic, but this works out well: we complement each other very well—his enthusiasm overcomes my skepticism, and my challenging questions help him think through problems."[15]

However, teams of more than two are often helpful in taking on complex and important problems with fresh perspectives, even though coordination overhead can get higher. From the 1950s to 2000 the average number of journal paper coauthors in science and engineering grew from 1.9 to 3.5 (Fig. 8.1).[16] This phenomenon becomes even more important when coupled with the result that in the 1950s two-author papers garnered 1.30 times as many citations as single-authored papers, soaring to 1.74 times as many citations in the 1990s. Working in teams of two probably produces better work and sends a stronger signal, which is more likely to be trusted, than work by a single person. The trust is heightened since having two authors working on a project signals a stronger commitment to a research result than a single person working alone, especially if one or both authors have strong reputations. I had a striking experience of this

CASE STUDY 8.1 EVIDENCE-BASED SOCIAL PROGRAM FUNDING

The story of medical research based on randomized clinical trials usually begins in 1747, when the Royal Navy Surgeon James Lind tested different treatments for scurvy with sailors on the *HMS Salisbury*. He found that eating citrus fruit, especially limes, relieved the painful symptoms, while the five other treatments had no effect. The successful outcome led to sailors being called "limeys."

Clinical trials grew as a feature in medical research after 1900, gaining momentum in the 1940s, and expanding dramatically in the 1990s, so that, by 2015, there were over 180,000 active registered clinical trials worldwide.[1] Experimental design and statistical analysis methods have been steadily refined, with features such as random assignment, placebo groups, double-blind testing (in which neither the participants nor the medical staff know which treatment group a participant is in), rigorous protocols, and standard statistical comparisons.

Clinical trials can last for years, have tens of thousands of participants, and cost hundreds of millions of dollars. All this effort by government, pharmaceutical companies, or research organizations is seen as worth doing because of the value of the new knowledge that is produced: practical guidance for clinicians, and refined theories of disease, body function, or pharmaceutical processes. Clinical trials are often seen as the "gold standard" against which other forms of evidence are compared. However, skeptics point out that biases include recruitment rules that limit participation and that treatment compliance is usually better than in normal situations.

Clinical trials are an attempt to bring medical research closer to the controlled experiments that physicists and chemists had used so effectively. Agricultural researchers, like Ronald Fisher in the 1920s, have also found ways to bring controlled experimental methods to the complex real-world situations of crops growing in differing soil, water, and sunshine situations. However, controlled experimental studies of social programs presents even greater challenges than either medical or agricultural experiments.

Studying social programs, such as additional training for poor grade-school readers, nurse home visits to low-income new parents, or job training programs for unemployed workers, take months to carry out and years for the impact to be seen. Furthermore, the significant variations in context make it difficult to ensure that the results from one study will predict future results. Often the initiators of new social programs have highly motivated, knowledgeable, and well-trained staff so their outcomes are strong, but follow-on programs with new staff may not be so effective. Differences in urban versus rural, low-income versus middle-income, or homogenous versus diverse populations, as well as from a hundred other variables, can easily affect outcomes.

However, with billions of dollars of government monies being spent on such programs, there has been a growing movement to provide evidence-based guidance in their selection, administration, and evaluation. In the past, commitments to large programs such as Lyndon Johnson's 1966 Child Nutrition Act were often based on presidential remarks such as "good food is essential to good learning"; but the pressure has grown to demonstrate efficacy, such as through improvements in health, school attendance, or learning outcomes.

A lively debate in Washington policy circles wrestled with the question of what constitutes rigorous evaluation.[2] Devotees of medical-style randomized clinical trials insisted on multiple site studies with careful controls and strict measurement protocols, with some patients receiving the proposed program treatment, and others receiving an alternate treatment or no treatment. Other researchers argued for quasiexperiment designs (QEDs), in which before and after statistical studies were enriched by in-depth ethnographic observations and interviews. Proponents of QEDs argue that these strategies contribute to understanding the causal basis for positive or negative outcomes, thereby advancing predictive theory formation.

By the early 2000s, dozens of evaluations of large programs had shown promise, so Congressional offices and executive agency staffers began to promote policies that would require evaluations. Even more dramatic was the initiative to shift from traditional policies of funding allocation by state population to requirements that major funding go to programs that have demonstrated efficacy. Of course, some funding was allocated to new programs so that fresh ideas could be tested and refined.

By 2013, this dramatic shift had spawned 700+ rigorous evaluations of social programs so as to provide evidence-based guidance for termination, revision, or expansion. Skeptics of government social programs supported these research efforts, since they believed that most programs would be shown to be failures, while advocates liked the idea of increased funding allocation for successful programs.

The compelling story of this historical transformation to evidence-based social program funding is told by former Republican policy analyst, Ron Haskins, who teamed with Greg Margolis to conduct 134 interviews of key decision-makers. The two are careful to support the Obama administration's adoption of evidence-based evaluations, while limiting discussion of whether they advocate increased or decreased government funding of social programs. Their courageous advocacy of rigorous evaluations for social programs could promote better practice and refined theories.

The shift to large-scale evaluations of long-term social programs is a powerful demonstration of the ABC principle (Applied and Basic Combined). These evaluations are conducted on large-scale interventions in "living laboratories" guided by foundational theories in social psychology. Basic science results are emerging about what motivates durable behavior changes in key areas such as parenting, learning, community participation, and nonviolent conflict resolution. Some evaluations have 5- or 10-year lifetimes, involving billions of dollars, but the outcomes provide evidence-based practical guidelines for program management, while justifying expansion for successes. In addition, the wealth of data from hundreds of different contexts supports theory refinement, which could lead to even more widespread successes.

---

[1] US National Institutes of Health, *ClinicalTrials.gov* (Accessed August 6, 2015) https://clinicaltrials.gov/.

[2] Haskins, R. and Margolis, G., *Show Me the Evidence: Obama's Fight for Rigor and Results in Social Policy*, Brookings Institution Press, Washington, DC (2014).

phenomenon when a paper I coauthored with a young star in information visualization attracted an astonishing 140,000 downloads in its first few months.[17]

An even more striking statistic reveals the warm reception for journal papers from five-person teams of coauthors, as in 2000 such teams had 2.62 times as many citations as single-author papers did. Coauthor team sizes have been growing over time, and their impact compared to solo authors is also growing larger. It seems teams are learning to be more effective, possibly because teamwork has been taught and technology support is better. By 2013, 90% of science and engineering papers in the Web of Science had two or more authors.[18]

Skeptics point out that papers with more authors are more likely to get citations from each of the authors; but, even after discounting this factor, the advantage of teams remains strong. More coauthors will know more colleagues, so they might spread the news further, but there is strong evidence that work by multiple authors is actually better work. This is the potent central claim: teams produce better work, because they take on more ambitious projects, bring complementary knowledge, and apply diverse research methods. Further advantages are that teams have larger social networks to collect input during research and disseminate results as they emerge.

Another confirmation of the benefits of teams came from a conference on knowledge discovery and data mining (the ACM-KDD), which in 2014 had an impressively rigorous acceptance rate of 14.6%.[19] The reviewer ratings of the 1000+ submitted papers increased steadily for papers with up to five coauthors and then remained level. Reviewer ratings may be imperfect, but this bit of evidence seems especially potent.

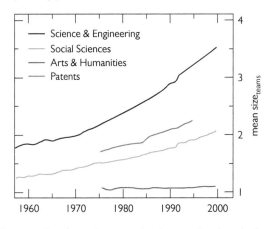

Figure 8.1 The mean size of coauthor teams in science and engineering journal publications has almost doubled in the years covered by this study. Social science and patent coauthor teams have grown more slowly, while arts and humanities teams have remained consistently small (Wuchty et al. 2007a).

While teamwork is growing in science research, it has long been a part of engineering research and even more so in design research. Design-studio training includes teamwork methods such as brainstorming and critiquing as part of the collaborative nature of design work, which is often conducted in open-plan environments so that social contacts are facilitated. Engineering training also involves teamwork to take on the complex and diverse components of many research projects, which is especially true in large business or government projects that may have thousands of engineers and designers. The growth of science research teamwork probably stems from the increasing complexity of contemporary challenges, and the improved technologies that support teamwork.

There are also substantial social and personal reasons that teams can be more effective. Working in a team, even a team of two, requires explicit coordination and puts pressure on each partner to deliver on time to satisfy stated expectations. In the best situations, teamwork promotes not only timely but also high-quality work, since there is a strong incentive to demonstrate excellence to partners who will recognize it. There is also strong social pressure to "pull your weight," an appealing industrial-age metaphor that means each team member contributes fairly. A further benefit of teamwork is the opportunity for all members to learn from each other, and sometimes to show off what they know. Junior members learn from research leaders, while senior members are exposed to new technologies and related disciplines from freshly trained students.

Teamwork has many other unstated, but substantial benefits, especially in creative work, that derive from and ethnic, racial, gender,[20] and personality diversity.[21] Diverse experiences and skills are clearly a benefit, but team members may also productively complement each other in the pressure for completion versus continuation to improve quality. They may balance breadth versus depth, basic versus applied research directions, and quantitative versus qualitative approaches. Resolving such conflicts or simply doing both is likely to improve research outcome quality.

Finally, researchers should remember that collaborations may prove to be more fun and fulfilling. Nobel Prize winner Daniel Kahneman goes to great lengths to describe the joyous intensity of his long-term collaboration with Amos Tversky in developing foundational principles of behavioral economics: "Amos and I enjoyed the extraordinary good fortune of a shared mind that was superior to our individual minds and of a relationship that made our work fun as well as productive."[22] Similarly, James Watson commented on "the fun of talking with Francis Crick" as they sought to understand the molecular structure of DNA.[23]

A linguistics colleague, Norbert Hornstein, describes the fun in his teamwork experience:

It's just more fun, especially when things are NOT working well . . . you see things from various points of view, something that working alone is very hard to do. And if you are lucky, the process lowers inhibitions and permits you to think differently than you normally do. You can be silly, clever, lead footed etc. and sometimes this kind of uninhibited thinking is just what you need to get around the problem. This has happened more than a few times for me in collaboration and when it happens it feels great: sort of like shooting the rapids after you've been becalmed. . . . as in most social things, it is possible to get energy from the other person. When I work alone, I can get at most 4 hours of serious work done in a day. When I am collaborating, there is really no limit. A friend and I once worked 26 hours straight to write a response to a paper of ours . . . True, we were punch drunk at the end, but that was part of the fun.[24]

Many team members report satisfaction and fun with team processes, but there is a dark side to teamwork. While mild respectful disagreements can be productive, forceful personality differences that lead to disruptive conflicts undermine team performance. The opposite effect is groupthink, in which team members all too quietly accept initial ideas without sufficient spirited discussion of alternatives. Vigorous discussions are also valuable during the initial project phases, when learning about other research methods, viewpoints, and variant terminology can smooth the way to future team success.

Teams also face difficulties of "free riding," which occurs when one or more team members don't contribute as much as others expect. There may be differences over project management decisions, but frequent differences center on the authorship order, credit for contributions, publication venue, choice of references, and writing style. In my experience, early open discussions of these issues enables amicable outcomes, but creative solutions such as writing two papers in different venues also produced a happy resolution while expanding our work in fresh directions.

Many teams fail to produce successful outcomes, but so do many individual projects. Researchers must learn to tolerate unsuccessful experiments, rejected proposals, and harsh paper reviews; perseverance and resilience are important personal characteristics. However, failures can sometimes lead to happy outcomes, such as new research directions. Also, there is heartening data that an unexpected experimental result or a paper rejection can actually trigger higher performance. One study found that rejected papers that were revised and resubmitted produced higher impact than papers that were accepted the first time.[25]

There is a growing research community, including an annual conference, around the topic of the Science of Team Science, but, in spite of the narrowly defined title, their studies, theories, and guidance apply to teams across science, engineering, and design.[26]

8.4 How to Do Team Research

To help ensure that these potential advantages of teams are realized takes thoughtful actions in forming the team and careful allocation of tasks; in addition, as teams grow larger, leadership and administrative skills are necessary. There are many theories about how to form teams,[27] and even books on forming research teams that collaborate over the Internet,[28] so these practical guidelines are just a starting point:

Previously successful collaborations: One of the strong correlates of team success is a history of fruitful previous collaborations. The practical application of this correlate in my work has been to first build a relationship and demonstrate compatibility by working together before writing a proposal or a paper together. Previous successful collaborations means that common ground (shared vocabulary and compatible working styles) has been found and that trust has been built. When companies or existing teams solicit our participation in working together, I like to start with some small collaboration before committing to a longer-term collaboration. I refuse to form a new collaboration under the tight pressure of submitting a proposal with a short deadline.

Balanced teams: Teams with mixtures of senior and junior members, women and men, or business and academic members are likely to produce higher quality work than homogeneous teams. Team members who bring knowledge of specific problems or research methods often provide an injection of fresh thinking that leads to high impact. But team members also need depth in their disciplines and proven successes on their own or in other teams. Teams with members of the same discipline can be effective when they have complementary skills, but team members from nearby or even distant disciplines can bring fresh problems, research methods, or analytic tools.[29] Scott Page's excellent book, *The Difference*, makes a strong case for the benefits of diversity, especially for the inclusion of women.[30]

Clearly defined goals and roles: As the team forms, important steps are to write a shared vision of the overall goals and to clarify individual roles, especially for large distributed teams. Then, an initial schedule can be developed that allocates tasks to be accomplished with deadlines to be met. These can be changed later, but having a clear specification of contributions from each team member is helpful, whether the plan is short-term work leading to a conference submission or multiple-year plans to deliver major breakthroughs, working systems, or mature products. Structured review processes in which some team members review work products of others helps. For proposal, report, or paper authoring, specializations may emerge; for example, some may be great at producing titles, abstracts, and introductions, while others may do excellent reviews of previous work. Team members may focus on evaluations or creating compelling and comprehensible figures. Finally, there may be social roles in teams, such as cheerleaders, gatekeepers, spokespersons, budget managers, or schedule keepers.

Credit for different roles can be spelled out at the end of the published paper, as is now required by an increasing number of journals.[31] Teams also have to decide on the authorship order, with the honored place of first author going to the major contributor. Discussion of authorship order should be held early in the project to ensure that expectations are clear to all. Sometimes strict alphabetic ordering by last name is kept as a tradition, but often senior researchers or lab directors take the last position. Disagreement about credit for ideas is one of the major reasons for research groups to break up. On one occasion we resolved a strong disagreement about author order by pushing the research further to develop the ideas into two strong papers.

Explicit statements of who does what by when: The overall vision sets shared expectations, and then there is the weekly management plan, which I convey to my research and course projects with the phrase "who does what by when" (see Chapter 11, Case Study 11.1). This strategy means that, for example, team members will commit to having Annette make the first draft of the screen design or first pilot implementation by 9 p.m. Tuesday evening, and Bharat provides feedback by noon Wednesday. Completing small commitments builds trust that leads to larger commitments.

Regular and open discussions: Teams are best when they hold regular and open discussions. Modest controversy is often healthy in choosing among alternative directions as well as in promoting trust among team members. Groups that have balanced speaking during meetings tend to perform better than teams in which one or two people dominate the discussion. Another commonly stated principle is acceptance of seemingly "wild" ideas that may offer unorthodox solutions or initiate new lines of thinking. Some creativity consultants develop systematic ways of promoting open discussions and diverse ideas.[32]

Good communication: Effective communication is not only the lifeblood of teams, but helps promote team success in contacts with others. Simply describing your work to other team members helps to clarify your intentions. Team members may have to learn how to speak to each other in constructive and positive ways during informal one-on-one discussions and in face-to-face group meetings. Often, getting team members to agree on terminology is a big step forward in forming common ground. Communication also includes respectful dialog, so replacing "your idea just won't work" with "I don't understand why you want to do it that way" changes the atmosphere in the room, raising the willingness of team members to contribute and inviting productive differences of opinion. When team members rehearse talks within the team, they not only promote team cohesion but probably produce better presentations to outsiders.

The team-working literature is filled with many variations and additions.[33] These provide useful guidance that may need to be tuned to local needs and sometimes violated because of other requirements. Leaders can use tools, such as the Collaboration Success Wizard, to help their team members collaborate more effectively.[34] Here are a selected few practical guidelines:[35]

Collaboration readiness: The team members are eager to work in the team and their management is supportive of team participation. Loners who are reluctant to work in teams are unlikely to become productive team members, and managers who allow but fail to encourage teamwork may undermine the team by providing inadequate resources or disparaging team successes. Some organizations promote a culture of collaboration by training for teamwork, making collaboration technologies readily available,[36] and celebrating successful teams.

Technology readiness for remote teamwork: The reality of contemporary teamwork is that inevitably some members will be traveling, while others are embedded in distant organizations, making regular face-to-face meetings difficult. Technology greatly facilitates collaboration at a distance, helping to bring team members closer together regularly to describe progress, share problems, exchange ideas, and forge agreements about future plans. Meetings by phone, Skype, or video conferences can help groups of 3 to 30 to coordinate their activities, learn from each other, and build trust. For larger groups, web conferencing tools like WebEx or GoToMeeting support presentations and discussions, while wikis, blogs, and deliberation systems provide durable records of substantive discussions including documents, links, data sets, videos, and more. To make such collaborations successful, team members need to have easy access to the right technologies, including network services, and be fluent users of their tools.

Technology readiness for collaboration: Many commentators remark about the power of body language in face-to-face meetings, which high-resolution low-latency conferencing seeks to achieve. However, there are virtues to slower technology-mediated collaborations, even with asynchronous tools such as email, shared calendars, blogs, and wikis. Some team members may be more effective when carefully composing text, which they can reread carefully before sending. Even controversial topics may be resolved by each party writing their position and then reflecting on their differences, possibly leading to thoughtful resolutions. Web-based sharing of data, draft reports, well-indexed published papers, and videos are often the core technologies for supporting team collaboration, while also enabling widespread dissemination.

Trained experienced leadership: Having a respected successful leader is a common component of success. Great leaders set visionary goals, inspire younger team members, push for high quality, and share the recognition and rewards. They also are attentive to and step in to resolve conflicts among team members, keep the project on schedule, deal well with setbacks, and even know when to remove someone from the team. In small teams, democratic management with no designated leader is possible, but as team sizes grow, leaders become valuable assets.

Adequate administrative resources and services: As teams grow larger, the successful teams have specialists to handle the administrative load of budgets, technology support, travel coordination, meeting planning, and human resource management (hiring, insurance, benefits, etc.).

Use of effective brainstorming strategies: Thousands of studies of brainstorming, usually in design and engineering, have shown that there are good and bad practices. While it can sometimes be helpful to have lively group discussions to develop new ideas, fresher and more diverse ideas emerge more reliably if individuals begin brainstorming on their own. Then team members can meet to present their ideas in a safe, nonjudgmental process that allows for clarification questions and refinements. Facilitated brainstorming sessions, with trained leaders, often elicit bold innovative ideas, which can be discussed and refined to gain support.

Team leaders who recognize that teams are continuously evolving may be able to make more effective interventions to promote collaboration. Tuckman's deftly described four stages of teams apply to many research teams: forming, storming, norming, and performing.[37] During team formation, building trust and learning about team members is key (forming); then, as activity picks up, intragroup conflicts may force changes in roles or goals (storming). After initial successes the team stabilizes (norming) and finally smoothly executes at a high level (performing). Some descriptions include a fifth stage, adjourning, to describe task completion or team dissolution.

One of the unsettled and controversial issues about teams is whether teams from a single discipline do better than those from distant disciplines. There is a growing awareness that collaborative work brings fresh opportunities based on novel combinations. There are even tantalizing data that point to the benefits of bringing together diverse knowledge and research methods. When Brian Uzzi and colleagues analyzed almost 18 million research publications in the Thomson Reuters Web of Science, they found that papers with what they called "atypical" citations produced higher citations counts than those containing only conventional citations.[38] However, the most successful papers also included high numbers of conventional citations, leading the authors to make the subtle but important comment that "novelty and conventionality are not factors in opposition; rather, papers that mix high . . . novelty with high . . . conventionality have nearly twice the propensity to be unusually highly cited."[39]

The thesis that high-impact research "draws on primarily highly conventional combinations of prior work, with an intrusion of combinations unlikely to have been joined together before" has appeal to many researchers who see themselves as pushing on boundaries or exploring frontiers.[40] The pattern of disruptive "intrusions" or maybe vivifying injections of fresh ideas reoccurs frequently in research histories where breakthroughs are the dominant metaphor. This breakthrough pattern is in harmony with reports from InnoCentive, the Web-based open problem site, that solutions often came from knowledgeable researchers from a nearby discipline who injected a fresh concept to an established domain.

The difficulties and opportunities for breakthroughs expand with more team members; but increasingly research projects are conducted by teams of dozens or hundreds of researchers, especially if they are distributed across organizations and are geographically remote. The US National Institutes of Health have launched many research centers to tackle complex problems such as cancer prevention, alcohol, drug, and tobacco abuse reduction, environmental health interventions, behavioral strategies to promote wellness, health disparity decrease, and so on.

Cummings and Kiesler point out that "policymakers in the research establishment must understand the difficulties of projects that cross distance and organizational boundaries, and decide if they are willing to invest in their extra coordination costs to make them successful."[41] However, even when adequate

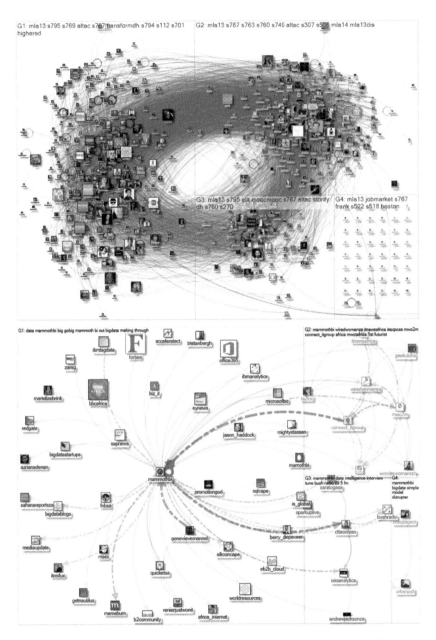

Figure 8.2 The upper network (made with NodeXL; www.codeplex.com/nodexl) shows three major clusters with thick bundles of connecting links indicating rich discussions within and across the clusters. The lower network shows a single major cluster that has just a few links indicating minimal discussion, while the small cluster to the upper right shows modest discussion.

funding is available, setting goals and managing large teams can be difficult. Engineering research teams for massive projects such as NASA missions or software projects also wrestle with coordination problems but often produce astonishing successes. In summary, teamwork in the small and the large can be difficult, but when done well it can be astonishingly productive, satisfying, and maybe even fun. Perseverance and resilience in the face of difficulties is just as important for teamwork as it is for individual work.

Many commentators on innovation point to larger networks as the source of fresh ideas and the stimulus to achieve high quality. Richard Florida and Stephen Johnson celebrate cities as the catalysts of large and high-density networks that promote fresh thinking and cross-pollination of ideas.[42] Physical meeting can be a big draw, as demonstrated by the success of the Meetup communities that hold meetings on emerging topics. However, it's not how big your network is, but how you use it. Large networks can be helpful in broadcasting ideas, but more potent networks are those that trigger discussions and provide productive feedback in response to well-defined questions. Managing the shift from audience counting to community building is a skill that many researchers are learning.[43] The growth of practical guidelines is matched by the efflorescence of theories of collective action, distributed intelligence, the wisdom of crowds, and so on. Visual representations of these networks clarify the distinction between a simple broadcast pattern and a spirited discussion (Fig. 8.2). In network analysis terms, low link density indicates inactive communities, while high link density indicates vigorous discussions. There is strong evidence that high-density communities are more successful.

8.5 Creating Successful University-External Partnerships

Overcoming the negative image of universities as "ivory towers" that are detached from the real world has been a long-term aspiration. In Ralph Waldo Emerson's famous speech "The American Scholar" in 1837, he argued strenuously for academics to engage in the real world: "Action . . . is essential . . . Without it, thought can never ripen into truth." That encouragement is still valid and still needed in today's academic environment to bring scholars into closer touch with civic, business, and global priorities. Partnerships are often difficult to initiate and maintain, but when they succeed they can produce large payoffs.

In more recent times, encouragement to work on real problems can be found in a potent *New York Times* op-ed piece by Nicholas Kristof, "Smart Minds, Slim Impact," in which the author complains that academic doctoral programs "have fostered a culture that glorifies arcane unintelligibility while disdaining impact and audience."[44] Kristof encourages research on current problems and public engagement through blogs, online lectures, and social media. Similarly, in their book *Everybody's Business: The Unlikely Story of How Big Business Can Fix the World*, Jon Miller and Lucy Parker present an enlightened view of how and why businesses should deal with global problems such as environment, health, education, energy, population, and human rights.[45]

The first reason for working with civic, business, and global partners is that they bring academics genuine problems in realistic settings, thereby clarifying requirements and providing a living laboratory to test candidate solutions. Fruitful collaborations steer practitioners to solve pressing problems and energize young researchers to make foundational breakthroughs that grow into widely applicable universal principles. Practitioners need to solve problems, while researchers need to publish innovative results, so synergistic collaborations blossom when there are strong opportunities to achieve both goals.

Beyond access to important pressing problems, there is a second reason for university researchers to work with civic, business, or global partners. These partners have access to data and living laboratories for testing hypotheses. Civic partners may be local, state, regional, or national government or citizen-led groups, who deal with education, community safety, transportation, environmental degradation, and many other problems. Business partners may be start-up companies with a bold idea, or mature companies with ample resources and large markets. Global partners may be international organizations (e.g., the World Health Organization, the International Monetary Fund, or Intelsat), regional associations (e.g., the European Union, the Organization of American States, or the Association of Southeast Asian Nations), or national governments with unique problems. These partners vary in size, sophistication, and resources, so developing appropriate expectations is important.

A major source of partnerships could be the large number of nongovernmental organizations (NGOs) that typically work on problems such as malaria, microfinance, or environmental protection or promote economic development in diverse nations. Some of these NGOs, like the Bill & Melinda Gates Foundation, have substantial resources and work on important problems, such as vaccine development, which will attract young researchers.

A third important aspect of many university-external partnerships lies in their asymmetric resources. Universities have energetic young researchers who are looking for challenges that will test, extend, and demonstrate their capabilities under the mentorship of accomplished professors. External partners have resources to support projects, which facilitates research partnerships.

More than 40 research projects in the University of Maryland's Human-Computer Interaction Lab have been sponsored by business partners, including large companies such as IBM, Apple, Google, or Microsoft as well as small companies, sometimes under innovation partnerships set up by the State of Maryland.[46] Other applied projects were supported by civic and mission-driven government agencies such as the Department of the Interior, the Census Bureau, or the National Institutes of Health.

Our experiences also revealed the difficulties that come from civic, business, and global partnerships. As in any partnership, there may be an initial period of simply learning each other's language and developing a common understanding of the problem. Then the work plan has to be negotiated so both sides have clear expectations of budget, schedule, and responsibilities.

The benefits of university-business partnerships are also demonstrated by the data from the ACM SIGKDD 2014 Conference on Knowledge Discovery and Data Mining.[47] The organizers found that the ratings for papers whose authors included a mix of academics and business practitioners were statistically significantly higher than those for papers whose authors were either all academics or all business practitioners. While more analyses like this one are needed, this evidence adds weight to the encouragement for university-business collaboration.

There are risks in university-business partnerships, so careful management is needed to ensure attention to business concerns for project confidentiality, data access restrictions, intellectual property rights, and publication plans. Successful collaboration depends on more openness than some businesses are used to for their internal projects. Universities typically are proud to report on their business partnerships, so even kick-off events need to be discussed to make sure business managers attend and support press releases.

Data access is a second concern, since companies have good reason to want to protect their customer, product, or service data. Universities have more open data access environments, so protecting corporate data can be difficult. Similar problems arise in dealing with medical histories and many government data resources. Since one of the academic goals is publication, clean data sets are essential, even if they are small versions that have been anonymized and de-identified to allow publication in figures and tables. In our research, we have developed a variety of strategies, such as having students hired as interns to allow them to see corporate confidential data. On other occasions, we tested our ideas and software on cleaned small versions of the data and then gave the software over to our partners for them to run on their confidential data sets. Data governance policies, such as assuring legitimate access while preventing malicious attacks, and long-term curation procedures take on increasing importance as data sets grow in size and value. Recognition for effective data curation is a growing issue in hiring and tenure cases and around the question of adequate citations or co-authorship in research papers that use valuable data sets.[48]

Some businesses start discussions by wanting to keep the partnership confidential, restrict access to their data, own the intellectual property produced, and limit publication of research results. These requirements go against university researcher expectations, so they need to be negotiated, but we have usually found ways to compromise, such as by sharing intellectual property rights or giving liberal licensing terms. We also give businesses a time-limited (2–4 weeks) right to review papers, so as to get the facts right and maintain confidentiality, before submission for publication.

A major advantage to businesses in collaborating and sponsoring research is their capacity to steer the work toward problems they find relevant, as well as the chance to be 6–12 months ahead of others in knowing the results.[49] Another advantage to businesses is the opportunity to offer internships or permanently hire students who work on their problems. Businesses who are listed as sponsors or who have coauthors for publications show their leadership in emerging topics. If companies cannot agree to terms that match university needs, that usually means they should find consultants for hire to do their work on their terms.

Working with businesses has many advantages for academic researchers, beyond funding, access to data, and use of test sites, but it has disadvantages, such as the mixed perceptions of colleagues. In some fields, work done for businesses is seen as constrained to narrow for-profit goals rather than as basic research. Even supportive reports recognize that "involvement in and support from industry remains a stigma for some investigators, as well as for some academic promotion and tenure committees."[50] Such critical attitudes inhibit valuable possibilities for many research groups, but sometimes such attitudes are merely the result of envy, which remains a disturbingly powerful force in academic communities.

A legitimate concern arises when faculty mentors have a financial or fiduciary relationship with a business that supports their research. In such cases, faculty have a conflict of interest in which they may steer student research toward work that promotes the business, and their own compensation, rather than the student's best interests. Disclosure of conflicts of interest, followed by effective independent oversight with regular reviews involving stakeholders, should provide protection for all.

Beyond small team partnerships with businesses, there are large-scale collaborative research centers,[51] which smooth the way for multiple businesses to join forces with larger university groups to promote a major research direction. These units face magnified versions of the challenges that small teams face, but some of the same guiding principles still apply: balanced teams, clear roles, clear goals, and good communication. The advantage is that the increased level of funding available for such centers can support seasoned management professionals.

Some collaborative research centers have local, state, or federal government involvement that brings new resources and challenges.[52] Etzkowitz has labeled these government, business, and university partnerships "the triple helix," to describe the intertwined efforts of universities to teach entrepreneurship, of governments to seek university involvement to drive regional economic development, and of businesses to join with universities in research partnerships.[53] Examples include the federally funded National Network for Manufacturing Innovation,[54] the US National Institutes of Health National Center for Advancing Translational Science,[55] and the State of California's Center for Information Technology Research in the Interest of Society (CITRIS; see Chapter 3, Case Study 3.1).[56] A unique collaboration is the Gulf of Mexico Research Initiative, whose $500 million funding from British Petroleum was provided in the aftermath of the Deep Horizon disaster and oil spill. This interdisciplinary community involving 130+ universities takes on applied and basic science, engineering, and design topics, already producing more than 500 papers in refereed journals and conferences (see Chapter 1, Case Study 1.1).[57]

The US National Science Foundation has made a strong effort to promote the NSF Innovation Corps (I-Corps) as a "public-private partnership program that teaches grantees to identify valuable product opportunities that can emerge from academic research."[58] While the goals are admirable, the initial efforts of this program seem too close to the discredited linear model that assumes basic research is done first then researchers are to "explore the transition of their technology concepts into the marketplace."[59] Earlier partnerships to define the research agenda, build trust with business partners, and test the ideas in the marketplace's living laboratory could yield higher payoffs. This linking of academic research with business needs is more in line with the popular "lean start-up" concept that advocates working with customers early on to define and develop products and services.[60]

Promoting collaborations is the mission of the Government-University-Industry Research Roundtable (GUIRR), which is a 30+ year old project of the National Academies.[61] The roundtable convenes several meetings a year on topics such as food safety, intellectual property, big data, social networking, and cybersecurity. The unique convening powers of the National Academies bring together leaders from government, university, and industry to have fruitful discussions and produce reports such as the one on "Guiding Principles for University-Industry Endeavors."[62] That report emphasized that the joint effort needs to be in alignment with the needs of both partners so that long-term relationships that lead to research results, market development, and exchange of personnel can be established.

The University Industry Innovation Network (UIIN) is a growing international community of academic and business leaders devoted to building partnerships and working hard to make them succeed. Their goal is to "exploit the full value of collaboration and cooperation, ultimately making an impact to academia, business and society."[63]

8.6 The Allure of Interdisciplinarity

During the past half-century, researchers, academic administrators, funding agency program managers, and many others have increasingly promoted the importance and power of interdisciplinarity and its variants: multidisciplinarity, transdisciplinarity, and crossdisciplinarity.[64] The traditional disciplinary boundaries have enabled hierarchically organized specialized communities of researchers to work on well-defined problems. However, early bridging disciplines such as physical chemistry, bioengineering, design science, or social psychology showed that there were substantial opportunities when collaborations could be formed to blend disciplines.

The growing discussion of interdisciplinarity (Fig. 8.3) is visible in reports from universities, professional societies, and national research agencies. The influential US National Academies issued a 2004 report that opened with this strong positive claim:[65]

Interdisciplinary research (IDR) can be one of the most productive and inspiring of human pursuits—one that provides a format for conversations and connections that lead to new knowledge.

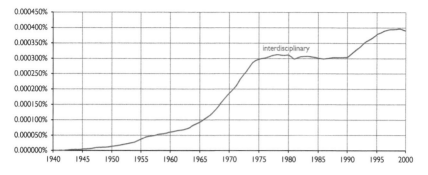

Figure 8.3 The Google Ngram Viewer for the term "interdisciplinary" shows the dramatic growth in its English language usage from 1940 to 2000. Created via Google Ngram, courtesy of Jean-Baptiste Michel, Yuan Kui Shen, Aviva Presser Aiden, Adrian Veres, Matthew K. Gray, The Google Books Team, Joseph P. Pickett, Dale Hoiberg, Dan Clancy, Peter Norvig, Jon Orwant, Steven Pinker, Martin A. Nowak, and Erez Lieberman Aiden. (2010) Quantitative analysis of culture using millions of digitized books. Science. Published Online Ahead of Print: 12/16/2010 DOI: 10.1126/science.1199644www.sciencemag.org/content/early/2010/12/15/science.1199644.

Their definition is broad:[66]

Interdisciplinary research (IDR) is a mode of research by teams or individuals that integrates information, data, techniques, tools, perspectives, concepts, and/or theories from two or more disciplines or bodies of specialized knowledge to advance fundamental understanding or to solve problems whose solutions are beyond the scope of a single discipline or area of research practice.

The National Academies report goes on to claim that interdisciplinary thinking is gaining ground because of the

1. inherent complexity of nature and society,
2. desire to explore problems and questions that are not confined to a single discipline,
3. need to solve societal problems, and
4. power of new technologies.

To buttress their claims, the authors include more than 40 case studies of institutions that have developed interdisciplinary programs. It is encouraging to read the optimistic findings, such as, "Successful interdisciplinary researchers have found ways to integrate and synthesize disciplinary depth with breadth of interests, visions, and skills."[67] On the other hand the authors warn that "the success of IDR groups depends on institutional commitment and research leadership. Leaders with clear vision and effective communication and team-building skills can catalyze the integration of disciplines."[68] In spite of this encouragement, junior researchers who clarify their mentors' attitudes to different forms of interdisciplinary research will have a better chance of making successful collaborations.

The respected American Academy of Arts and Sciences ran a follow-up conference (ARISE 2) entitled "Advancing Research in Science and Engineering, Unleashing America's Research & Innovation Enterprise."[69] Then the National Academies released a 2014 report that used the term "convergence" and "transdisciplinarity" in its push for collaborative research, especially in the physical sciences and engineering and in the life sciences and medicine.[70] The authors reiterate and document the dramatic changes taking place in many universities that broaden the sources and increase the frequency of collaborations:[71]

Convergence represents a cultural shift for academic organizations that have been traditionally organized around discipline-based departments. The overall ecosystem needed to foster and sustain convergence draws not only on academic contributors but increasingly also on the cross-fertilization of ideas with stakeholders and partners from national laboratories, industry, clinical settings, and funding bodies, as well as insights from economic, social, and behavioral sciences.

The growth of interdisciplinary programs has been documented in many reports, including an extensive analysis of American colleges and universities during 1975–2000; the latter showed that especially strong growth occurred in environmental studies and biomedical sciences.[72]

The practicalities of making interdisciplinary teams work are similar to those required to make any team work, with the additional necessity of understanding different research methods, reporting standards, and reward structures. Junior researchers who want to form interdisciplinary teams would do well to check with their senior mentors to get guidance and secure approval, possibly in writing. A good interdisciplinary teamwork strategy is for members to get early agreement as to what aspects of their research will be publishable in each discipline as well as in emerging interdisciplinary publications. Interdisciplinary projects will especially benefit from networking with like-minded teams to validate their strategies for themselves, their peers, and their mentors.[73]

While interdisciplinarity is increasingly widely accepted, those who still prefer traditional disciplinary boundaries are vocal opponents. The case for interdisciplinarity is made by Julie Klein in her book *Creating Interdisciplinary Campus Cultures*: "Interdisciplinarity is associated with bold advances in knowledge, solutions to urgent societal problems, an edge in technological innovation, and a more integrative educational experience."[74] She provides solid foundations and successful strategies for promoting interdisciplinarity on campus and warns of the difficulties that may emerge in individual decisions around hiring, tenure, and promotion, as well as administrative decisions around funding, space allocation, and recognition.

Jerry Jacobs responds with a thoughtful defense of disciplines, pointing out that disciplines have clear useful functions, such as promoting quality, coordinating curricula through professional societies, and providing clear career paths for young scholars.[75] He believes that those researchers who are eager for interdisciplinarity are free to explore it through research centers, labs, and institutes, which far outnumber the departments on most research campuses.

Jacobs and others are not convinced that interdisciplinarity more consistently generates breakthrough ideas or even that interdisciplinary research outcomes have higher impact. However, the complexity and variety of interdisciplinary research team strategies makes it difficult to prove or disprove these hypotheses. Early evidence shows fewer citations for interdisciplinary journals than single discipline journals, but interdisciplinary fields may need time to mature and grow.[76] Those who believe in the power of interdisciplinary research could provide evidence for it by documenting processes and outcomes, so convincing comparisons can be made. Two helpful insights would be to identify the sweet spots of which disciplines benefit by working together and whether nearby or distant disciplines produce more productive collaborations.

In spite of the criticisms, government funding agencies increasingly believe in the power of collaboration across disciplines. The US National Science Foundation uses the term "cross-cutting" research to describe funding programs that require participation from faculty representing two of its eight divisions. For example the "Cyber-Enabled Discovery and Innovation" program often brought partners from the physical sciences to work with computer scientists or engineers in developing new tools to support advanced research. Other recent topics included disaster response, Learning Health Systems, and educational analytics.

The European Union issued a 2004 report on interdisciplinary research, celebrating its potential for major breakthroughs "at the boundaries or intersections of disciplines."[77] The report warned that "interdisciplinary research proposals tend to 'fall between the cracks,'"[78] since senior research reviewers favor traditional disciplinary topics, but laid out detailed recommendations to accelerate interdisciplinary research.

British funding agencies also stepped forward with innovative programs to encourage interdisciplinary collaborations around new problems. For example, the Engineering and Physical Sciences Research Council lists these interdisciplinary research themes that go beyond traditional disciplines: digital economy, global uncertainties, energy, living with environmental change, healthcare technologies, and manufacturing the future.[79]

A clear testimonial for collaborative research between computer scientists and other disciplines comes from David Patterson's review of his 30 years running research labs on computer systems:[80]

The psychological support of others also increases the collective courage of a group. Multidisciplinary teams, which increasingly involve disciplines outside computer science, have greater opportunity if they are willing to take chances that individuals and companies will not.

This raises the question about whether there is an optimal distance in backgrounds of partners. For example, do computer scientists who are algorithm designers and systems builders produce high-impact research just as often as computer scientists who work with mechanical engineers or landscape designers? Supportive evidence about fresh thinking from outsiders comes from studies of the InnoCentive open innovation platform, which brings "solvers" to work on challenge problems. Winning solutions were positively correlated with distance from the source problem discipline, and women solvers were statistically significantly more effective.[81]

One of the advantages of interdisciplinary work is that it usually involves teams, often with different backgrounds, necessitating dialog to explain ideas. The dialog required in teamwork may play as large a role as the interdisciplinarity, since it forces team members to formulate and present their ideas clearly. Team members will have to agree on terminology, goals, roles, work schedules, and much more, which might trigger more thoughtful explanations and fresh solutions.

Interdisciplinary research should remain a personal choice, which attracts open-minded researchers because of the opportunities to learn something new, the fun of discovering colleagues with complementary thought processes, and the chance to do something distinctive. Although the attractions of well-understood disciplinary boundaries remain strong, the interest in interdisciplinary research continues to grow.

8.7 Skeptics' Corner

There are undeniable attractions and advantages to working alone.[82] Within the bounds of conference and funding agency constraints, individuals can choose topics they like, set their own schedules, and follow their personal agendas. Their claims to fame are clear, especially with observers such as managers, journalists, and patrons who recognize the familiar narrative of the lone genius. It remains true that academic tenure and promotion are granted on an individual basis, and awards such as the MacArthur Fellowship recognize individual accomplishments.

Individuals who prefer to work and write papers on their own are nonetheless likely to build close relationships with savvy mentors, helpful colleagues, and a supportive spouse or friends. Mentors and colleagues are sounding boards for ideas and sources of reality checks as intermediate results and fresh directions emerge. Spouses and friends have a well-defined but different role. They provide loyal and sympathetic encouragement, often as simple as "Don't worry, you've had hard times before. Stay with your research, you'll find a way forward. You always do. I believe in you."

Teamwork does take additional time, especially during team formation, when team members need to first learn about each other's terminology and research directions and then formulate a work plan and coordinate schedules. However, joining existing successful teams to integrate research methods can benefit all members and improve their publication portfolios.

The shift to team research is an opportunity for many but is not welcomed by all. Dysfunctional teams are painful parts of many research careers, often attributed to well-intentioned superiors who had political reasons to create teams but failed to provide the training or resources needed for success. Critics have complained about European Union projects in which collaborations across member countries were sometimes valued more than research needs. Critics also point to an ill-formed incentive model as undermining collaboration in the US National Cancer Institute's $350 million effort to create a software and data sharing community.[83]

Teamwork strategies are a growing part of training in many disciplines, but it may take some practice and a few failures to recognize when it is appropriate and when solitary work is best. Cummings and Kiesler summarize the difficulties thus: "There is tension between the benefits to innovation of working across disciplinary and organizational boundaries versus the risks that arise from the costs of coordination and relationship development in these collaborations."[84]

Working with industry partners may be seen as selling out to business, just as working with local or national governments or global partners may be seen as service rather than research. These are legitimate concerns that deserve respect. Similarly, some colleagues may disapprove of work with interdisciplinary partners, leading to difficulties when a researcher is reviewed for hiring, promotion, or recognition.

8.8 Summary

Teamwork is an increasingly popular way of doing research, probably because of the urgency of contemporary problems and the potential for high-impact work. Some funding agencies encourage or even require teamwork in their program announcements. However, teamwork is a complex strategy with many variations and occasionally goes badly, producing acrimonious fights and failed projects. While individual struggles may go unnoticed, team discord becomes public, so willingness to listen and compromise is vital. Perseverance and resilience in the face of the struggles are important since the benefits of teamwork, when done right, are large.

A key strategy for effective teamwork is to build on previously successful teams with familiar trusted partners. Balanced teams with a healthy mix of personalities, gender representation,[85] skills, and experiences are more often successful, especially if there is clear agreement on the goals and roles. Detailed management plans that gain agreement about "who does what by when" keeps team members moving forward rapidly. Successful outcomes are more likely when teams have a culture of open discussions where nascent ideas can be aired and meetings have roughly equal participation by team members. Other social processes such as well-designed brainstorming sessions, sometimes run by a professional facilitator, can lead to fresh ideas, as design schools have taught for decades.

Verbal communications skills are vital, especially for discussions among team members. Writing skills enable teams to successfully convey their results in ways that increase their impact. Similarly teams that practice presenting results with slide talks and video presentations are likely to produce better research and higher impact than those that do not. The complexity of teamwork means that there are many other ingredients to success, such as excellent leadership and administrative support, especially as teams grow larger.

Beyond teamwork strategies, there are two major issues for teams to resolve. The first is how to partner with civic, business, or global organizations so as to learn about important problems, balance the applied and basic research agendas, and have living laboratories to test their ideas. The central tenet of this book is that working on real problems with real users produces better applied and better basic research.

The second major issue is to decide on the degree of interdisciplinarity to include in the team. While there is broad enthusiasm for working across disciplines, even distant ones, there is legitimate resistance from those do not appreciate the benefits and pleasures of collaborations with diverse colleagues. Junior researchers would do well to gain support from their senior mentors in joining team and interdisciplinary projects.

CHAPTER 9

Test Ideas and Prototypes with Realistic Interventions

Prototyping helps you get ideas out of your head and into something more tangible—something you can feel, experience, work through, play with and test. . . . you can't afford not to prototype on your next project.

Todd Zaki Warfel, *Prototyping*

9.1 Introduction

Taking on ambitious decade-long projects that address substantial civic, business, and global priorities requires large teams of diverse researchers. It also requires wisely chosen research strategies that start small with proof of concept studies and then employ scaling up (increased size) and scaling out (increased diversity) to ensure validity and generalizability of the applied and basic research goals.

Successful strategies include progressive investment of effort and resources in (1) agile processes for iterative prototype refinement as theories and practical guidelines are refined, (2) big data analysis for pattern detection and predictive models, (3) case study reports to seek causal clarity through qualitative data analysis, and (4) visual analytics for exploration, discovery, and innovation.

The New ABCs of Research. First Edition. Ben Shneiderman.
© Ben Shneiderman 2016. Published in 2016 by Oxford University Press.

Throughout the research process, team leaders who have well-developed internal communication plans with both text and diagrams can promote team cohesion and continuously refine goals. Similarly, a well-developed external communications plan can elicit peer network feedback and promote stakeholder support. These practices are more common in engineering and design research, so shifting science research practices to more regularly apply pilot and prototype testing could accelerate their progress.

> **Test Ideas and Prototypes in Increasingly Realistic Ways**
>
> Rigorous and realistic testing of ideas and prototypes brings quantitative and qualitative feedback to scale up for size and scale out for diversity.

9.2 Agile Processes for Iterative Prototype Refinement

Going to the moon was a major accomplishment for applied and basic research in science, engineering, and design. Moving from President Kennedy's 1961 vision to the 1969 success produced worldwide excitement plus dramatic advances for each discipline. The rapid success benefited from substantial resources, national commitment, and swift movement from small to larger prototypes, in many parallel projects. The scaling up from the one-person Mercury capsule, to the two-person Gemini vehicle, to the much larger three-person Apollo spacecraft was matched by the scaling up of the launch rocket system from the Atlas, to the larger Titan II, to the massive Saturn V. These were also exercises in scaling out, as each system had to deal with more challenging contexts from short-term to long-term earth-orbit missions, and then lunar landing. Dozens of other major components, such as spacesuits, steering rockets, and computer displays, were prototyped and tested in earth-based environments and then in suborbital, earth-orbit, and moon-orbit conditions, leading up to the momentous moon landing in July 1969.

Few projects will ever be as ambitious or dramatic as the first moon landing, but every project can learn from the engineering and design prototyping processes that provide early, quick, and low-cost tests that speed refinements, so as to support movement to larger, more diverse, and more ambitious tests. Prototypes help experimenters refine their measurement techniques, theoreticians to validate their predictive models, and managers to build confidence in their teams. Designer Todd Warfel writes that "One of the fundamental values of prototyping is that it is generative, which means as you work through the proto-typing process, you're going to generate hundreds, if not thousands, of ideas. . . . prototyping often leads to innovation and a significant savings in time, effort, and cost."[1]

Most research and practitioner organizations have some prototyping strat-egy; these strategies have diverse names that describe the type of models used, including scale model, concept car, test bed, breadboard, or mock-up. Other prototypes can be in the form of a quick drawing, textual description, or com-puter simulation, with names such as sketch, scenario, storyboard, or wire-frame. The goal of all these strategies is to use quick, low-cost methods that allow researchers and other stakeholders to refine their ideas and demonstrate the successes necessary to gain funding and approval, so as to move on to the next stage. Google's hybrid model of research is based evolutionary growth of projects tested in vivo with live users: "We have structured the Google envir-onment as one where new ideas can be rapidly verified by small teams through large-scale experiments on real data, rather than just debated" (see Chapter 1, Case Study 1.2).[2]

Researchers conducting hypothesis testing experiments may design prelim-inary experiments, with names such as a feasibility study, vanguard experiment, pilot test, pilot study, pilot experiment, and so on. These varied terms are often tied to larger concepts such as agile development, iterative design, technology demonstrator, or rapid prototype, all designed to produce a trial balloon, proof of principle, or proof of concept that will then need scaling up, ramping up, scal-ing out, and so on.

Prototype testing has many benefits to the research team, such as enabling the early, quick, and low-cost tests already mentioned. Prototypes, in their varied forms, are helpful in communicating with others in ways that are usually much more powerful than a written plan for a scientific controlled experiment, an engineering specification sheet, or a design requirements document. As Mike Davidson, Vice President of Design for Twitter reportedly quipped, "A proto-type is worth a thousand meetings."

Multiple hand-drawn sketches are especially attractive, since not only are they quick, but their incomplete, unformed style invites commentary and sug-gestions. Colleagues, managers, users, funders, potential customers, and other stakeholders feel comfortable, maybe even eager, to comment on sketches ra-ther than a single polished working model since they can easily ask clarifying questions, make outrageous comments, or propose alternate directions, without fear that they will undermine a substantial effort. In short, using multiple prototypes is a high-payoff strategy that is also fun.

Prototype testing is common in engineering and design disciplines. In automotive design, concept car sketches lead to 3D computer renderings and clay models, all of which are designed to quickly gain feedback from colleagues, managers, and others. Increasingly, 3D printed models enable designers to make tangible models that can be painted, passed around, and replaced by still more realistic models. Then, a handcrafted car is built and tested before the manufacturing process is scaled up to the assembly-line level. Similarly, architects go from sketches, to precise drawings generated with computer-assisted design tools, and then to foam models. Likewise, aircraft manufacturers develop elaborate computer models of new aircraft; the use of such models dramatically speeds up development and enables wind tunnel simulations until, eventually, a prototype is constructed for actual flight testing.

User interface design researchers and practitioners have been leading proponents of several innovative prototyping techniques, especially sketching, scenario writing (sometimes with impressive videos), mock-ups, and paper or functional prototypes.[3] The electronic environment for building user interfaces makes it convenient for varied prototyping tools that allow rapid construction and easy testing of multiple interfaces for desktop, Web, and mobile applications. The user interface and user experience design culture strongly supports usability testing, which is also scaled up from testing a few users in an hour to testing hundreds of users over a few days, collecting performance data and satisfaction ratings. Usability testing with varied user groups helps ensure that novel designs will be effective with skilled computer users, novices, users with disabilities, culturally diverse users, and even low literacy users.

E-commerce Web and mobile device designers are even more ambitious, often testing millions of consumer users through A/B experiments in which varying designs with different layouts, colors, wording, images, and so on are tested with actual users who are randomly assigned to the A versions (maybe small product photos with longer descriptions) or B versions (maybe large product photos with short descriptions) to see which version produces the most sales.[4] Ron Kohavi, who reports that Microsoft has approximately 200 A/B experiments running every day,[5] refined his methods by scaling up from small studies to experiments involving tens of millions of users, while scaling out to compare the responses from diverse user communities. Similarly, Amazon, Netflix, eBay,

Etsy, and most other e-commerce websites start with small studies and then scale up to multiple large studies and scale out to diverse user communities.

In similar ways, usability tests and massive online experiments accelerate design evolution as well as contribute to publishable design research. Small, well-controlled, human-subject experiments are favored by researchers who are developing foundational theories. Using combinations of methods helps build confidence in the results, clarify user intent, lead to new hypotheses, and make for a convincing case for fellow researchers.

The use of business-related experiments is also supported by innovation consultant Michael Schrage, who claims that "the more simply and creatively you can experiment, the more simply and creatively you can learn to add value."[6] His "5×5" strategy, which he describes as "a rapid methodology emphasizing lightweight, high-impact experimentation," directs a team of 5 people to work for 5 days to design 5 business experiments that could be done in 5 weeks for less than $5000 each.[7] The goal is to try new ideas, develop appropriate measures, and lay the foundation for scaling up and scaling out. He wants more than good ideas; he wants demonstrated, measurable, and repeated successes that can be widely applied in large organizations by nonresearchers whose motivation needs to be raised to deliver reliable products and services. Schrage supports the combination of applied and basic research, seeing successful application as more challenging than abstract theories. He admonishes intellectual property lawyers who talk about "reduction to practice," suggesting that they talk about "elevation to practice."[8]

Another form of prototyping is to release an "alpha version," that is, a rough early form, of a new software product or service to a small number of users. Once it is refined, it can be released as a "beta version," which is a high-quality product or service that is actively being refined.

Scientists are rarely taught about prototyping their experiments, but the idea of turning initial efforts into more mature experiments is frequently passed on from mentors to their students. Publication of results of prototype tests is usually difficult, since peer-reviewed journals expect well-controlled and complete experiments, possibly with replications.

Beveridge's classic book *The Art of Scientific Investigation* makes a useful comment on pilot experiments in science: "One type of preliminary experiment is the 'pilot' experiment, which is often used when human beings or farm animals are the subjects. This is a small-scale experiment often carried out at the laboratory to get an indication as to whether a full-scale field experiment is warranted."[9] Medical tests usually start with small cohorts to check for safety and efficacy before scaling up to large randomized clinical trials.

In speaking to science researchers about informal processes, cardiology researcher Guy Salama described how he first tried a hormone test on a few rats to determine the impact of varying doses on atrial fibrillation. Then studies were conducted with more rats, and a controlled study with rats verified the results against placebo injections. Then Salama described scaling up to more expensive studies with rabbits and even more elaborate studies with dogs. Failed studies took only limited time and costs but helped collect evidence and refine procedures for the results they were seeking to prove. The resulting cleansed narrative in a peer-reviewed journal presented early phases of the testing in a single sentence, while reporting at length on the successful results with dogs.

A major example of scaling up from initial efforts in physics research is the Laser Interferometry Gravitational-Wave Observatory (LIGO) project. The LIGO goal is to detect gravitational waves, originally predicted by Einstein in 1916, with extremely precise measurements at distant points on the earth. This attempt at validating gravitational theories is the most expensive project funded by the US National Science Foundation, involving hundreds of researchers supported by multiple international partners. Starting in 1992, the project managers have gone from small devices meant to develop measurement techniques to 2.5-mile-long devices with increasing accuracy but have not yet detected the elusive gravitational waves. A further doubling in accuracy, now underway, could bring the promised results. The long scaling-up process has produced valuable scientific research and impressive engineering accomplishments, which could improve research in other arenas.

Taking risks is well accepted in design, studied in engineering, and should be part of training in science. Risk is part of research. Most government research agencies encourage high-risk projects, which speed learning from failures while keeping costs low. These policymakers can steer funding to promising directions. Unfortunately, failed research directions are rarely publishable, but they can add credibility to papers that present successful outcomes. The "lean startup" concept for forming innovative businesses is closely tied to testing early prototypes with customers to define and develop successful products and services (see Chapter 8, Section 8.5).

9.3 Big Data Analysis for Pattern Detection and Predictive Models

The remarkable growth in data collection and dissemination techniques by way of Internet-supported distributed databases continues to produce grand opportunities for analytic insights that further accelerate the growth of data resources. While most commentators see this as a flood, deluge, inundation, tsunami, tidal wave, or firehose, I prefer to shift these watery metaphors to happier thoughts about the thirst-quenching streams, life-giving irrigation, and playful splash pools of data.

I think these happy metaphors would better serve the big data discussions that address the value, velocity, variety, and validity of data sources. The value of big data is in providing fresh insights to complex important physical, business, environmental, and social processes. For the first time in history, much of what we do is online and, for the first time in history, we have the tools to analyze these streams of data. Social media discussions, e-commerce transactions, and sensor outputs produce an ever more complete image of human and natural activity. The benefits from the massive data sets collected by private businesses and government agencies are attractive, but threats to privacy remain serious concerns.[10] The positive outcomes from big data are well-designed consumer products and services, environmentally protective agricultural practices, efficient energy use, and effective healthcare delivery. The downside is the broad violation of privacy by corporations and government agencies,[11] resulting in a reduced willingness of individuals to speak out on controversial issues, and a heightened fear of repressive leaders, malicious criminals, or annoying spammers.

Advocates of big data predictive models claim that the strong correlations between behavior patterns and meaningful outcomes are sufficiently interesting and reliable to support productive interventions. In simple cases, supermarkets that identify growing purchases of a product can increase their stocks of desired products. In a more ambitions case, New York City big data analysts correlated the occurrence of major fires with building age, type, size, construction materials, and so on to help fire inspectors best use their scare resources to look for dangerous violations. The New York City Fire Department hopes that this strategy will lead to a reduction in the number of severe fires, as well as in fires overall, as it will enable them to remove inflammatory materials and implement safe practices at high-probability fire locations.[12] Similarly, social media companies make predictive models to suggest potential friends to follow or interesting postings, while music websites suggest new album releases that correlate with your listening pattern. Mistaken recommendations are usually harmless. Viktor Mayer-Schönberger and Kenneth Cukier argue for "a move away from the age-old search for causality . . . instead we can discover patterns and correlations in the data that offer us novel and invaluable insights . . . we don't always need to know the cause of a phenomenon; rather we can let the data speak for itself."[13]

The engineering challenge is to deal with the volume of big data that flows from the still growing millions of daily traffic reports, billions of stock market transactions, and trillions of Internet packet transfers. Collecting the terabytes, petabytes, and exabytes of data requires new hardware and software architectures, but that is only the starting point.

Cleaning the data and transforming it into useful resources is still a manual process for the wide variety of big data, which can range from once-a-second logs of a patient's body temperature, to hourly river level reports provided by arrays of sensors in a vast region, to the daily logs of a billion Facebook users. The cleaning process has to account for errors from instruments, changing collection practices, failures of networks, and bugs in software. In addition, when the sources include text data, the validity of results derived from analytic tools may be jeopardized by the presence of malicious content, terminology inconsistencies, or even simple typos.

The basic strategy is to seek for data patterns that can guide decisions, as is done in recommender systems that use previous patterns to suggest films to watch, music to purchase, friends to follow, or hotels to stay at. Other systems seek to ferret out credit card fraud by spotting purchasing patterns that are common to fraudsters yet unusual for a given customer, for example, a large purchase from a country that a customer has never visited or a small purchase from a gas station that a customer has never used. Since 3%–4% of all credit card charges are fraudulent, there is a large database from which to extract common patterns for fraud.

On the other hand, the use of big data methods to search for terrorists needs to be seriously questioned, since there are rarely sufficient numbers of consistent patterns available to build reliable predictive models.[14] The central concern is the large number of false positives, which may lead to invasive investigations of normal citizens who occasionally do something out of the ordinary, such as sending money to a needy friend in an unstable foreign country. These false positives can undermine the culture of freedom and privacy in ways that weaken strong communities and reduce trust in government.

With these cautions in mind, the growing sophistication of data scientists, software engineers, and visual analytics designers can harness big data for productive purposes; even so, constant awareness is necessary. For example, in 2009, the enthusiasm over the capacity of the Google Flu Trends to predict outbreaks up to 2 weeks in advance of hospital reports was seen as an early triumph of big data: by analyzing search logs for terms such as "flu" and "fever" or products such as "Tylenol," researchers found that regional increases in the number of search queries for these terms were strong signals of flu outbreaks and that these signals could be detected before hospital and clinic reports from the Center for Disease Control and Prevention confirmed the outbreaks.[15] However, the predictive models diverged from reality, producing misleading estimates that had misled health planners in allocating resources. Changes to search algorithms, as well as a lack of continuous monitoring, meant that the predictive models were no longer effective.[16]

Similar slips in high-frequency trading models or econometric models have led to costly mistakes; so, the methods used for the analysis of big data require further refinement. In the preface to their data mining book, Ian Witten, Eibe Frank, and Mark Hall warn that "exaggerated reports appear of the secrets that can be uncovered by setting learning algorithms loose on oceans of data."[17] Similarly, a National Academy of Sciences report warned that "attempting to bring statistical principles to bear on massive data . . . may yield results that are not useful at best or harmful at worst."[18] So the qualified message is that the value of big data remains promising in dealing with complex problems that were previously beyond analysis, but care is necessary.

The greatest care should be for the use of big data in life-critical or high-cost applications that can lead to dangerously wrong recommendations if only correlational models are applied without understanding the complexity of real-world decisions. Understanding causal factors and the implications of mistakes can be advanced by coupling big data correlations with closer examination through case study reports, which may lead to causal clarity. Another way to improve the efficacy of big data is to add visual analytics methods that provide the capacity to better understand unusual distributions, clusters, outliers, and other patterns.

9.4 Case Study Reports: The Path to Causal Clarity

The scale of big data is impressive, but in their enthusiasm for it, some analysts forget that these new techniques can be deceptively incomplete. Having every tweet or online purchase from a person may not be enough to understand his or her motivations, decision-making paths, temporary exceptions, or mistaken actions. Furthermore, Twitter or Facebook users are a biased selection of the population of any country, so using that data to predict shopping, elections, or support for political decisions is risky. Social media postings do provide rapid

CASE STUDY 9.1 A VIENNESE VERSION OF BLENDING DISCIPLINES

Professor Dr. Werner Purgathofer

Reproduced with permission from Robert F. Tobler—rftobler.at.
http://austria-forum.org/af/Wissenssammlungen/
Wissenschaftler/Purgathofer,_Werner

Even in the elegant streets of traditional Vienna, which produced great scientists like Doppler, Boltzmann, Schrödinger, and Freud, and famed composers like Haydn, Mozart, and Beethoven, there is the rumble of change. While its leading universities largely adhere to disciplinary boundaries, there are visionary thinkers who see novel interdisciplinary possibilities.

Professor Dr. Werner Purgathofer heads the renowned Institute of Computer Graphics and Algorithms at the Technische Universitaet Wien (Vienna University of Technology). The institute is located downtown in a renovated nineteenth-century building, behind whose five-story, rectilinear, unadorned facade are respected academicians who work on basic computing theory problems. However, this group also includes some 25 applied researchers who work on scientific visualization, computer graphics, and virtual environments. But Purgathofer pushes toward even bolder possibilities that stem from applied problems driven by the needs of industrial partners.

To realize his ambitions of high-impact research, Purgathofer found it helpful, and maybe even necessary, to be president and scientific director of the VRVis Research Center, which he founded in 2000.[1] He received initial funding from the Austrian government and the City of Vienna, which has enabled him to grow this group to 60 researchers devoted to strengthening Austria's capacity for innovation and competitiveness. Located in the modern high-tech center of Donau City, on the outskirts of Vienna, the TechGate center is in a high-rise glass-fronted tower, across the street from the Vienna International Center, which hosts the United Nations Office in Vienna, and the International Atomic Energy Agency.

The VRVis Research Center's website has a clear statement of its goals: "Transfer of technology from science to industry is not an empty phrase but rather the daily agenda of VRVis. With a solid foundation in basic research, VRVis sees itself as a bridge between academia and industry and conducts applied research for its company partners which lead to joint product development."[2] The bridge to industry includes more than 30 partners, who provide funding as well as pressing problems whose solution could have immediate application in the form of new products or better services for customers.

The partners are roughly grouped into the automotive industries, urban infrastructure, medical/biotech, and cultural heritage or creative industries. I found the visualizations of urban scenes, transportation systems, and historic buildings to be innovative, as were the medical data visualizations, such as one that showed a 3D reconstruction of a human heart from MRI images to show damage following a heart attack.

Purgathofer's quiet style is deceptive, but he reveals his quest for diversity in the hobbies he lists in his home page: orienteering, jogging, skiing, tennis, playing piano, reading, trying to learn Spanish, and ballroom dancing. His traditional academic strengths provide a solid foundation for leading others in what are clearly bold directions. Getting continuing government support and doing corporate outreach successfully over more than a decade testifies to his skills. Equally important is his growing success in getting traditional researchers to integrate design and engineering practices into their scientific work.

When asked about how he measures the impact of his integrative strategy he says: "Our biggest success is when companies actually incorporate results in their processes or products. But to be valuable for industry we also need to stay at the forefront of scientific research, i.e. the researchers have to successfully publish papers in the top scientific media. In this context it is a challenge to keep the main goal of the center in our focus: to transfer scientific results into the real world! This is quite different from solving the problems researchers assume are out there."[3]

[1] VRVis, *Forschungsthematik: Visual Computing* (Accessed August 8, 2015) www.vrvis.at.
[2] VRVis, *VRVis Forschungs GmbH* (Accessed August 8, 2015) http://www.vrvis.at/about?set_language=en.
[3] W. Purgathofer, personal communication.

---

feedback and provocative quotes, making them irresistible to journalists and others seeking to comment on breaking news stories.

However, another gift of social media, email connectivity, and nearly ubiquitous phones is that personal contacts are possible. Anthropologists and journalists have long valued face-to-face interviews to deeply understand human actions, assess context, collect memorable stories, and spot surprising patterns, all of which contribute to an ethnographer's "thick descriptions." Pat Bazeley describes qualitative research as focusing on "observing, describing, interpreting, and analyzing the way people experience, act on, or think about themselves and the world around them." She claims that qualitative data derived from personal contacts can be "intense, engaging, challenging, non-linear, contextualized, and highly variable. It is potentially productive of fresh insights and deep understanding."[19]

Qualitative data analysts also know that interviewees and informants may have reason to deceive. Remembering that all human actions are situated in a rich environment of physical, social, and cultural phenomena could guide researchers to be more cautious but also to collect evidence to make more generalizable theories and valid practical guidelines. Trained ethnographers are aware that a small number of qualitative case studies can leave a biased impression, so they are cautious about making overly broad claims.[20]

Rigorous qualitative data analyses are a valuable part of case study research methods, which are gaining acceptance in some fields, for more than ways to generate hypotheses. Advocates, such as Robert K. Yin, assert that repeated case studies are a way to collect evidence that supports hypotheses, especially if care is taken to collect data for both sides of rival hypotheses.[21] This bold claim is controversial with quantitative researchers, who see statistically significant differences from replicated controlled experiments as the gold standard. As rigorous case study methods are developed to answer questions about complex social or environmental systems, researchers are gaining confidence that replicated case studies provide valuable evidence to support hypotheses. The benefit of carefully collected case studies is that they can provide in-depth analyses, reveal unexpected behaviors, and expose sequences of events that suggest cause and effect.

For researchers who are combining applied and basic research, a mixed-methods strategy may provide a good balance for capturing both controlled experimental and authentic case study data, thereby gaining multiple confirmations to please diverse audiences. For our work on developing novel visual analytics tools for use by domain experts, we balanced quantitative controlled experiments of specific design features with ethnographic-style, qualitative, 4–8-week case studies of domain experts solving their own problems. The controlled experiments with 20 participants gave convincing evidence of the advantage of one design feature over another, with quantitative evidence for faster performance and increased accuracy. The case studies gave compelling stories of domain experts who found the new visualization tool gave a clearer picture of their data, leading them to make more confident and detailed statements of their results in published papers. Additional quotes about how our tools changed their problem-solving strategies were encouraging, as was the manager who reported that the data visualization led to direct changes in a commercial product. An additional perspective came from a short survey that was emailed to our users and produced 57 responses that confirmed the feedback from our case study users.[22] Our growing confidence in and fluency with case studies led to increasing the number of case studies from 3–5 up to 10–12 per project.[23] The key feature is having real users, from outside our development team, working on real problems with real data.

One reason for the growing interest in case studies and qualitative data is that both quantitative data from controlled experiments and that from big data collections are also seen as flawed.[24] Controlled experiments can be far removed from reality, with constraints that facilitate measurement but raise serious questions of validity and generalizability. Medical randomized clinical trials are usually seen as the "gold standard" for evidence-based medicine, a strategy in which stresses the importance of quantitative data in medical decision-making. However, each patient is unique and may not match the set of patients selected for a clinical trial. Typically, clinical trial patients have a single disease, are selected for age, gender, or other attributes, and are highly compliant in their adherence to the experimental protocols. The patients treated by doctors may suffer from multiple diseases, have complex medical histories, and be resistant to adhering to the treatment requirements.

The prestigious *New England Journal of Medicine*, which typically focuses on controlled trials and other experiments, urged a return to the acceptance of case studies in medicine. The lead article offered a three-generation case study which acknowledged the controversy by stating, "Data are important, of course, but numbers sometimes imply an order to what is happening that can be misleading. Stories are better at capturing a different type of 'big picture.'"[25]

Peter Kramer, a renowned clinical psychiatrist and best-selling author, spoke up in support of case studies: "vignettes can do more than illustrate and reassure. They convey what doctors see and hear, and those reports can set a research agenda. . . . I want to venture a radical statement about the worth of anecdote. Beyond its roles as illustration, affirmation, hypothesis-builder and low-level guidance for practice, storytelling can act as a modest counterbalance to a straitened understanding of evidence."[26]

Many independent researchers have developed varied forms of case studies, field studies, and ethnographic reporting strategies. The popular term "action research" was coined by social psychologist Kurt Lewin to describe an interactive inquiry process between researchers and practitioners to change an existing situation into an improved situation. He is credited for making the comment, "If you truly want to understand something, try to change it." Action research invokes applied research to produce change with a theory foundation to guide and interpret results so that they can be more widely applied.[27]

Designers thrive on rich observational data from case studies, while big data scientists prefer voluminous automated activity data. Observations and interviews can be biased, just as automated activity data can be selective. What does a problem-solving domain expert do? Maybe, just maybe, combining the two strategies can produce more realistic and widely applicable insights that both guide practitioners and support theorists.

9.5 Visual Analytics for Exploration, Discovery, and Innovation

The remarkable growth of visual analytics tools and methods has dramatically reshaped the possibilities for exploration, discovery, and innovation.[28] However, broad adoption of these transformative tools could be accelerated by national efforts to raise awareness, promote visual literacy, and stimulate usage across science, engineering, and design.

The benefits of visual analytics have been validated by rigorous empirical and field studies, demonstrated in key industry applications, disseminated by selected journalists and bloggers, and championed by some government agencies. The substantial payoff of visual analytics is that it reveals vast evolving networks, in which dramatic local changes anticipate cascading chain reactions of human activity. These potent chain reactions are often constructive, but they can also be destructive. Other success stories include pharmaceutical drug discovery, cheminformatics, healthcare delivery, oil-gas discovery, manufacturing production management, national intelligence analyses, and financial data analyses.

Acting promptly to develop powerful data gathering, analysis, and visualization tools will lay the foundation for prosocial constructive actions by individuals, communities, corporations, and governments. A central intellectual contribution is to ensure that statistical algorithms, with their dangerously incomplete predictive models, are not the only methods used to make critical decisions. By introducing visual analytics tools, analysts can make deep insights that lead to meaningful universal principles, causal explanations, more reliable predictions, comprehensible prescriptive guidance, and generalizable theories that, in turn, spawn new insights.

Visual analytics users have demonstrated that buried in big data are big insights. However, for big data resources to be more than larger haystacks in which to find precious needles, the massive data centers will need to support humans trying to make sense of it all. Fortunately, innovations in visual analytics are demonstrating that a good user interface is worth a thousand petabytes.

Even the White House press release on the national big data initiative (mentioned in Chapter 7, Section 7.6) emphasized "developing scalable algorithms for processing imperfect data in distributed data stores" and "creating effective human-computer interaction tools for facilitating rapidly customizable visual reasoning."[29] These well-crafted challenges put visual analytics and user interfaces solidly on the national agenda, ready to work with devotees of automated strategies for influencing academic, business, and government efforts.

Three possible applications of visual analytics address the White House challenges and clarify human participation:

1. *Cleaning error-laden data,* such as the 6300 emergency room admission records in which statistical analyses had failed to detect the 8 patients who were entered as being 999 years old. Information specialists will recognize this as a code for "age unknown," but the programs that calculated ages of admitted and discharged patients accepted this as a normal value, thereby distorting the results. A simple bar chart of the ages would have led any viewer to gasp with surprise. There are an unlimited number of errors that may be missed by algorithms but spotted by experts, such as the patient who was admitted to the emergency room 14 times but discharged only twice. The variety of data errors is astonishing, such as, for example, when a stock that normally trades in the $60–$70 range has a reported trade of $655, or when the annual marketing data report shows no results for the month of April, which normally has strong Easter sales. A quick glance at an appropriate visual display enables users to confirm the expected and detect the unexpected, especially errors.

2. *Supporting exploration and discovery.* Users typically begin with identifying the questions they wish their data to address; these questions then lead them to choose a particular visualization, such as line charts, timelines, size- and color-coded scattergrams, and maps. Sophisticated visual representations enable users to compare hierarchies, treemaps, and networks to spot emerging trends or shrinking communities. These users may immediately spot surprises or errors, but typically they split a medical data set to see men or women in separate displays, group by age, and then maybe focus on overweight or hypertensive patients. Multiple simultaneous coordinated views mean that an interesting cluster can be selected in one view to produce highlights in every view. The interactive control panel is the driver's wheel for the visualization engine, allowing users to explore overviews, filter out unwanted items, zoom in on interesting areas, and then click for

details-on-demand. Insights can lead to bold decisions in medicine, business, and national security, or compelling stories about sports teams and the social networks of Hollywood stars.

3. *Presenting results to policymakers, business managers, and news media viewers.* Election-night television hosts present striking graphics of red and blue states with demographic voting differentials. The following morning newspapers show detailed data by county or Congressional district, with meaningful comparisons to previous elections or highlights about exceptional outcomes. Similarly, public health analysts distill millions of reports into a few cogent visualizations to guide policymakers and inform the public about the extent of spreading epidemics or the success of cancer treatments.

The development of technology that simplifies production of high-quality static graphics, animated weather maps, video presentations, and interactive websites has lowered the barriers to entry. Some great designers have produced compelling visualizations for publication in books and websites, museum exhibits, or animated videos. However, we are just at the early stages of broadening visual literacy and training a new generation to create effective visualizations, so there are still too many flashy-trashy uninformative visualizations that receive too much attention.

If visual analytics tools that integrate powerful statistical techniques are made commonly available to visually literate viewers, the benefits could be as potent as the use of graphical user interfaces. There will be resistance by those who prefer text and tables, but a populist visual analytics movement could accelerate discovery in every discipline and support more informed decisions from business and government.

9.6 Skeptics' Corner

Some applied and basic researchers believe so strongly in the clarity of their plans for science experiments, engineering projects, or design concepts that they resist the idea of pilot testing or prototyping. These skeptics see the idea of a small pilot experiment or prototype test as a waste of time and energy. Their confidence in their plans is admirable, but I believe misplaced. Small prototype tests of initial ideas have generally proven to be a fruitful process that speeds work, avoids costly mistakes, and increases quality. Furthermore, the tools for making pilot tests, sketches, models, and simulations have grown more sophisticated, further lowering the cost and time to make and test prototypes. Nonetheless, critics of prototyping believe that time is better spent in more literature study or analysis than in developing prototypes.

This chapter also covers data collection and analysis techniques that may be new to some researchers. Big data methods require new skills and ways of problem-solving, which may be more than a traditionally trained researcher can accept. The idea of a predictive model based on previous patterns seems like a valuable idea, but there are many legitimate dangers to using such models, especially if the underlying cause and effect is not well understood. Skeptics of big data are right to be concerned about the stability of the predictive models, invasion of privacy, and increased power of well-heeled, highly skilled adopters.[30]

Similarly, skeptics of case studies and qualitative data analysis have legitimate reasons for concerns over choice of case study participants and the inclination of researchers to "cherry-pick" examples that favor their pet theories or hypotheses. The classic guide to experimentation by Donald Campbell and Julian Stanley dismisses case studies as having "such a total absence of control as to be of almost no scientific value."[31] One defender of case studies characterizes the criticisms as "(a) theoretical knowledge is more valuable than practical knowledge; (b) one cannot generalize from a single case, therefore the single case study cannot contribute to scientific development; (c) the case study is most useful for generating hypotheses, while other methods are more suitable for hypotheses testing and theory building; (d) the case study contains a bias toward verification; and (e) it is often difficult to summarize specific case studies."[32]

Visual analytics requires training, engaged designer-analysts, and effortful exploration to remove errors, resolve missing data, deal with anomalies, and account for unusual patterns. It takes judgment to derive insights, and conversations with colleagues and stakeholders to decide what to do. There is also the danger of allowing poorly chosen axes or color palettes, deceptive size coding, or cluttered displays to mislead decision-makers. In short, the many problems with real data that are usually invisible or ignored by statistical programs become apparent when using visual analytic tools. Some analysts welcome this clarity that requires discussion with domain experts, while others find this to be a difficult process.

Every research method has its strengths and weaknesses, so keen awareness of the limitations is needed.

9.7 Summary

Contemporary research projects, which address immense problems, would do well to start small with pilot tests of experiments and prototypes of software, systems, and services. Rapid, low-cost, low-risk pilot tests and prototypes are increasingly important as teams take on more ambitious projects that satisfy applied and basic research goals.

Collecting data from these small studies helps refine plans, improve measurement, and clarify goals. The principle of "something small soon" leads to early failures but with the chance to promptly reformulate directions. It also leads to confirmation of successful ideas, a chance to share promising results with colleagues so as to collect feedback and with stakeholders to gain support. Scaling up from small studies to large ones and scaling out to cope with diverse contexts refine practical guidelines and foundational theories, both of which help to strengthen nascent ideas.

Big data analyses from social media, Web logs, e-commerce transactions, and sensors offer new possibilities for researchers to understand social dynamics in natural and made-world systems. The capacity to take large volumes of data and extract insights based on statistical techniques is a dramatic advance that promises many improvements in making reliable predictions and contributing to understanding the relationship among underlying variables. Big data analysis techniques with natural language processing can be applied to large text corpora, such as document collections, blog postings, or Twitter streams. Then, sentiment analysis can detect changing patterns of preferences across time and location. All these methods have limitations, which should be understood, but their value is great.

Case studies with in-depth observations and interviews with real users dealing with real problems provide a different perspective that promises valuable insights to complement big data analyses. While big data analyses give more objective measures, the qualitative and subjective analyses from case studies offer the chance to get closer to the users, see deeper into problems, and be more open to new possibilities. Guidelines for rigorous case studies are emerging in diverse disciplines, so acceptance is growing for repeated case studies as a way of collecting evidence to support theories and hypotheses.

Visual analytics has emerged as a set of maturing technologies that also provide fresh opportunities to understand both the natural and the made worlds that we live in. These tools enable exploration in novel ways that can lead to discovery of important trends, while also leading to compelling presentations. When a state governor was shown a map that highlighted counties having distinctly high cancer rates, he instituted new rules that called for more screening tests, which led to a decrease in mortality. Visual presentations can lead to important changes. Education beginning in elementary schools could raise visual literacy and train the next generation, who are already entranced by interactive gaming, to be interactive data explorers.

CHAPTER 10

Promote Adoption and Assess Impact

You don't succeed as a scientist by getting papers published. . . . Having your work matter, matters. Success is defined not by the number of pages you have in print but by their influence. You succeed when your peers understand your work and use it to motivate their own.

Joshua Schimel, *Writing Science: How to Write Papers That Get Cited and Proposals That Get Funded*

10.1 Introduction

Sometimes ideas need the right boost to take off. For example, the idea of having electronic encyclopedias on personal computers was growing in the mid-1980s, when we developed author and browsing tools based on highlighted, clickable, textual links embedded in sentences. This hypertext variant, which allowed links among articles on a single computer, was presented in academic papers and disseminated with a commercial spin-off, while competing with a growing set of alternate products.[1] Our group showcased the idea in 1988 by producing a scientific journal issue, which contained seven papers, as a disk for personal computer use. This technology demonstration was sold by ACM, the leading computing professional society, as a disk called *Hypertext on Hypertext*.[2]

That applied research project, which showed how hypertext scenarios could transform academic publishing, was seen by Tim Berners-Lee while he was working to help particle physicists share documents. His spring 1989 manifesto

The New ABCs of Research. First Edition. Ben Shneiderman.
© Ben Shneiderman 2016. Published in 2016 by Oxford University Press.

for the World Wide Web cited our hypertext demonstration, adding the term "hot spots" to describe the highlighted, clickable, textual links.[3] Within a few years, this link-based user interface strategy became a global standard for Web authoring and browsing tools. Berners-Lee's breakthrough idea was to allow links to reach articles on networked computers, a world-changing step forward that boosted our link strategy in ways we never anticipated.

Researchers are embedded in social networks that enable small ideas from many sources to be combined into major breakthrough ideas. Research teams can activate their networks by creating inspirational prototypes and compelling narratives to gain recognition among peers, or they can promote their ideas directly to civic, business, or global partners. Tailoring the message to each audience requires sensitivity to their needs and an understanding of their background knowledge. Then, the choice of media to tell the story can include personal face-to-face contacts, polished videos, public presentations, or written papers. Researchers can also engage with knowledge entrepreneurs, such as journalists, consultants, conference organizers, and business gatekeepers, to spread ideas through their broad networks of strong and weak ties that reach across industries and countries.

The familiar line about academic life is "publish or perish," but now researchers who shift to "publish and publicize" will become the leaders in their fields. With more than a million new research papers being published each year, getting attention and gaining mindshare in the knowledge marketplace requires more than passive admiration of the printed or Web version of a recently published paper.

Spreading ideas is a turbulent imperfect process, so vigorous promoters can influence the attention to their work. The best form of promotion is still good writing with striking visuals. Once this foundation is laid, spin-off presentations can be produced through slide decks, podcasts, videos, blogposts, and other media. These "transmedia" products enable researchers to reach diverse audiences in formats they like best. Then, publicity to community listservs, personal emails, Facebook posts, tweets, and dozens of other services are possible. The goal is to do more than to reach large audiences; the goal is to trigger discussion, gain feedback, and form new collaborations.[4]

Write Well, Promote Thoughtfully, and Assess with Care

Telling compelling stories to the right audiences by using effective media honors your work and increases impact.

The good news is that researchers can now track promotional efforts through download counts of their papers, data sets, or software. They can also track website visits, social media mentions, and citations from other research papers. In addition to these metrics, researchers can collect an evidence-based portfolio by recording stories that indicate influence on colleagues, adoption by business, or controversy surrounding a research result. While a growing number of online services track research impact, researchers are the best judges of what stories to tell about their impact.

This chapter is a guide to good writing that promotes adoption of research results, which in turn leads to increased recognition, chances to be hired, possibilities for tenure, and so on. The traditional dependence on objective metrics such as citation counts and subjective letters from leading researchers is being supplemented by alternative objective metrics and new forms of subjectively gathered story portfolios. Hiring and tenure committees are rewriting their rules to account for the large shift in scholarly communication. The key to success is to have a good story to tell.

10.2 It Starts with Clear Writing

Clear writing leads to clear thinking. Some may say that I have inverted the order, but the growing evidence is that writing well promotes thinking well. Many researchers have a flash of a new idea while showering, walking in a forest, or in the dreamy passages into and out of sleep, but turning those enchanted moments into a clear statement that can be communicated to others takes writing skills. Writing helps researchers turn ideas into action.

The action is the research, whose trajectory from idea to impact is often an engaging story with challenges, tension over decisions, uncertainty about outcomes, and questions about the future. At its best, research is an adventure story of mythic heroes striving to have high impact by solving a specific meaningful problem, while producing mind-opening theories with the promise of broad applicability. However, the traditions of research writing are to subdue the mythic proportions, report on facts, and use unemotional language that shows unbiased objectivity. These traditions also wash out the struggles, early prototype testing, setbacks, and failed hypotheses, leaving a clear linear story with little drama. While the majority of research paper submissions are rejected, the final published papers rarely report on these painful episodes; in fact, I can't think of one.

Contemporary advisors about research writing stress the importance of story arcs and storytelling, both of which adapt writerly notions of clear challenges, tension, and satisfying resolutions to engage readers. Joshua Schimel advises that "the papers that get cited the most and the proposals that get funded are those that tell the most compelling stories."[5] He offers a standard story template called OCAR:

Opening (O): Broad vision of importance of the quest, followed by a specific list of the key actors (molecules, species, materials, devices, algorithms, etc.).

Challenge (C): Clear statement of what your actors can accomplish and what uncertainties need to be resolved; lucid research questions and testable hypotheses.

Action (A): Precise, replicable description of what happened during the research.

Resolution (R): Report on the outcome for your actors and what it means for practitioners, theoreticians, and future researchers (much like the two parents, three children concept presented in Chapter 1).

Schimel suggests four strategies of how to tell the story, depending on the audience, goals, and length, but each variation has a beginning, middle, and end that clarify what happened and why the outcome is important. He stresses careful research reporting, while keeping the story elements of clear challenge (triggering curiosity), tension (uncertainty about results), and outcomes that engage readers and leave them satisfied.

Schimel encourages researchers to apply Chip and Dan Heath's six-factor writing formula to make ideas "sticky" in readers' minds, called SUCCES:[6]

S: Simple ideas have power. Simplicity brings clarity to conquer complexity.

U: Unexpected results fill in knowledge gaps and make memorable impacts.

C: Concrete examples make abstract ideas comprehensible.

C: Credible reports on previous work and links between data and conclusions.

E: Emotional writing in research is tied to curiosity and excitement.

S: Stories have modular structures with logical sequence from beginning to end.

The combination of OCAR and SUCCES gives researchers guidance for the overall structure; then, every paragraph and sentence has to be crafted to keep the reader's attention from the introduction to the conclusion. Beyond the structure and style, research report authors who learn to compose well-crafted paragraphs and sentences will increase their impact. There are hundreds of rules for good writing to engage readers, including using consistent terminology, correct use of active versus passive voice, cause-effect phrasing, simple wording, and parallel construction.

Even small issues draw spirited debates. Most writing guides suggest limiting the use of pronouns such as "I," "my," "we," or "our" so as to put the emphasis on the research. For example, changing "We split the samples into five quintiles based on our ranking of performance, which enabled us to compare the highest to the lowest groups" to "Quintile splits enable comparison of high to low performing groups" focuses attention on the work while trimming the word count from 24 to 10 words.

One of my personal issues is to assert human agency in use of computers. For example, changing "The algorithms in SystemX enable it to discover relevant images" to "Users of SystemX can discover relevant images" clarifies that users are in control.

However, researchers' goals are more ambitious than writing well. Schimel focuses on the traditional research goals of getting other researchers to cite journal or conference articles and getting granting agencies to fund proposals. However, in the social-media-rich world of high-impact research, great articles also activate discussions that lead to more downloads, trigger inquiries from those who want to apply the results, and spawn further research to validate the theory. But application by practitioners and refinements by peers is only the starting point. The best research can have hundreds of impacts, including patents, improvements to industrial processes, start-up companies, government policy changes, revisions to educational curricula, and attention in the popular media.

The linkage between writing style and increased dissemination was made clear in a study by Katherine Milkman and Jonah Berger. They found that the research results are more likely to be shared by nonresearchers when the summary "(i) evokes stronger emotion, (ii) increases perceived usefulness, (iii) draws greater interest, or (iv) is more positive."[7]

The growing number of guidebooks and technical writing courses provide helpful guidance to young researchers.[8] Personal experiences through writing workshops "organized by graduate students for graduate students" is a hopeful sign, but many more are needed.[9]

In addition to well-organized, clear writing with memorable examples that provoke curiosity and excitement by way of unexpected results, research papers benefit from two other components: (1) compelling figures that clearly present the results or captivating visual imagery, such as photos of tissue cells, unusual plants, intriguing animals, or fascinating devices, and (2) supplementary websites with more figures, downloadable source data, informative videos that reveal dynamic processes, and background information with links to related work.

In an increasingly visual world, readers' attention can often be engaged by well-crafted animations with explanatory commentaries that can be replayed, accompanied by interactive information visualizations that allow further data exploration. In an increasingly social world, readers' reactions can be captured by allowing comments, facilitating social media postings that promote dissemination, or providing an email address that invites discussion.

Well-written and well-illustrated papers are crafted to suit a specific audience at a conference or journal. Specialized conferences or even narrowly focused smaller workshops mean that readers are likely to be familiar with the terminology and previous work.[10] Broad journal papers and wide-ranging review papers meant for diverse audiences require background explanations and clarifications of the impact of the results. Most researchers desire to publish in high-profile journals such as *Science, Nature*, or the *New England Journal of Medicine*, in part because these are widely read and highly cited, but the thousands of other, specialized journals are also good candidates.[11] These established respected journals have been joined by a proliferation of low-quality journals that are eager to find new authors by offering rapid publication and minimal reviewing. Journals published by prominent professional societies are usually high quality, and there are also respected for-profit journals. The concern here is with for-profit journals that have poor quality control and charge authors excessive publication fees. There is a similar range in conference quality that varies greatly across disciplines. Almost every journal and conference now includes publication on the Web, but many require payment by readers. Open access publishing (see Sections 10.4–10.8) often produces higher download counts and possibly more citations, but some tenure and promotion committees have yet to appreciate their value. Researchers should consult with senior mentors, check with colleagues, and study where related work is published before they decide where to submit their own work.

10.3 How to Promote Research

Those who learn how to promote their work have a distinct advantage in the increasingly competitive research world. Graduate education now often includes training and opportunities to present research through live lectures, podcasts, and videos, plus experience in building websites, writing blog posts, formatting posters, or composing Wikipedia pages. The capacity to broadcast new results or the URLs of freshly published papers using Twitter, Facebook, or other social media tools opens up new possibilities for receiving feedback from fellow researchers, influencing practitioners, attracting journalists, and learning about potential new collaborators.[12]

The social media possibilities for self-promotion are growing rapidly, so their impact is likely to increase. But some researchers are uncomfortable with broad promotion of their own work. They still have many possibilities, such as engaging with professional intermediaries on their campus, at professional societies, or research funding agencies, whose job depends on telling research stories. More energetic researchers may develop personal contacts with new media writers, traditional print journalists, and others who are eager to report on fresh stories.

For researchers to make effective use of social media or to develop connections with intermediaries, they will have to adopt fresh attitudes about shaping and presenting their work. In his book on *Marketing for Scientists*, astrophysicist Mark Kuchner encourages researchers to learn "the craft of seeing things from other people's perspectives, understanding their wants and needs, and finding ways to meet them."[13] This shift of perspective from reporting on what the researchers did to describing why it is important to others is at the heart of promoting research to diverse audiences. Interpreting results for research peers, industrial leaders, government policymakers, or high-school students requires sensitivity to the knowledge and needs of each audience. For some researchers, this shift comes easily, while others will have to practice to achieve it. Promotion is not about boasting; it is about thoughtful development of "takeaway messages" that are tuned to the needs of others.

10.4 How to Build Your Pathways to Impact: The Becker Model

The Becker Medical Library team at Washington University in St. Louis has a website on how to enhance research impact by making research more visible.[14] Their strategies begin with 13 recommendations for how to prepare research for publication; then they offer 27 ways to promote published work and 5 ways to keep track of research so as to make it more discoverable. They steer researchers to write complete abstracts, provide keywords to promote searchability,

Box 10.1 How to Build Your Pathways to Impact: The Becker Model

The Becker Model emphasizes social connections to enhance the impact of a research contribution.

- Ideas travel through networks and relationships.... Develop expertise in your field and be a trustworthy source.
- Address areas of policy interest.
- Build relationships and networks.
- Get decision makers involved in the research.
- Join relevant committees and insert your findings into decision making.
- Consider Action Research designs.
- Don't wait for publication. Disseminate early.
- Cultivate champions.
- Be opportunistic.
- Present, Present, Present.

Source: Becker Medical Library, *Strategies for Enhancing the Impact of Research* (2015) https://becker.wustl.edu/impact-assessment/strategies.

engage with social media, create project websites, visit leading research centers, and present work at conferences (Box 10.1). Well-made, one-to-five-minute videos can also clarify research results and reach new audiences. Following all their suggestions would leave little time for future work, so researchers have to choose which strategies to use.

The need to promote research is apparent, since the volume of new papers and active scientists is so high that gaining attention and influencing the research directions of others requires persistence and creativity. There is a role for academic departments and institutions, since they have professionals whose job is to promote research results of junior and senior researchers within the research community, to practitioners, and beyond. Improved writing and storytelling can turn a useful research result buried in an academic journal into an international news event that draws wide attention. The journalistic skills of identifying the human interest aspects, making the business case, and presenting the results in a comprehensible manner are helpful in successful outreach.

The goal is always more than mere dissemination and reaching a large audience. Meaningful impacts produce active community discussions, changes in research directions, and applications in the made world.

CASE STUDY 10.1 THE WEB SCIENCE TRUST: THOUGHT LEADERS FOR BLENDED RESEARCH

Tim Berners-Lee's 1989 manifesto for the World Wide Web was driven by the need to improve communication among physicists working at CERN in Geneva and elsewhere. He sought to manage the large volume of information across many countries with a rapidly changing community of researchers. Driven by this practical problem and his awareness of the inadequacy of existing solutions, Berners-Lee turned to the idea of linked information and the nascent hypertext concepts with selectable hot spots, which he later called the "World Wide Web."

The remarkable impact of his work took only 3–4 years to spread widely and only another decade to achieve worldwide impact, which is still growing. The applied goals he identified launched a large community of researchers who have since developed mathematical theories of networks, scientific studies of performance, engineering projects to achieve scalable systems, social and political analyses, and a large design community that creates appealing comprehensible websites.

Elevated to Sir Tim Berners-Lee, he is admirably devoted to continuously refining the underlying Web technologies through the community activities of the World Wide Web Consortium (W3C), which "develops open standards to ensure the long-term growth of the Web."[1] The W3C is devoted to making sure that the Web is accessible to all with its mission statement, "The social value of the Web is that it enables human communication, commerce, and opportunities to share knowledge. One of W3C's primary goals is to make these benefits available to all people, whatever their hardware, software, network infrastructure, native language, culture, geographical location, or physical or mental ability. . . . W3C's vision for the Web involves participation, sharing knowledge, and thereby building trust on a global scale."[2]

The admirable statements and commitments to social aspects of the Web are guiding researchers to frame their work in ways that align with the social science agendas, engineering aspirations, and design goals. The continuing stream of position papers from Berners-Lee and close colleagues repeatedly use the terms "socially embedded" and "interdisciplinary."[3]

These thought leaders are firmly devoted to science and engineering, but they also see a clear role for many forms of design. The Web Science Trust, which seeks to shape thinking about Web research, represents a global network of laboratories, publishes articles in leading scientific and general media, convenes conferences, and organizes summer schools.[4] Another bold initiative is the Web Observatory, a system created to facilitate the sharing of data about what is happening on the Web and the tools developed to analyze that data.[5] Over time, this system will enable exploration of the entire history of the Web and more accurate forecasts of its future development.

Dame Wendy Hall and Sir Nigel Shadbolt, who are both Web Science Trustees, launched the Web Science Institute at the University of Southampton to promote blended research. They obtained British government funding to create an educational and research community devoted to their aspiration to blend science, engineering, and design. The Web Science Trust's other prominent trustees, such as James Hendler, Noshir Contractor, and Daniel Weitzner, promote these new research directions in academic, industrial, and government circles.

The independently organized World Wide Web conference has become a strong computer science conference,[6] so the Web Science Trust felt it helpful to start a Web Science conference series that would ensure a respected forum for the computer science and social science work that they identified as being vital.[7] Researchers have tracked the Web Science conference publications to understand which related domains have been most influenced by and attracted to the Web Science theme.[8]

Sir Tim Berners-Lee was a cofounder of the Web Science Trust but is mainly affiliated with the W3C host site located at MIT in Cambridge, MA, and the World Wide Web Foundation.[9] His influence in the World Wide Web community is enormous, and his annual keynote talks at the World Wide Web Conferences provide detailed updates on what is happening while sustaining the grander vision of building a social system to benefit everyone. The recent 25th anniversary of the World Wide Web gave yet another occasion to reaffirm the belief in the social embeddedness of the Web, when a Web Science Track was launched at the 2014 WWW Conference.[10]

The bridging of computer science and social science is a clear goal for many, but the majority of computer scientists and computer science departments are still devoted to traditional topics.[11] However, some highly respected computer scientists working in traditional departments are taking on these new topics. A major article in the influential journal *Nature* quoted Cornell University's Professor Jon Kleinberg as saying, "I realized that computer science is not just about technology, it is also a human topic."[12] Wider acceptance of this premise would demonstrate an important shift.

[1] W3C, *World Wide Web Consortium (W3 C)* (2015) http://www.w3.org.

[2] W3C, *W3C Mission* (2015) http://www.w3.org/Consortium/mission.html.

[3] e.g., Berners-Lee, T., Hall, W., Hendler, J., O'Hara, K., Shadbolt, N., and Weitzner, D., A framework for Web science. *Foundations and Trends in Web Science* **1**, 1 (2006), 1–130, p. 1; available at http://www.nowpublishers.com/article/Details/WEB-001; Shadbolt, N., Hall, W., and Berners-Lee, T., The semantic Web revisited, *IEEE Intelligent Systems* **21**, 3 (2006), 96–101; Shadbolt, N. and Berners-Lee, T., Web science emerges, *Scientific American* **299**, 4 (October 2008), 32–37; Berners-Lee, T., Hall, W., Hendler, J. A., Shadbolt, N., and Weitzner, D. J., Creating a science of the Web, *Science* **313**, 5788 (2006), 769–771; and Hendler, J., Shadbolt, N., Hall, W., Berners-Lee, T., and Weitzner, D., Web science: An interdisciplinary approach to understanding the Web, *Communications of the ACM* **51**, 7 (2008), 60–69.

[4] Web Science Trust, *The Web Science Trust* (Accessed August 11, 2015) http://webscience.org.

[5] Web Science Trust, *Web Observatory* (Accessed August 11, 2015) http://wstweb1.ecs.soton.ac.uk/web-observatory.

[6] International World Wide Web Conferences Committee, *Welcome* (2015) http://www.iw3c2.org/.

[7] ACM Web Science Conference 2014 (WebSci14), *ACM Web Science Conference 2014 (WebSci14)* (Accessed August 11, 2015) http://www.websci14.org/.

[8] Hooper, C. J., Millard, D. E., Fantauzzacoffin, J., and Kaye, J. (2013) Science vs. science: The complexities of interdisciplinary research, in CHI'13, *CHI'13 Extended Abstracts on Human Factors in Computing Systems*, ACM, New York, NY (April 2013), pp. 2541–2544; Hooper, C., Dix, A., Web science and human-computer interaction: When disciplines collide, in WebSci '12, *Proceedings of the 4th Annual ACM Web Science Conference*, ACM, New York, NY (2012), pp. 128–136.

[9] World Wide Web Foundation, *World Wide Web Foundation* (2015) http://webfoundation.org.

[10] 23rd International World Wide Web Conference, *WWW2014 Call for Web Science Track* (2014) http://www2014.kr/calls/call-for-web-science-track/.

[11] Shneiderman, B., Web science: A provocative invitation to computer science. *Communications of the ACM* **50**, 6 (June 2007), 25–27. doi: 10.1145/1247001.1247022.

[12] Giles, J., Computational social science: Making the links, *Nature* **488**, 7412 (August 23, 2012), 448–450, p. 448; available at http://www.nature.com/news/computational-social-science-making-the-links-1.11243.

10.5 Promotion by Social Media

Researchers who make their work visible in their desired communities can trigger increased downloads and desired impacts. Academic research portals have been organized as for-profit companies, such as Academia, which claims 26 million members who share papers "to accelerate the world's research."[15] Another such portal, ResearchGate, claims 7 million members who share papers, discuss research, and form collaborations.[16] Nonprofit registries such as ORCID provide a unique identifier for researchers so publishers, funding agencies, and others can track the work of individuals, especially those with common names.[17] Another approach is the VIVO alliance of 100+ institutions to enable the "discovery of researchers across institutions."[18] Larger issues of scholarly publishing and data curation are addressed by the FORCE11 (Future of Research Communication and e-Scholarship) "community of scholars, librarians, archivists, publishers and research funders that has arisen organically to help facilitate the change toward improved knowledge creation and sharing."[19]

Dozens of Web-based research support sites, such as Mendeley,[20] Zotero,[21] and CiteULike,[22] are among the growing family of social bookmarking or reference management tools.[23] These tools can help researchers identify relevant papers and colleagues, as well as to promote their work by uploading, tagging, and discussing papers. For some isolated or introverted researchers, these social media sites provide welcome contacts with widely distributed fellow researchers who share their interests.

These technology-mediated approaches can help reach a broad audience, but a heightened aspiration should be to trigger discussions within a networked community. Bloggers who comment on research articles catalyze further discussions, create interest, and encourage follow-up research by others.[24] Similarly, having a large number of Twitter followers is good, but the goals should be to trigger retweets, replies, mentions, and other discussion-provoking actions.[25] Eventually these discussions could influence industrial or government applications and research citations.

A study led by Gunther Eysenbach examined the impact of tweeting about journal articles and found that "tweets can predict highly cited articles within the first 3 days of article publication."[26] However, he cannot separate the impact the tweets had on the citations approximately 2 years later from the inherent qualities of the article which might attract tweets and citations. Still, this positive correlation suggests that, all things being equal, tweeting about your article or ones you like will increase the number of readers and citations.

Web-based and social media sources such as blogs, Facebook, Twitter, and Wikipedia provide other ways to reach relevant audiences. My colleague Michael Hicks received a warm response for his informative blog post "What Is Probabilistic Programming?"[27] A reader posted a link on the reddit Web aggregator site,[28] generating a healthy 4600+ readers within a few weeks. Then Hicks reports that "something happened . . . and it received 8,300 pageviews" on a single day, with further peaks as other readers posted the link to new communities, attaining 22,000+ page views within a few months.[29] For a focused topic with specialized readers, that is a strong impact. Hicks also received a keynote invitation for a conference on this topic, which will trigger even more page views.

Newer forms of academic publishing provide fresh opportunities to disseminate an idea. The unrefereed and free arXiv website enables researchers to post their papers to a widely viewed location (two million downloads/week) to quickly gain feedback for their work.[30] Many established researchers have used the arXiv mechanism to plant their flag with a new idea. After 25 years, there are more than a million manuscripts, triggering lively discussions among readers. One astronomer told me he made sure to read the arXiv postings in his field each morning, so as to participate in spirited lunch discussions with colleagues. It takes some courage to post a paper, since mistakes or missing references are often noticed and publicly discussed in a few hours.

Another expanding possibility is to publish via an open access journal, many of which are issued by the nonprofit, 10-year-old PLOS (for Public Library of Science),[31] which charges authors a publication fee so as to allow free access to their refereed paper. This approach has the virtue of democratizing access to research and can lead to increased readership and citations counts.[32]

10.6 Promotion by Personal Connections

Beyond using technology-mediated approaches, researchers who build personal connections with relevant prominent researchers or practitioners can promote their ideas and raise their reputation. Email discussions with leaders are a good start, but repeated personal visits still have powerful impacts in building an effective network.[33] There are many paths to research recognition, but the social experiences of being on conference program committees and journal editorial boards are likely to help aspiring researchers. Workshops and conferences present other opportunities to meet colleagues, ask thoughtful questions, and present fresh ideas at panels or breakout groups.

With interdisciplinary research, there may be several possible media directions and a variety of stories to tell. Visual presentations, great photos, engaging animations, and lively videos add to the attraction for a research result. The US National Science Foundation prepares well-written reports termed "Discoveries" several times a month, with engaging short stories and attractive images or videos.[34] The US National Institutes of Health,[35] NASA,[36] and other agencies promote their supported research projects in a similar fashion, showing the US Congress that their funding produces results that advance research and may lead to economically important innovations.

Publishing reports in the AAAS *Science* or in *Nature* is also a powerful way to gain the attention of journalists, who are eager for fresh story ideas. Our 1-page article with the simple title "911.gov" called for a Web-based social media communication system to "provide better reporting on disasters, coordination of responses, dissemination of information, and social networking to deliver assistance."[37] Email and phone inquiries began 48 hours before publication and, when the embargo was lifted, more than 20 media organizations, including the BBC, *Discovery Channel, New Scientist, Newsweek,* and *Nature*, disseminated this idea.

Similarly, a well-coordinated effort by the Pew Internet and American Society offered science bloggers, traditional journalists, and Web-based reporters personal teleconferences with the authors to promote our new report on six distinct network patterns in Twitter discussions. The personal interviews gave the writers unique quotes and allowed them to generate very diverse reports for varied audiences, thereby producing a record-breaking number of report downloads.[38]

Publishers are eager to promote the work of their authors, so researchers should tap their publicity services and professionals. Another approach is to work with publicity directors in the hundreds of professional societies in the United States, United Kingdom, Europe, and beyond. These professionals are responsible for promoting the work of the society's members, so sending them a well-crafted abstract written for broad audiences can trigger their efforts. A related idea is to cultivate relationships with writers for online magazines, as they are often hungry for content. It takes persistence on the part of researchers to build contacts and maintain them with regular stories, but mentions on popular websites can yield tens of thousands of readers.

Even in the era of Web-based dissemination of knowledge, the physical appearance of a researcher to make a presentation can yield high payoffs. A practiced speaker who engages audiences, thereby making personal connections with fellow researchers and students, can influence others to do follow-up research, which extends a successful contribution. Personal contacts remain a powerful way to build trust and convince others that a result has value.

10.7 Send Five and Thrive

When completing a research paper, one approach to gaining attention from relevant researchers is to extract five key authors from the list of references. Then, send them an email that has a fact-based introduction, such as "Dear Dr. Rockstar, I'm a doctoral student at the University of Maryland, working with Prof. Ben Shneiderman, who sends his regards." Then, the heart of the message has two points: "Your work was an inspiration for this paper, so I wanted to check with you to (1) see if we have been fair in citing your papers, and (2) know if you have published any more recent work on this topic." While young researchers may be daunted by the idea of writing to senior researchers, such emails usually produce helpful responses quickly. Even senior researchers are pleased to know that their work inspired new efforts, thereby validating their contributions.

This "Send Five and Thrive" idea has additional benefits, such as compelling authors to consider whether they have cited the key previous papers and encouraging them to think about whether they have given fair and positive descriptions of previous work. For example, shifting from a negative comments such as "previous work by Rockstar failed to . . ." to positive ones such as "the pioneering work by Rockstar can be extended by . . ." increases the likelihood of making a favorable impression.

10.8 Assessing Impact: Citation Counts

The traditional approach to measuring research impact is to count the number of articles published in high-quality refereed journals or conferences. Approval by journal editorial boards and conference committees is taken as testimony to quality. However, as Schimel, among others, asserts, the durable and broader impact is seen only 2–6 years later, when future journal and conference articles cite the original article that contains the discovery, invention, or innovation.[39]

For decades, the citation counts assembled by trusted commercial sources such as the Thomson Reuters Web of Science have been seen as a reliable measure of research impact. This plausible and well-developed strategy is based on the assumption that influential work is cited by future researchers. Unfortunately, the number of citations from the first 1–2 years is not a good predictor of the number of citations in the following years, so it may take 4–6 years till a journal article becomes recognized as having high impact.

This scenario has many assumptions embedded in it, so even an optimist must face troubling realities. Authors are not always fair or accurate in citing all the work that influences them. Active researchers read or scan approximately 400 papers a year, so they may not remember all the work that influences them, or they may prefer to cite related work from close colleagues or those who already have a substantial reputation. Famed sociologist of science Robert K. Merton called this the "Matthew Effect,"[40] basing the name on the biblical passage about how "the rich get richer and the poor get poorer." In some fields, there are fierce competitors who cite work within their group but do not cite work from rival groups. Many authors simply are more aware of and give greater respect to colleagues from the same institution than those from other institutions, so researchers from prominent large institutions may have a strong advantage over struggling newcomers from smaller institutions.

Citation counts are a convenient quantitative measure that is appealing to many researchers because of its presumably objective approach. However, the dangers in counting citations include the different numbers of papers written per year across disciplines. Since some disciplines or subdisciplines may have larger numbers of papers, it is difficult to compare citation rates across them. Since some prolific author teams heavily cite their own work, many counting schemes remove such self-citations. Still, big author teams may have more colleagues and students who could be encouraged to cite a certain paper. These and other ways of gaming the system have been studied carefully, in efforts to develop reliable impact metrics.

In spite of these problems, the lure of citation counts is strong, since they invite simple ranking strategies for papers and researchers. The prominent research journal *Nature* asked Thomson Reuters to produce a "Top 100" list drawn from the 58 million papers in the Web of Science since 1901. Then, the *Nature* editors provided a thoughtful analysis of what leads to high citation counts.[41] The surprise was that some of the great scientific breakthroughs, such as the discovery of high-temperature superconductors, the structure of DNA, or the fact that the universe is expanding, are not on the list. The top three entries, with more than 100,000 citations each, described laboratory methods that are widely used in multiple research areas; for example, one was a 1951 paper on how to measure protein in a solution. Less than 15,000 papers got more than 1000 citations, 14 million got 10–999 citations, and 18 million got 1–9 citations. The remaining 25 million papers got no citations, a fact which indicates the difficulty of getting attention for published research, even in the respected set of peer-reviewed journals. In addition, *Nature* editors generated an alternate Top 100 list by working with Google Scholar. This list includes books, which make up about two-thirds of the list, but the topics still emphasize laboratory, statistical, and research methods.[42]

Some journals are more prestigious and more widely read than others and therefore attracting more submitted papers, especially from leading researchers. The Journal Impact Factor (JIF), based on the average number of citations to articles, was created as a measure of journal quality, thereby providing something of an objective guide to authors about where their work might attract more citations. JIFs under 1.0 are considered to be low, while world-famous journals such as *Nature* and *Science* have JIFs over 30. As the JIF metric gained prominence, journal editorial boards coaxed colleagues and students to cite papers in their journal, thereby undermining trust in this metric. Challenges were also raised, since the JIF is an aggregate measure of a journal rather than a way to assess the contribution of a single author or paper.

Reaction against the JIF has become so strong that a major cell biology society developed a 3-page Declaration on Research Assessment that argued strenuously against use of any form of journal impact factor, stating that "journal-based metrics, such as Journal Impact Factors" should not be used as "a surrogate measure of the quality of individual research articles," encouraging "a shift toward assessment based on the scientific content of an article rather than publication metrics of the journal in which it was published."[43] Unfortunately, judgments of contributions are highly subjective and variable, depending on who is doing the evaluation. Senior researchers working on established problems are less likely to be sympathetic to junior researchers who take on new directions or use new research methods.

Rather than complain about JIF flaws, three enterprising librarians at the Becker Medical Library at Washington University in St. Louis, Cathy Sarli, Ellen Dubinsky, and Kristi Holmes, offer the 16-page Becker Model for assessment of research impact.[44] The complementary sections "Advancement of Knowledge" and "Clinical Implementation" are close to this book's focus on promoting basic outcomes (e.g., influence on or recognition by other researchers) and applied outcomes (e.g., use by clinical care practitioners in industry or government). The sections "Community Benefits" and "Legislation & Policy" include long-term impacts tied to use of research results in public health or to influence federal, state, local, or nongovernment policy. The fifth section, "Economic Benefits," covers diverse sources such as license agreements, start-up companies, and cost reductions in healthcare delivery or disease prevention. Since the Becker Model's orientation is toward medical research, versions are needed for other fields, but the wide scope is a valuable reminder of the rich diversity of research impacts beyond citation counts.

Another complaint against citation counts is that they miss the impact on the growing number of practitioners who may be eager readers but less frequent writers and citers of previous work.[45] Many researchers are proud of their impact on industry, especially their influence on successful products or services or on government efforts and projects.

10.9 Assessing Impact: Alternate Metrics

The rebellion against citation counts has triggered many other approaches. Since so many articles are read on the Web rather than from paper journals, several groups propose counting the number of downloads as a measure of impact. This metric has the distinct advantage that these counts begin to appear within hours of posting of a new article, so download counts provide rapid understanding of what topics researchers care about. Furthermore, download count advocates emphasize that their measures include practitioner activity, which is an indicator of research result applications, rather than papers containing citations. A key community formed around the term "altmetrics" explores and develops alternative metrics to assess impact.[46]

The immediacy of Web download counts is satisfying for authors, who may check daily to see how much attention their work is getting. Naturally, tweets (with links to the articles), Facebook mentions, blog posts, or other forms of social media recognition trigger a cascade of downloads, but these may be true indicators of interest in the research results. Critics complain that energetic or well-connected researchers from prominent universities can use their tweeting and blogging friends to generate high download counts. Once again, the rich may be getting richer, and the path to high reputation for new scholars may be as difficult as it has ever been.

So, if the critics of objective measures such as citations, downloads, or tweets are right, then how might research impact be assessed? The Becker Model offers a strong set of examples appropriate for the medical field but useful as a guide to all researchers. It covers conference and other presentations, publications, and grants received. It values alternative research products, such as curated data sets, and training materials, such as textbooks, software, and informative websites. The Becker Model also includes commercial spin-offs such as patents, license agreements, consultancies, advisory boards, and industrial partnerships. A further category of research impact is from media attention by trade press, general publications, newspapers, radio, television, and Wikipedia descriptions. Certain scientific publications have annual lists of "Breakthroughs of the Year" (AAAS *Science*) or "Top Scientific Discoveries" (*WIRED*), and there are Web-based lists of "Hot Papers" (*Thomson Reuters Essential Science Indicators*).

Other recognitions are also important, such as the "Best Paper Awards" given by many conferences or professional societies.[47] Variants such as "Best Student Paper" or "Best 10-Year Old Paper" (sometimes called "Test of Time Awards") also signal research importance.

Recognition of research contributions is one important form of assessment, but many researchers are more concerned about their overall personal reputation. For that, they can use broad services such as Google Scholar, which counts Web-based citations of an author's work and provides aggregated summaries that are often used to compare one scholar to another.[48] Once again there are dramatic differences across disciplines, troubling questions about those who may have gamed the system, and the Matthew Effect, through which senior researchers from prominent institutions will stand out especially strongly.

One novel approach to individual assessment is the h-index and its many variants.[49] If a researcher has 5 publications, each with at least 5 citations, that researcher has an h-index of 5. If a researcher has 20 publications, each with at least 20 citations, that researcher has an h-index of 20. The h-index is meant to count breadth and depth of contributions, so as to present an overall measure that may be harder to game. But once again, variations in the size of disciplines and extreme values for some leaders raise questions of fairness, and utility in predicting future performance.[50]

Reputations for research groups, departments, and universities are also important, so list makers seek to apply metrics at every level. Rating services such as that for the *US News and World Report* will rate departments and universities, usually on an annual basis, using a mix of objective measures and ratings from university administrators. The use of subjective ratings does turn this into a popularity contest, again favoring strong and large universities.

Honors received for individuals are a less frequent but still impressive indicator of overall impact. Nobel Prizes garner immediate worldwide attention, while national medals of science, engineering or design excellence raise the stature of recipients. Some awards, such as those from the MacArthur, Sloan or Guggenheim Foundations, help build the careers of young researchers. Similarly, honorary doctorates, prominent invited lectures, or biographies in prominent media outlets burnish the reputation of those fortunate enough to receive them.

There are many lesser recognitions, such as "Best Paper" accolades at conferences, "Top Ten Download" certificates from journals, professional society awards, and campuswide research prizes. Testimonial letters from prominent leaders about young researchers can be helpful for tenure review cases or for other promotions. Such letters are often detailed and personal, citing specific contributions, but skeptics point to the high variability in letter-writing style from flamboyant to cautious.

The difficulty in getting reliable objective and subjective measures is a disturbing reality, but it also indicates the rich variety of ways scientists, engineers, and designers make contributions. Many people still hope that a big data strategy will produce a single objective measure to judge their own work and assess others, but the inescapable reality is that discovery and invention do not have a simple metric. On the other hand, neither does health or happiness.

The multidimensionality, subtlety, and volatility of creative life defy simple metrics. Last year's novel research contribution becomes merely a template for the also-rans, who produce worthwhile but lesser contributions. The rising stars who publish their repeated discoveries and innovations will usually be honored appropriately and they may at least have the personal satisfaction of feeling that they have done great work. Scientists, engineers, and designers who have a strong internal sense of confidence in their work may appreciate the outside recognition, but they are the best judges of their contributions. The self-confidence to keep going, take criticism, and do better is a vital source of success.

10.10 An Economic Theory to Guide Assessment

The STAR METRICS (Science and Technology for America's Reinvestment: Measuring the Effect of Research on Innovation, Competitiveness and Science) project was spurred by the American Recovery and Reinvestment Act of 2009.[51] This large economic stimulus funding program required job creation statistics, including those for academic research projects, to be carefully collected. The Federal Demonstration Partnership was the sponsor,[52] and the initial science agencies were the US National Institutes of Health, the US National Science Foundation, and the White House Office of Science and Technology Policy; they were later joined by the US Department of Agriculture and the Environmental Protection Agency.

The long-term goal of STAR METRICS, whose primary audience was the US Congress, was to "document the outcomes of science investments to the public."[53] By using standardized measures from funding agencies and research institution grant recipients, the promoters sought to measure impact in terms of contributions to scientific knowledge, societal benefits, workforce improvement, and economic growth.

One of the key features of STAR METRICS was that the theory of change was people centered—so the focus was capturing data on the engine of change (principal investigators, postdocs, graduate students, etc.) at the most granular unit of analysis possible (individual grants at granular time periods). One way of conceptualizing the people-centered framework is to consider researchers as firms, which seek success by measuring documented expenditures on capital, labor, energy, materials, and services to produce successful products, which are ideas and students. Idea production can be tracked by papers, patents, or presentations, while student production is measured in numbers of graduates who bring the ideas to academic, industrial, or government organizations. The key, however, is that the transmission of ideas comes from the interaction of individuals—and mechanical links between grants and documents are misleading. The framework can be used for researchers to examine a variety of different questions, ranging from the impact of individuals, teams, or projects to the impact of entire research agendas or funding strategies.

For example, researchers could examine how research grant funding changes outcomes in terms of advancing knowledge, developing social networks, and disseminating knowledge. Another application of the STAR METRICS data would be to track the paths of students who move to business or start-up companies and hence contribute to economic growth. STAR METRICS followed many of the high-impact research strategies described in this book through working with program managers and six research institutions to develop a set of measures that were reliably collected during the administration of grants. Interdisciplinary collaborations and partnerships helped refine the design of models and metrics. In addition, publications and presentations, sometimes to Congressional committees, generated feedback that led to additional refinement of those designs.

In many ways, the STAR METRICS project reflects new research directions that focus on the design of sociotechnical systems based on theoretical foundations, while producing a practical technique for management and assessment. STAR METRICS does not currently cover all aspects of impact assessment, since it currently includes only a fraction of the items in other methods, such as the Becker Model. However, the community is collecting new data and building models to expand the current infrastructure from the bottom up.[54] In sum, STAR METRICS shows a promising direction based on reliable objective data that are hard to manipulate, making it a step forward in assessing the efficacy of funding agencies and research groups.

10.11 Skeptics' Corner

The core ideas of this chapter—good writing, research promotion, and impact assessment—are still widely seen as a distracting waste of time that could be better spent on new research. Skeptics fear that if research papers have to be made readable by wider audiences, it will water down scientifically accurate or technically complete descriptions. There is a prevalent belief that serious research papers require careful reading on the part of specialists, so the niceties of good writing are seen as undermining the rigors of research. One colleague gave me a backhanded compliment by declaring that he could understand my research papers, while he was proud that his papers were widely known to be difficult to read.

Most researchers consider efforts to disseminate research as a time-wasting distraction and sometimes frown upon it as unprofessional self-promotion. Skeptics think that their work speaks for itself, and therefore they do not see the value of project Web pages, video explanations, Facebook postings, tweets, or blogs. One skeptical colleague felt that tweets, even by two respected colleagues, simply added to the unproductive "cacophony." Several colleagues found talking with journalists to be problematic, since journalists were seen to have their own agenda, which sometimes included disparaging reports on what journalists saw as esoteric research projects. One or two bad experiences can make researchers retreat into relative silence.

However, researchers are eventually reviewed for hiring, tenure, or promotion, and their grant proposals must be approved by peer-review panels. For such occasions, indications of success of their past work is necessary; so, making their work comprehensible and visible helps to generate a portfolio of stories, colleagues who will write supportive letters, and quantitative reports of publications, citations, downloads, and media mentions.

Critics of download counts rightly point out that inflated counts can be purchased from services whose collections of machines can be programmed to download articles repeatedly. These unethical schemes have pushed download services to monitor for unusual spikes in downloads, but dangers remain. However, citation counts can also be unreliable or manipulated.[55]

10.12 Summary

The enormous, worldwide growth of research makes for a highly competitive marketplace of ideas. In this environment, researchers and teams who take the time to write well-crafted papers as well as develop public presentations and videos can gain greater visibility, feedback, and recognition. A wide variety of Web-based and social media tools enable researchers to disseminate and promote their ideas. Other tools facilitate discovery of new research collaborators, support effective teamwork, and promote spirited discussions. Since each researcher and team has many options, explicit discussions will be helpful in formulating an acceptable level of social media outreach effort.

Another challenge for teams is to decide on how much effort to devote to different impacts. Those who want academic citations will need to reach out to relevant colleagues, encourage follow-up work, and build their network of research peers. Those pursuing tenure or promotion would do well to cultivate personal connections with research leaders who can write supportive letters and with senior faculty who will be on their evaluation committees. Researchers with commercial aspirations, who build partnerships with business leaders, establish personal connections with technical professionals, or speak at trade conferences, are more likely to see their work applied by existing or start-up companies.

PART IV

Making It Happen

Since this book values theory and practice, it seems reasonable to sum up with a theory of how the research ecosystem functions, and practical recommendations for change. Inspired by Kurt Lewin's belief that, if you want to understand something, try and change it, I make my initial theory of how the research ecosystem functions explicit. Then I use this theory to describe practical recommendations for change, which I hope will feed back into a refined theory. Some changes will be easy; others will be hard.

CHAPTER 11

Recommendations for Action

Knowing is not enough; we must apply. Willing is not enough; we must do.

Johann Wolfgang von Goethe, *Maxims and Reflections*

11.1 Introduction

My life in research has been very satisfying, but I've begun reconsidering what I and my fellow researchers have been doing during our careers. Could we have been more successful and had greater impact than we did? I wondered how it could be different for today's researchers: (1) how could students and junior researchers enjoy their careers more than we did and be more successful than we were, and (2) how could senior researchers and policymakers change the research ecosystem of academia, business, government, and others, to increase the payoffs for stakeholders?

These large questions are what drove me to write this book, but the process of writing clarifies thinking (see Chapter 10, Section 10.2). Writing chapters forced me to consider how the research ecosystem worked and how its processes might be improved. I've always had an interest in reading what others wrote about science, engineering, and design, as well as mathematics, art, creativity, and much more.[1] On top of that background, I read more than 500 articles and 50 books while working on this book. I'm still not a philosopher or historian, but I am richer for the experience. As a participant in the research ecosystem, I can now see the water I am swimming in.

The New ABCs of Research. First Edition. Ben Shneiderman.
© Ben Shneiderman 2016. Published in 2016 by Oxford University Press.

The New ABCs of Research serves two purposes within the research ecosystem for science, engineering, and design: it is (1) a guide to students and junior researchers and (2) a manifesto for change, particularly for senior researchers and policymakers. I believe that promoting an emphasis on combining applied and basic research (the ABC principle) will increase productive outcomes in both applied solutions and basic theory. But change is hard; so, beyond setting a personal role model, guiding my students, and encouraging colleagues, how can I trigger changes in the research ecosystem? This book achieves the first step in the change-agent playbooks: create awareness of the current situation and offer a clear alternative.

Then the hard work begins, of promoting adoption, measuring outcomes, refining plans, and persisting over time.[2] When the practical goal of effective intervention is guided by theories of organizational design, then change agents have a chance to succeed. My strategy is to prototype the change process in my own classes and research, convert colleagues in my academic department, and then seek to influence my campus. I've accomplished some of that, and now I am scaling up and scaling out to influence other relevant actors in the research ecosystem.

11.2 Seeing the Research Ecosystem

Travelers benefit from having a map, as do those who would cut new paths or reroute rivers. Similarly, those who wish to navigate the research ecosystem for science, engineering, and design would benefit from a map, as would those who wish to restructure it.

My simplified map of the research ecosystem and how it functions is meant to help change agents understand what interventions they could make to gain support for the ABC and SED principles. As with any complex ecosystem, there can be many maps, each tuned to the needs of different users. Ecosystems evolve over time, so revisions are needed to keep up. There may be other relevant maps of the research ecosystem, but let's start with a simplified map of *actors* and actions in the core academic research environment map (see Fig. 11.1).

The upper left side begins the story with *universities* that contain departments. Departments are the disciplinary centers of activity, with the budgetary power to hire and reward *faculty*. The faculty have many responsibilities, on campus and beyond, but a central role is mentoring and teaching *students*. Faculty form *research teams* to pursue diverse goals, and then students join the

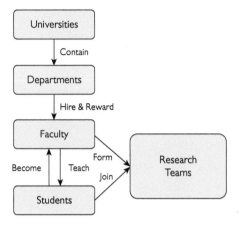

Figure 11.1 Map of the actors and actions in the core academic research environment.

research teams. Eventually some students <u>become</u> faculty members. Of course, there are more actors and actions in a university, but this map is a starting point to tell the story of what happens.

The bigger picture is represented in the detailed map in Figure 11.2, which shows how universities participate in the world. The research teams work to pursue their diverse goals, including their effort to <u>produce</u> *papers*. Papers are important, but an upgraded model would include outcomes in the form of solutions to problems, and refined theories, as well as patents, databases, software, scientific experiment results, engineering systems, and design products and services. As the Becker Model reminds us (see Chapter 10, Sections 10.3 and 10.4), other outcomes could include start-up companies, changes to education, guidelines for practice, changes in government policy, new research directions for others to follow, and much more.

Some research teams <u>collaborate</u> with *businesses*, who may supply funding as part of the collaboration. Other teams get <u>funding</u> from *government agencies*, nonprofit organizations, or philanthropic foundations.[3] When research succeeds, the research teams produce papers that get <u>submitted to</u> *journals or conferences* for review, with the hope of being <u>published by</u> *professional societies* or *commercial publishers*. *Journalists* may bring the ideas in these papers to wider audiences by <u>describing</u> the work in stories they prepare for print, Web, video, or other media outlets. The large number of published papers <u>influences</u> other research groups, who may extend the original work further. Another outcome of research is that businesses and government agencies may <u>hire</u> the students

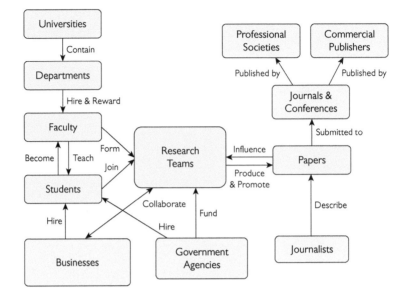

Figure 11.2 Simplified map of the research ecosystem as a guide to interventions designed to raise support for the ABC and SED principles.

who were involved in the research as they pursued their undergraduate and graduate education.

The map in Figure 11.2, with 12 actors (boxes) and 17 actions (arrows) is a reasonable start, but many other actors and actions could be included. A major addition would be the wide variety of research team products beyond papers, such as patents, data, research, and so on. Some research teams are self-funded, because the team members find a compelling idea or problem they want to address immediately rather than pursue the often-lengthy proposal-process. Self-funding is necessary for ideas that do not fit with existing funded programs. Businesses may have internal research teams that submit papers for publication.

Other actions that could be added to the map include the presentations researchers give at other universities, at businesses, for government agencies, and in public forums. An increasingly powerful force is the steady stream of research-related emails, tweets, Facebook posts, blog posts, Wikipedia entries, YouTube videos, and many other communications. These signals trigger chain reactions of human engagement through richly connected networks, building or tarnishing reputations, shifting interest to new topics, or initiating new collaborations.

Faculty members have many more roles than are shown in Figure 11.2, such as paper reviewing for journals and conferences, consulting for companies or government agencies, and occasionally writing books. Faculty also can have strong allegiances beyond their departments to research institutes within the university, and these institutes also compete for resources and recognition. In addition, while departments are important, they are usually organized into colleges or schools, which may have powerful and influential deans who can play key roles in academic life.

The research ecosystem is as vibrant as a tropical coral reef, with swirling currents, established coral beds, invasive organisms, and swarming schools of fish who take on roles as predators and prey. Small temperature changes or changes in the acidity of water can shift the balance, altering the network of relationships. Occasionally earthquakes, tsunamis, or drilling rigs can radically shake the ecosystem, forcing those who can to find new homes. Some see safety in a familiar research ecosystem, but dramatic paradigm shifts regularly punctuate the equilibrium.

For a more complete understanding of the research ecosystem, two major additions are needed: (1) social, economic, and political pressures that shape government and business research agendas as well as what constitutes an acceptable topic in academic circles, and (2) the impact of research on individuals, universities, businesses, and government organizations. In short, research is embedded in a large societal system which is only now becoming the subject of research programs, such as the US National Science Foundation's Science of Science and Innovation Policy.[4] That program's goals include "the study of structures and processes that facilitate the development of usable knowledge, theories of creative processes and their transformation into social and economic outcomes" and "the collection, analysis and visualization of new data describing the scientific and engineering enterprise."[5] I fervently hope that future programs will also include design research themes.

Another way to understand the research ecosystem is to follow the trajectory of individuals, such as students, who take courses and then join a research team. Students may become a coauthor of a paper and present at a conference, another university, or a business. Then students may become faculty members or take jobs at a business or government agency.

Familiar trajectories for faculty members are to seek tenure and promotion, while consulting for businesses or government agencies. Faculty members often become members of conference program committees or journal editorial boards, where they review submitted papers.

Radical changes sometimes alter this research ecosystem, such as the open publication strategies that avoid review of papers, allowing researchers to publish their own work on the Web (see Chapter 10, Section 10.5). Philanthropic foundations are playing a growing role by funding research, giving prominent prizes, and running research centers of their own.[6]

With this simple map of the research ecosystem, we can explore how different actors can be successful living in it and changing it to produce positive responses to the immense challenges of this century.

11.3 Guidance for Students and Junior Researchers

Students and junior researchers who embrace the ABC and SED principles will do well to find sympathetic mentors who can guide them to success and help them cope with the inevitable setbacks. These students and junior researchers will thrive in academic environments that are supportive of interdisciplinary education and multiple research methods.

The US National Research Council report *Convergence: Facilitating Transdisciplinary Integration of Life Sciences, Physical Sciences, Engineering, and Beyond* encourages interdisciplinary approaches, suggesting that students should develop

- "intellectual capacity to deal with real, complex problems";
- "confidence and willingness to approach problems from multiple perspectives";
- "ability to communicate with scientists from other disciplines";
- "ability to make decisions in the face of uncertainty (reflective judgment)"; and
- ability to "understand strengths and limitations of different disciplinary perspectives."[7]

The report continues by recommending that "learning should be goal-directed, exciting, and personal. A problem-solving approach . . . can also be an effective way to help students learn how to work in teams."[8] These recommendations are well aligned with the goals of innovative educational programs in engineering or design, such as those at Olin College, the iFoundry, the Stanford d.school, or OCAD University (see Chapters 4 and 5). Unfortunately, there are still only a few universities that offer students a chance to learn these strategies, as signaled by the 30+ mentions of "barriers" in the report.

However, enterprising students at many universities may find sympathetic faculty who seek to teach undergraduate and graduate courses with team projects addressing real, complex problems. Summer or semester internships with business or government agencies offer opportunities for students to work with practitioners on real problems. Northeastern University is famous for its 100-year-old required undergraduate co-op program that "integrates rigorous classroom study with real world experiences to create a powerful way to learn."[9]

Students have to find their own balance of building disciplinary strength while acquiring interdisciplinary breadth. An increasing number of universities have interdisciplinary programs in emerging fields such as sustainability, neuroscience, human-computer interaction, or bioinformatics and also offer opportunities for students to define their own program, possibly as a double major with courses in two or more disciplines.

Some universities offer multiyear team research projects, such as the University of Maryland's Gemstone Program.[10] It gives undergraduate honors students a chance to develop their research, teamwork, communication, and leadership skills by working with selected faculty on substantial projects that lead to a thesis report. Each year, a dozen Gemstone teams are formed; each team consists of 8–15 students who work together for four years with a faculty mentor and staff leaders who build local connections, provide resources, and help resolve problems. Current projects include studying how antidepressants affect prenatal neural development, how age-related macular degeneration can be prevented, and how toxins and oils are absorbed by plants in lakes and seas. When the students have completed their projects, they make a public presentation and then can show their research results, in the form of reports, websites, or videos, to employers or graduate admissions committees, to demonstrate their research experience and capacity for teamwork.

In most university programs, graduate students pursuing research-oriented masters or doctoral degrees have an unusual amount of freedom to choose their direction, but they must gain the support of their faculty mentors and the dissertation committees that validate their work. Enterprising graduate students often take on ambitious projects to produce breakthrough results. In the best cases, energetic junior researchers, guided by senior mentors, produce results that neither could do on their own.

The lessons of Chapter 10 are likely to be easily taken up by students and junior researchers, who are well versed in using social media. However, they will have to shift their posting strategies to reach professional groups, compose research-related entries, and sign up with research communities such as

ResearchGate, Academia, or VIVO. The difficult decision will lie in choosing which papers to publish in traditional journals and when to try open venues such as PLOS and arXiv.

Junior researchers are often attracted to follow the ABC and SED principles, but the challenges of seeking tenure and promotion often pressure them to pursue traditional goals. Tenure and promotion committees consisting of senior researchers often have traditional expectations about research topics and methods, leaving junior researchers with the challenge of demonstrating the validity and value of nontraditional outcomes. Savvy junior researchers know that having research results published in leading journals and conferences are central to career advancement. They ensure that they have a balance of collaborative papers in which they often hold the prestigious first-author position, and some single-author papers in which they show their personal strengths. These savvy junior researchers will also have strong testimonials from leaders in their fields, plus evidence of impact through citation or download counts, patent applications, media coverage of their work, and presentations at major research centers. In addition, they will have strong portfolios of professional service, such as serving on conference program committees, and of teaching success, such as developing popular new courses.[11]

A growing number of interdisciplinary programs are sympathetic to the ABC and SED principles, so students should study examples of research from the programs they apply to and ask faculty and current students about their experiences. However, this openness to new research topics and methods could limit the career choices of graduates.

While students and junior researchers mostly must learn to live within the research ecosystem, changing it is part of the agenda for senior researchers and policymakers.

11.4 Guidance for Senior Researchers and Policymakers

Senior researchers and policymakers who seek to promote the changes implied by the ABC and SED principles have many choices about how to intervene. The National Research Council *Convergence* report has long lists of action items, starting with simple ideas of lecture series, informal lunch gatherings on specific research topics, and research paper "clubs" to discuss a weekly paper. The report encourages making small changes, such as hosting lectures from outside

CASE STUDY 11.1 TEACHING TEAMWORK WITH REAL USERS

Relate-Create-Donate

My ideas about high-impact research strategies emerged and were tested and refined over two decades of teaching. The strategies drew on earlier education technology ideas in the "Relate-Create-Donate" concept: students working in teams to produce something ambitious for someone to use outside the classroom and which would survive beyond the semester.[1] This concept became my guiding principle in every course I taught, but it became especially effective in my 30-student graduate computer science course on information visualization.

The University of Maryland's 15-week semester gives me enough time to include smaller team projects early on, so that students develop the communication skills necessary for working in teams of 4 or 5 students over an 11–12 week project. The students also have individual homework, a midterm exam and a final exam, so I can obtain enough information to provide a final grade for each individual. In teaching this course, I learned that random assignment of students to teams produced greater diversity than allowing the students to choose their own teams did; in addition, it simulated the professional world, in which employees usually are assigned to teams.

To generate real problems embedded in "authentic" projects, I invite campus colleagues and Washington, DC, area business and government professionals to visit my course and give 10-minute pitches for projects that they want done. Then the student teams contact the presenters to negotiate doing the project, so as to prepare a 1-page proposal that describes the work and names the outside mentor/client. The fact that these are authentic projects, with engaged client/mentors, raises their importance, since someone other than the students cares about the project's completion. I provide guidance in refining the proposals, often trimming overly ambitious ideas.

The second deliverable, which is due within a week of the first, is a list of 15–20 papers, websites, or reports about previous work on the chosen problem, with sentence-long annotations about why each item is relevant. I tell students that I expect the team members to become the world's leading experts on their problem and to read every paper ever written about their topic. This bold requirement is designed to force them to narrow and define their project, as well as to learn about what published work entails. I explain the two parents, three children strategy (see Chapter 1, Fig. 1.5) to clarify the commitment to basic theory and applied problems in planning and outcomes.

The third deliverable consists of three rough prototypes of the user interface. These prototypes can be made using Photoshop or PowerPoint, or they can be paper-and-pencil sketches, and they are to be made by individual students rather than teams, so as to encourage the production of diverse designs. Then, in design-studio fashion, they are presented to the class and the mentor/clients for review, so as to promote convergence of opinion onto the best design, with refinement based on the other designs.

Within two more weeks, the first working version of the user interface is required, written in traditional programming languages or newer toolkits. The rapid prototyping tools and agile programming methods now available have dramatically raised my expectations of what students can accomplish.

Next, a midsemester report to the class forces teams to decide on their directions and practice presenting their projects. These presentations ensure that everyone in the class knows about the other projects, enabling them to learn what tools are being used, see what problems are addressed, and measure their ambition against others. The presentations also show the first versions of what the visualization, including the control panel, would look like and describe the usability test plan with the list of required tasks.

All the deliverables, including an annotated bibliography, early designs, and slide presentations, are put on our class wiki for everyone to see. This form of open work is novel and disturbing to some students, but I just present it as the normal expectation, so everyone quickly gets used to the idea. They like seeing each other's projects, and where possible I encourage teams to help each other. Our class discussion board enables me to post reminders about deadlines, notes about new tools or lectures, and links to great examples. It also enables students to ask each other for help. They are often reluctant to ask for help publicly, but once they see a few examples of supportive comments about design problems, software glitches, or helpful Web resources, activity picks up. It also helps that I comment on especially helpful students and thank them in class or online.

The semester races ahead rapidly, so the teams are soon testing their user interfaces with four to eight realistic users or a smaller number of expert user case studies, and turning in an evaluation report with recommended improvements. At this point, I am sometimes discouraged by what I see, but the last three weeks are a remarkably transformative time.

Peer Reviews to Improve Project Reports

The final report is due in draft form on the class wiki 2 weeks before the semester's end, followed by a 3-day review period and 3-day revision period. Students sign up to do a review, which is delivered as an email to the team and copied to me, stating what they liked in a paragraph and then giving high-, middle-, and low-level suggested revisions that could be accomplished in time. I grade these reviews based on how effective each student has been in giving helpful advice for other teams to improve their final reports. Reviews can cover presentations of problems and solutions, descriptions of related work, references, figures, evaluations, and future work, as well as writing style, spelling fixes, grammar, and so on. Five percent of each student's final grade depends on how much they have helped their classmates improve their work. About half the class takes me up on the extra-credit opportunity to review a second project report, so that each team of four to five students generally get five to seven reviews. Another benefit of this process is that, having reviewed another project's draft report, students are likely to reflect more carefully about their own.

This peer-review strategy is meant to raise every team's report quality, but it has many other benefits. When students realize that classmates are going to read their reports, I believe they take more care in writing them. The students are invariably generous in sending supportive overall comments, and the best reviews will have 2–3 pages of deep, thoughtful commentary with valuable suggestions for revisions that can be accomplished in the remaining days. This idea of having peer review only works because I explicitly reject the idea of grading on a curve. I promise students that it is possible for everyone to earn an

A grade. I've occasionally gotten close to that happy state, but there are often students who have worked less diligently and who wind up with B grades, or worse. However, I believe that one of the big payoffs of this teamwork approach is that the dropout rate is very low in my course. Once the students get past the drop/add period, it is rare for me to lose a student or assign an incomplete. I believe that team projects keep the students engaged in a powerful way so that they do their share and proudly produce a polished project.

The last week of the course involves 15-minute presentations of each project in a festive atmosphere with client/mentors, other students, and my colleagues attending. Good questions and hearty applause prevails. Every team also has to post a 3–5 minute demo video on the Web, so that gives them another chance to practice communications skills and to tell their story. Student teams are regularly invited to repeat their presentations at the client/mentor facilities, often leading to some follow-on work, and possibly a summer internship or permanent job offer.

Teaching Teamwork

Early in the semester, I describe teamwork strategies, focusing on two aphorisms: "Something small soon" and "Who does what by when." The first is aligned with my frequent deliverables, to push the project along, and the second is the clear assignment of goals and roles, such as "Gina will produce a code module by 9 pm Tuesday and Miguel will provide feedback by noon on Wednesday."

Even with all the structure and encouragement I provide, I tell the students that I expect two out of eight teams to get into trouble and that one of those will wind up in my office. The problems are typically between the high-aspiration students who are eager to get an A and the overwhelmed students who have other courses that they care more about or family/health problems that undermine their commitment to my class. We discuss ways to give the overwhelmed students a chance to take on tasks they could handle, and I get to learn who the strong or weak students are. This usually, but not always, gives me what I need to know about individual contributions to projects, but I still require the team project reports to have a credits section, in which the percent effort of each team member is listed for each project component. Composing the credits section can be controversial; however, since they know in advance that this is required, it gives additional encouragement for each student to "pull his/her weight."

Computer science students don't automatically seek to work in teams, but I think that, by doing so, they are learning valuable professional skills in a relatively safe environment. My best measure of success is that many of the team project reports go on to be published papers in conferences and journals. I used to say that one in ten student projects could lead to a publishable result; but these teamwork methods (external client/mentors, multiple deliverables, open posting, internal reviews, etc.) and the support technologies (class wiki, Web access to previous work, discussion board, shared code repositories, etc.) have enabled a much higher rate than that. In my best semester, five out of seven teams published papers in respected conferences and journals. Students have a strong portfolio item to show future employers and, if their work is published, they can proudly add it to their resumes.

Some student projects have been featured in media reports, blogged by industry leader Tim O'Reilly, turned into a cover story for *LINUX Magazine*, or triggered commercial applications. Students may build on their work in a master's or doctoral dissertation or get hired by colleagues and companies. Not every student likes the pressure of working in teams on authentic projects, but I'm encouraged by the students who go on to do excellent work and check back with me many years later.

---

[1] Shneiderman, B., *Leonardo's Laptop: Human Needs and the New Computing Technologies*, MIT Press, Cambridge, MA (2002); Shneiderman, B., *Relate-Create-Donate: An Educational Strategy* (2002) http://www.cs.umd.edu/hcil/relate_create_donate/.

---

speakers on new topics, coffee- or pizza-fueled discussions of research plans, and weekly journal clubs to read papers on an area of common interest.[12]

Social occasions for students and junior researchers may trigger fresh thinking, new collaborations, and awareness of work beyond their current focus. As a visiting researcher, I have strong memories of lively afternoon coffee discussions at the top floor of New York University's Courant Institute, snack breaks in the gardens of the Weizmann Institute, and midmorning tea parties at Canterbury University. The camaraderie of fellow researchers, the opportunity to learn about something new, and the chance to try out my new ideas made these occasions worthwhile. Researchers are often competitive, but they appreciate being part of a thriving community.

The *Convergence* report dwells on educational changes, such as revising courses to include new topics, including research results that address current issues, allowing students to shape their degree program, and encouraging project-oriented courses. External interactions are encouraged, through inviting speakers from business, developing collaborations with other universities, and facilitating student summer internships in businesses.[13]

Substantive changes include cluster hires to bring in several faculty at once who might work together in an emerging area. Cluster hires have become a popular mechanism and often include both junior and senior hires, who form a natural team that is then given ample resources to support its research plan. This reduces the isolation and struggle of a single junior faculty member trying to develop a new research area.

The report encourages joint appointments across departments and schools, but this is a well-known problem for junior faculty, who consequently will be reviewed by two units. Each unit will have to hear a compelling story of how the research advances the home discipline while reaching out to important new collaborators. Department deans, college deans, and campus provosts will need to address this important issue if change is to be made. One role model is the

University of Southern California, which has developed guidelines to emphasize a variety of forms of collaborative scholarship and to introduce attribution
standards for contributions to larger projects.[14]

Leadership from chairs, deans, and provosts can do much to adjust hiring,
tenure, and promotion policies so that junior researchers who choose new directions and methods are warmly received. One simple strategy is that the contract for new hires includes a clause indicating expected research and teaching
topics; such a contract forces the discussion early on and gives some protection
to new hires when their promotion or tenure review occurs. While disciplinary
rigor is a virtue, many researchers are open to revising the boundaries of their
discipline and the acceptable research methods. Sometimes new trends such
as big data, neuroscience, proteomics, or design for sustainability become so
widespread that junior researchers who address these topics will have a strong
advantage.

Innovative educational programs that combine disciplines, take on applied projects, require teamwork, and work with internal and external mentors often provide life-changing experiences for students. The Olin College's
engineering education (see Chapter 4, Section 4.2) and its partnership with
the University of Illinois show how new small colleges and established big
universities can take on new directions. Similarly, the University of Maryland Gemstone Program (Section 11.3) and the century-old requirement for
cooperative internships at Northeastern University show how teamwork and
business involvement produce great student experiences. Stanford University's new d.school (Section 5.6) and the Rhode Island School of Design show
that new programs and long-existing institutions are changing to accommodate contemporary topics.

Campus leaders can provide top-down encouragement and rewards for those
who teach or take on new topics or methods. At the same time, bottom-up attitude shifts and recognition from peers are important to spread changes to the
culture of research. This changing culture means that new courses might be
introduced, but equally important is the revision of existing courses to include
the new research topics, challenges, and terminology. Changing long-held attitudes that gave senior researchers their success is very difficult but is possible.
The case study examples show how individuals, campuses, and large institutions
have produced significant changes.

In many cases, academics will quickly shift their interests if government
funding agencies open new programs or require certain kinds of teamwork. The
US National Science Foundation triggered strong interest in new topics such as
digital libraries, cyberinfrastructure, and visualization by launching research

programs with funding in these areas. A recent program announcement, "Algorithms in the Field," went further in suggesting specific collaborations:[15]

Algorithms in the Field encourages closer collaboration between two groups of researchers: (i) theoretical computer science researchers, who focus on the design and analysis of provably efficient and provably accurate algorithms for various computational models; and (ii) applied researchers including a combination of systems and domain experts.

While engineering is an established component of the National Science Foundation's portfolio, the increasing appearance of design in the National Science Foundation's program announcements signals a change. The Secure and Trustworthy Cyberspace program had more than 40 mentions of design in its announcement.[16] Funding, as well as the stature of National Science Foundation or National Institutes of Health funding, accelerates the shift to fresh research topics and methods among academics, but it can be helped by other forces such as business needs and professional society reforms.

11.5 Guidance for Business Leaders and Professional Societies

Business leaders, especially research managers, often lead shifts to new topics because they see competitive advantages and market opportunities. The desire to lead a disruptive innovation and the fear of missing it drives contemporary businesses to make bold investments in some research topics. Businesses may enlist academic consultants, hire recent graduates, and retrain their staff. The top-down nature of business means that research managers have more power than academic leaders in shifting the research priorities of their staff, especially when a prominent customer makes specific requests.

However, the very competitive nature of businesses means that they are more likely to keep their results secret, file for patents, and be restrictive in sharing data. This approach is understandable, but various open innovation strategies suggest new ways for businesses to adopt external innovations and new motivations to share their research.[17] Sometimes the successful model set by InnoCentive, which enables business to post awards for solutions, has produced significant outcomes, but the more common approach is direct support and partnership with academic researchers. Many businesses provide gifts and contracts to academic teams to work on business problems, often with a liberal policy toward publication and shared ownership of intellectual property.

Data sharing can be a problem, but strategies such as finding an open data set that has characteristics similar to the business data set or creating a sufficiently anonymized version of the data are effective. In our projects, we have often formed partnerships where we developed and tested our software on an open data set, and then our partners ran it on their protected version. We've made similar arrangements with healthcare providers, who must protect patient privacy, and government agencies, which also needed to protect their data. Some businesses have creatively opened massive data sets to academic researchers via a nondisclosure clause that prohibits further dissemination. In short, there are ways that businesses, as well as nonprofit organizations, government agencies, community organizations, and consumer groups, can creatively work with academics to benefit from the fresh ideas and methods that they bring.

Professional societies are often bound by traditions and influenced by advisory boards of senior researchers, but they can be a source of forward-looking thinking, because they survive in a competitive environment as well. Competition among professional societies pushes their leaders to follow emerging trends, initiate workshops and training programs, and launch new journals or conferences.

Journal and conference program chairs and committees seem to have more influence than many others in approving new topics and research methods. The mere listing of a fresh term from a hot topic invites potential paper authors, especially ambitious junior researchers, to reframe their work to fit the journal or conference call for papers. The challenge then is to ensure that the review committees are sympathetic to the new topics and research methods.

Journal and conference organizers can also address the need to recognize and reward teamwork. An increasingly required approach is to require paper authors to include credits at the end of the paper to clarify which coauthor lead the way with different components of the work. Research papers may eventually resemble Hollywood films with detailed credits scrolling by at the end. Revealing the complexity of collaboration and the many tasks required helps junior researchers to appreciate all that goes into successful teamwork and helps senior researchers in hiring, tenure, and promotion decisions.

Another strategy for journal and conference organizers is to make "Best Paper," "Test of Time," or "Most Downloaded" awards, to direct attention to notable work. "Best Paper" and "Honorable Mention" awards reflect the impressions of program committees but have not been shown to correlate strongly with future citation papers. "Test of Time" papers are given for the most cited paper from 10 or 20 years ago, often offering the authors a chance to reflect on the history of their work. "Most Downloaded" awards are an early indicator to the community about which papers are generating unusual interest.

11.6 Skeptics' Corner

The refrain "You can't fight city hall" suggests that large systems are hard to change, which is true, but change is possible. Another sharp quip, usually attributed to physicist Max Planck, is that "disciplines change one funeral at a time." This strongly worded belief is often true, but thoughtful interventions can produce changes by engaging with the senior researchers to gain their sympathy or by creating new communities with shared interests. In fact, the novel uses of the World Wide Web, social media, and visual communication tools are already producing rapid changes in how research is done, published, and promoted. The question is, who will steer the changes with enough persistence to achieve meaningful reforms in conservative university administrations, massive government funding agencies, and established professional societies?

Skeptics see that the research ecosystem is controlled by senior people in universities, government agencies, and professional societies. Since they made their career successes according to old rules, they may be slow to accommodate new challenges, emerging technologies, and rising ambitions. Junior researchers are less willing and able than senior researchers to organize and assert pressure for change, thereby inhibiting the introduction of new policies that they want.

11.7 Summary

The immense problems of our century, the new technologies to support research, and the increased ambition of researchers mean that change is needed. Solving the applied problem of changing the research ecosystem is facilitated by having a theory of how it works (see Fig. 11.1). Next, targeted interventions can be prototyped locally and then scaled up and out, while the evidence that productive changes are being made can be tracked.

Resisting change will be difficult, since new business and nonprofit organizations are rushing in to provide alternative publishing venues and to develop researcher communities that transcend professional societies. At the same time, individuals and philanthropic foundations are funding a greater fraction of research than before, while businesses adopt new strategies such as open innovation.

To participate in the inevitable changes, students, junior researchers, senior researchers, policymakers, business leaders, and professional society directors can adopt the ABC and SED principles and then apply the five research life cycle strategies. The research ecosystem participants who keep aware of what is happening around them will have a better chance to succeed than those who do not.

CHAPTER 12

Change Is Hard, but Possible

The credit belongs to the man who is actually in the arena . . . who strives valiantly; who errs, and comes short again and again, because there is no effort without error and shortcoming; but who does actually strive to do the deeds; who knows the great enthusiasms, the great devotions; who spends himself in a worthy cause; who at the best knows in the end the triumph of high achievement, and who at the worst, if he fails, at least fails while daring greatly.

Theodore Roosevelt, "The Man in the Arena" Speech at the
Sorbonne, Paris, France, April 23, 1910

12.1 Introduction

The first step in making substantial change is to understand the status quo; the next is to offer a clear path forward to an attainable destination. In most established communities, devotion to tradition is strong, so gaining consensus for change is difficult; but dialog is a healthy process for refining ideas and gaining buy-in to make change.

I claim that the context for research is changing (Part I) because of (1) the immense problems of the twenty-first century, (2) the widespread use of novel Web-based libraries, open access publishing, social media engagement, and visual communication tools, and (3) the raised ambitions of research teams. Combining applied and basic research and blending science, engineering, and

The New ABCs of Research. First Edition. Ben Shneiderman.
© Ben Shneiderman 2016. Published in 2016 by Oxford University Press.

design have the potential to raise impact. Then, researchers who choose action-able problems and collaborators with civic, business, or global priorities can establish teams and conditions for successful applied research and foundational basic research. The set of five research life cycle strategies (see Fig. I.1 in the Introduction to this book) provide guidance for conducting research, present-ing results, and measuring impact. The goal is to contribute to the solutions of major problems while developing refined theories that have broad implications. There are many difficult steps along the way, and many opportunities for failure, but that is the nature of research.

With these ideas in mind, and with the changes to the research ecosystem de-scribed in Chapter 11, there is an opportunity to set ambitious research agendas for the coming decades and beyond. Chapters 3, 4, and 5, which have sections on roadmaps and challenges for science, engineering, and design, provide sug-gestions for valuable starting points for near-term research projects. However, there are also long-term research visions that may be useful in reshaping aca-demic education, business directions, and government policies.

Scientists, engineers, and designers have been central in making discoveries and innovations in the industrial age, the electrical age, and the information age. I believe they are ready to lead the way on yet another great journey of dis-covery and innovation, seeking new knowledge and understanding of how in-dividuals, organizations, and communities form policies, build consensus, and work together, while overcoming threats from internal conflicts and external challenges.

While every human era has been social, it may be that the hypersociality made possible by social media will dramatically lower barriers to collaboration. The leaders of the social media age might paraphrase the enthusiasm of NASA's roadmap authors thus: Remarkable discoveries will address three defining ques-tions: What motivates individuals to act? How can expectations and behaviors of individuals, organizations, and communities be changed? How can conflict resolution and management bring a more harmonious world? As stated by the roadmap authors, "Seeking answers to these age-old questions are Enduring Quests of humankind."[1]

It seems possible that the generations of hierarchically organized societies with emperor-like leaders who worked top-down in an imperial manner to pur-sue economic or military success may give way to network-organized societies in which power can rise bottom-up from multiple individuals and organiza-tions. Often this decentralized approach leads to spirited innovation, competi-tion, and collaboration that accelerate idea formation, testing, and refinement.

While many future scenarios are tied to technology advances such as genomic interventions, carbon sequestration, 3D printing, or nanotechnology, the significant transformation now underway is the shift to social media technologies, which enable behavioral economics solutions, collaboration, citizen action, and entrepreneurship. The social media age already has it success stories of Facebook, Twitter, YouTube, and blogging. Fresh thinking has also brought open-source success stories such as Linux and Wikipedia. Web-based medical information and social media health tracking are building patient knowledge and resources. The move to precision healthcare based on personalized genomic analyses will be increasingly important. However, the determinant of success will be how well innovations can be disseminated through the massive learning health community, where the influential variables will be the capacity to create trust, empathy, responsibility, and privacy at scale.

The social media age is a grand opportunity for new kinds of science, engineering, and design research. The scientific method, engineering prototypes, and design thinking will all be valuable in making discovering and innovations that promote human welfare while preserving our planet.

One research project would be to develop a "Handbook of Human Needs and Desires," analogous to the valuable *Handbook of Anthropometry*, which contains measurements of human physical properties such as height, weight, and body mass index, as well as hand size, reach, lifting ability and much more, for young, adult, and elderly people.[2] The 3000 pages of the *Handbook of Anthropometry* provide valuable information to guide designers of cars, furniture, medical devices, games, and so on. It covers gender and age differences, as well as healthy and diseased individuals. It might be equally valuable to have a detailed "Handbook of Human Needs and Desires," to guide researchers in choosing topics that could lead to deeper understandings as well as better products and services than are currently available. A starting point would be Abraham Maslow's hierarchy of human needs, which is usually depicted as a pyramid with the broad base being physiological needs for survival, such as food, water, clothing, and shelter. The next level is safety, which is followed by love/belonging, which followed by esteem. The top of the pyramid is self-actualization, which is described as aspiring to become the best person you can be.[3] This widely used hierarchy provides a clear message, but it has been challenged as falsely suggesting that there is a clear hierarchy of needs and criticized for lacking sensitivity to different cultures. While Maslow spells out some of the details, a full "Handbook of Human Needs and Desires" would constitute a periodic table of motivation, a guide for both researchers and practitioners.

While there are mature research communities in science and engineering, with structures defined by national bodies such as the US National Academy of Science and the US National Academy of Engineering, there is currently only one national organization for design, the DesignSingapore Council, which seeks to develop the design sector as a distinguishing feature of the business community in Singapore.[4] Currently, the New York-based National Academy and the London-based Royal College of Art School of Design provide some leadership in the design community.[5] In addition, multiple European schools of design are providing fresh thinking and leadership in the growing global community of designers.

I think a key ingredient for promoting the establishment of national bodies in design would be for the existing design research communities to unify and possibly produce a "Design Research Roadmap" with a 10–30-year vision and milestones such as the following:

- Design research guidelines: What are the best practices for conducting and reporting design research? Is there a list of exemplary design research papers?
- Visionary scenarios: How can designers best influence colleagues, industry, and the general public with visionary video scenarios, inspirational prototypes, written concept papers, or staged performances?
- Natural selection in product and service design: The evolution of mature designs takes thousands of adaptations. Could this process be improved or accelerated?
- Design of creative ecologies: What are the design principles for studios (containing 1–100 people), companies (containing 50–5000 people), cities (e.g., see Richard Florida's views on talent, tolerance, and technology in cities),[6] and regions (e.g., Silicon Valley)?
- Understanding expertise: How are experts different from novices, and how can these differences be measured/assessed? What are the different forms of expertise? How do we best train novices to be experts?
- Origin of communities: How do communities evolve, split, merge, compete, or decay? Can community design improve this process? Can metrics/indicators be developed to monitor participation and leadership?
- Community development: How do communities grow? Is it best to start with a small tight group and grow the network with similar thinkers (i.e., strong ties), or does a broad reach to diverse audiences (i.e., weak ties) help?

- Community governance: How can leaders promote change, moderate disputes, and encourage participation?
- Understanding of levels of expertise in science, engineering, and design. How can educators and managers agree about the levels of training and assessment across disciplines?

Another approach would be the establishment of "Design Research Grand Challenges," such as

- make it possible to provide affordable personally tailored health/wellness regimes to everyone;
- increase the number of affordable family-friendly homes and communities for parents and children;
- design objects and living spaces that enable and assist senior living;
- design objects, living spaces, and caretaking processes for life completion, legacy, and remembrance;
- create sustainable energy strategies for living, working, and recreation;
- develop wilderness and urban environment design to encourage protection;
- develop design principles for community safety;
- design scalable responses to natural and made-world disasters;
- create citizen science strategies to support learning and research;
- design for a quieter world; and
- design for compassion, mindfulness, self-confidence, tranquility.

12.2 Skeptics' Corner

The emphasis on social media and design may be too radical for many science and engineering researchers. They have a full list of research topics and see little chance that disruptive changes will force them to change their directions. Of course, social media is not the only worthy research topic, as there are many important science, engineering, and design challenges (see Chapters 3, 4, and 5) that remain viable and valuable.

There is a danger that is more pernicious than research failure. Research can also come from malicious actors with destructive goals, including tyrants, terrorists, and criminals. There is no guarantee that research will be used in positive, prosocial ways to benefit the largest number of people. However, I believe that, when research directions are discussed openly and results are publicly available, there is a better chance that long-term outcomes will be constructive.

The recommendations of this book range from short-term modest and realistic changes to long-term big disruptions. Readers can choose their favorites.

12.3 Summary

The great successes of science, engineering, and design have created a vibrant civilization, with problems and new challenges. Blending these disciplines with ambitious projects that combine applied and basic research agendas is a fresh way of thinking. It requires diverse knowledge and skills that are probably best realized through teamwork. Reorienting the research community to these new principles and getting them to integrate new ways of thinking is a continuing challenge.

NOTES

INTRODUCTION:

1. Swaby, R., *Headstrong: 52 Women Who Changed Science—and the World*, Broadway Books, New York, NY (2015).

   Hargittai, M., *Women Scientists: Reflections, Challenges, and Breaking Boundaries*, Oxford University Press, Oxford (2015).

CHAPTER 1:

1. Vansteenkiste, M. and Sheldon, K. M., There's nothing more practical than a good theory: Integrating motivational interviews with self-determination theory, *British Journal of Clinical Psychology* **45**, 1 (2006), 63–82.

2. Rabin, C., Labs Are Told to Start Including a Neglected Variable: Females, *New York Times* (May 14, 2014) http://www.nytimes.com/2014/05/15/health/nih-tells-researchers-to-end-sex-bias-in-early-studies.html.

3. Bush, V., *Science, The Endless Frontier: A Report to the President on a Program for Postwar Scientific Research*, Office of Scientific Research and Development, Washington, DC (1945).

4. Zachary, G. P., *Endless Frontier: Vannevar Bush, Engineer of the American Century*, MIT Press, Cambridge, MA (1999).

5. Edgerton, D., The linear model did not exist: Reflections on the history and historiography of science and research in industry in the twentieth century, in K. Grandin and N. Wormbs (Editors), *The Science–Industry Nexus: History, Policy, Implications*, Watson, New York, NY (2004), pp. 31–57.

6. Narayanamurti, V., Odumosu, T., and Vinsel, L., RIP: The basic/applied research dichotomy, *Issues in Science and Technology*, **29**, 2 (2013), 31–36.

7. Allen, T. J., *Managing the Flow of Technology: Technology Transfer and the Dissemination of Technological Information within the R&D Organization*, MIT Press, Cambridge, MA (1977).

8. Gertner, J., *The Idea Factory: Bell Labs and the Great Age of American Innovation*, Penguin Press, New York, NY (2012).

9. Medawar, P. B., *Advice to a Young Scientist*, Harper & Row, New York, NY (1979).

10. Stokes, D., *Pasteur's Quadrant: Basic Science and Technological Innovation*, Brookings Institution, Washington, DC (1997).

11. A similar concept was proposed with the term "vision-inspired basic research" to capture the idea of bold advances triggered by divergent thinking: Roco, M. C., Bainbridge, W. S., Tonn, B., and Whitesides, G. (Editors), *Convergence of Knowledge, Technology, and Society: Beyond Convergence of Nano-Bio-Info-Cognitive Technologies*, Springer, New York, NY (2013).

12. The RAND Corporation, *Discovery and Innovation: Federal Research and Development Activities in the Fifty States, District of Columbia, and Puerto Rico, Appendix B: Government-Wide and DOD Definitions of R&D* (2000) http://www.rand.org/content/dam/rand/pubs/monograph_reports/MR1194/MR1194.appb.pdf.

13. DARPA, *About DARPA* (Accessed July 31, 2015) http://www.darpa.mil/about-us/about-darpa.

14. Branscomb, L., The false dichotomy: Scientific creativity and utility, *Issues in Science and Technology* **16**, 1 (2007), 66; available at http://www.issues.org/16.1/branscomb.htm.

15. Candy, L. and Edmonds, E., *Interacting: Art, Research and the Creative Practitioner*, Libri Publishing, Faringdon (2011); Edmonds, E. A. and Candy, L., Relating theory, practice, and evaluation in practitioner research, *Leonardo* **43**, 5 (2010), 470–476.

16. National Science Foundation, *Directorate for Computer and Information Science and Engineering (CISE), Grant Proposal Guide: GPG* (Accessed July 24, 2015) http://www.nsf.gov/funding/pgm_summ.jsp?pims_id=503,641&org=CISE.

17. Shneiderman, B., Creativity support tools: Accelerating discovery and innovation, *Communications of the ACM* **50**, 12 (December 2007), 20–32.

18. Shneiderman, B., Dunne, C., Sharma, P., and Wang, P., Innovation trajectories for information visualization: A comparison of treemaps, cone trees, and hyperbolic trees, *Information Visualization Journal* **11**, 2 (2011), 87–105.

19. Shneiderman, B., Tree visualization with tree-maps: A 2-dimensional space filling approach, *ACM Transactions on Graphics* **11**, 1 (January 1992), 92–99; Shneiderman, B. and Plaisant, C., *Treemaps for Space-Constrained Visualization of Hierarchies Including the History of Treemap Research at the University of Maryland* (2014) http://www.cs.umd.edu/hcil/treemap-history.

20. President's Council of Advisors on Science and Technology, *Transformation and Opportunity: The Future of the U.S. Research Enterprise* (November 2012) http://www.whitehouse.gov/administration/eop/ostp/pcast/docsreports.

21. Spector, A., Norvig, P., and Petrov, S., Google's hybrid approach to research, *Communications of the ACM* **55**, 7 (July 2012), 34–37.

22. MIT Committee to Evaluate the Innovation Deficit, *The Future Postponed: Why Declining Investment in Basic Research Threatens a U.S. Innovation Deficit* (April 2015) http://dc.mit.edu/sites/default/files/innovation_deficit/Future%20Postponed.pdf.

CHAPTER 2:

1. schraefel, m. c. and Churchill, E., Wellth creation: Using computer science to support proactive health, *IEEE Computer* **47**, 11 (November 2014), 70–72.

2. The Center for Urban Science and Progress (CUSP), *NYU Center for Urban Science and Progress* (Accessed July 28, 2015) http://cusp.nyu.edu/. New York University's CUSP is a unique public-private research center that uses New York City as its laboratory and classroom to help cities around the world become more productive, livable, equitable, and resilient. CUSP observes, analyzes, and models cities to optimize outcomes, prototype new solutions, formalize new tools and processes, and develop new expertise/experts.

3. IBM, *Smarter Cities* (Accessed July 28, 2015) http://www.ibm.com/smarterplanet/us/en/smarter_cities/overview/.

4. McLuhan, M., *Understanding Media: The Extensions of Man*, McGraw-Hill, New York, NY (1964).

5. Thompson, C., Smarter than You Think: How Technology Is Changing Our Minds for the Better, Penguin Press, New York, NY (2013).

6. Rainie, L. and Wellman, B., *Networked: The New Social Operating System*, MIT Press, Cambridge, MA (2012).

7. Illinois Institute of Technology, Center for the Study of Ethics in the Professions (CSEP), *Codes of Ethics Collection* (Accessed July 28, 2015) http://ethics.iit.edu/ecodes/introduction.

8. ICSU, *Freedom & Responsibility Portal* (Accessed July 28, 2015) http://www.icsu.org/freedom-responsibility.

9. e.g., see 4th World Conference on Research Integrity, *Background* (Accessed July 28, 2015) http://www.wcri2015.org/background.html.

10. e.g., 3rd World Conference on Research Integrity, *Montreal Statement on Research Integrity in Cross-Boundary Research Collaborations* (2013) http://www.cehd.umn.edu/olpd/MontrealStatement.pdf; World Medical Association, Inc., *WMA Declaration of Helsinki: Ethical Principles for Medical Research Involving Human Subjects* (2015) http://www.wma.net/en/30publications/10policies/b3/. The World Medical Association developed the Declaration of Helsinki as a statement of ethical principles for medical research involving human subjects, including research on identifiable human material and data.

11. National Society of Professional Engineers, *Ethics* (2015) http://www.nspe.org/resources/ethics. "Professional engineers take seriously their responsibility—not just for the quality of the jobs they work on—but for the safety and well-being of the public at large."

12. e.g., see AIGA, *Design for Good Resources* (2015) http://www.aiga.org/designfor-good-get-involved/; dozens of "Design for Good" organizations and projects are described at this site.

13. Brad Hesse, personal communication by email, February 17, 2015.

14. Virginia Polytechnic Institute and State University, *Scieneering: Learning, Discovery, and Engagement at the Intersections of Science, Engineering, and the Law* (2015) http://www.undergraduate.provost.vt.edu/scieneering/index.html.

CHAPTER 3:

1. Merriam-Webster, Incorporated, *Dictionary: science* (2015) http://www.merriam-webster.com/dictionary/science.

2. Wikipedia, *Science* (2015) https://en.wikipedia.org/wiki/Science.

3. Wikipedia, *List of Dewey Decimal Classes* (2015) http://en.wikipedia.org/wiki/List_of_Dewey_Decimal_classes.

4. National Academy of Sciences, *Mission* (2015) http://nasonline.org/about-nas/mission/; American Association for the Advancement of Science, *About AAAS* (2015) http://www.aaas.org/about-aaas.

5. Proceedings of the National Academy of Sciences, *Proceedings of the National Academy of Sciences* (2015) http://www.pnas.org.

6. Thomson Reuters, *Web of Science* (2015) http://wokinfo.com/citationconnection/; formerly Web of Knowledge, produced by the Institute for Scientific Information.

7. Stokes, D., *Pasteur's Quadrant: Basic Science and Technological Innovation*, Brookings Institution, Washington, DC (1997).

8. Further support for Stokes comes from those who take a cognitive technology view: Fiore, S. M., Power and promise: Cognitive psychology and cognitive technology, *Cognitive Technology* **13**, 1 (2008), 5–8, and Fiore, S. M., Cognition and technology: Interdisciplinarity and the impact of cognitive engineering research on organizational productivity, in S. Kozlowski (Editor), *Oxford Handbook of Industrial and Organizational Psychology*, Oxford University Press, Oxford (2012), pp. 1306–1322.

9. Rutgers University, The Thomas Edison Papers, *Edison's Patents* (2012) http://edison.rutgers.edu/patents.htm.

10. Kuhn, T., *The Structure of Scientific Revolutions*, University of Chicago Press, Chicago, IL (1962; third edition, 1996).

11. Bush, V., *Science, The Endless Frontier: A Report to the President on a Program for Postwar Scientific Research*, Office of Scientific Research and Development, Washington, DC (1945).

12. Horgan, J., *The End of Science: Facing the Limits of Science in the Twilight of the Scientific Age*, Broadway Books, New York, NY (1996).

13. Horgan, J., What Thomas Kuhn Really Thought About Scientific "Truth," *Scientific American* (May 23, 2012) http://blogs.scientificamerican.com/cross-check/what-thomas-kuhn-really-thought-about-scientific-truth/.

14. Pentland, A., *Social Physics: How Good Ideas Spread: The Lessons from a New Science*, Penguin Press, New York, NY (2014).

15. American Committee for the Weizmann Institute of Science, *About Us: Meet the American Committee and the Weizmann Institute* (2015) http://www.weizmann-usa.org/meet-the-institute.aspx.

16. The Rockefeller University, *About the Rockefeller University* (2015) http://www.rockefeller.edu/about/.

17. National Science Foundation, *Proposal and Award Policies and Procedures Guide*, National Science Foundation, Arlington, VA (2014), pp. III–2. http://www.nsf.gov/pubs/policydocs/pappguide/nsf15001/nsf15_1.pdf (Accessed October 19, 2015).

18. Ibid, pp. II–12.

19. Kamenetzy, J. R., Opportunities for impact: Statistical analysis of the National Science Foundation's broader impact criteria, *Science and Public Policy* **40**, 1 (2013), 72–84.

20. National Academies, Committee on Facilitating Interdisciplinary Research, Committee on Science, Engineering, and Public Policy, *Facilitating Interdisciplinary Research*, National Academy Press, Washington, DC (2004), p. 2.

21. Stevens Institute of Technology, *Center for Innovation in Engineering and Science Education* (Accessed July 29, 2015) http://www.ciese.org/.

22. University of Maryland PERG, *University of Maryland's Physics Education Research Group* (2011) http://www.physics.umd.edu/perg/; NARST, *NARST Mission Statement* (2015) https://www.narst.org/about/mission.cfm.

23. National Science Teachers Association, *National Science Teachers Association* (2015) http://www.nsta.org/.

24. The White House, *The White House Science Fair* (Accessed July 29, 2015) https://www.whitehouse.gov/science-fair.

25. Bargmann, C., Newsome, W., Anderson, A., et al., *BRAIN 2025: Brain Research through Advancing Innovative Neurotechnologies (BRAIN) Working Group Report to the Advisory Committee to the Director, NIH* (June 2014) http://www.nih.gov/science/brain/2025/BRAIN2025.pdf.

26. NASA, *About Us* (2015) http://nasascience.nasa.gov/about-us/science-strategy.

27. Ibid.

28. NASA, *Enduring Quests, Daring Visions: NASA Astrophysics in the Next Three Decades* (2013) http://science.nasa.gov/media/medialibrary/2013/12/20/secure-Astrophysics_Roadmap_2013.pdf.

29. European Strategy Forum on Research Infrastructures, *Strategy Report on Research Infrastructures: Roadmap 2010* (2011) http://ec.europa.eu/research/infrastructures/pdf/esfri-strategy_report_and_roadmap.pdf; Science Europe, *ScienceEurope_Roadmap* (December 2013) http://www.scienceeurope.org/uploads/PublicDocumentsAndSpeeches/ScienceEurope_Roadmap.pdf; Science & Technology Facilities Council, Science and Technology Facilities Council, *World-Class Research, World-Class Skills, World-Class Innovation: Annual Report and Accounts 2013–2014* (July 2014) https://www.gov.uk/government/uploads/system/uploads/attachment_data/file/330866/Science-and-technology-facilities-council-annual-report-and-accounts-2013–2014.pdf; Ministry of Business, Innovation and

Employment, *National Science Challenges* (Accessed July 29, 3015) http://www.mbie.govt.nz/what-we-do/national-science-challenges; Kuroda, M., *Challenges to Redesign Science for Science and Technology Policy in Japan* (2014) http://www.apo-tokyo.org/publications/wp-content/uploads/sites/5/Prof.-Kuroda-APO-KEIO.pdf.

30. National Academies, Science of Science and Innovation Policy, *Principal Investigators' Conference Summary*, National Academy Press, Washington, DC (2014), p. 47.

CHAPTER 4:

1. Petroski, H., *To Engineer is Human: The Role of Failure in Successful Design*, Vintage, New York, NY (1992).

2. Wikipedia, Engineering (Accessed July 30, 2015) http://en.wikipedia.org/wiki/Engineering.

3. National Society of Professional Engineers, *What is a PE?* (2015) http://www.nspe.org/resources/licensure/what-pe. To become licensed, engineers must complete a four-year college degree, work under a Professional Engineer (PE) for at least four years, pass two intensive competency exams, and earn a license from their state's licensure board. Then, to retain their licenses, PEs must continually maintain and improve their skills throughout their careers.

4. Arthur, B., *The Nature of Technology: What It Is and How It Evolves*, Free Press, New York, NY (2009).

5. Petroski, H., *The Essential Engineer: Why Science Alone Will Not Solve Our Global Problems*, Knopf, New York, NY (2010).

6. Queen Elizabeth Prize for Engineering, *Queen Elizabeth Prize for Engineering Winner 2015: Dr Robert Langer* (Accessed 2015) http://qeprize.org/.

7. *What is Engineering?* (2012) http://whatisengineering.com/.

8. Wikipedia, *Engineering* (Accessed July 30, 2015) http://en.wikipedia.org/wiki/Engineering.

9. National Academy of Engineering, *Engineering Sections* (2015) http://www.nae.edu/MembersSection/Sections.aspx.

10. National Academy of Engineering, *Awards* (2015). http://www.nae.edu/Activities/Projects/Awards.aspx.

11. Dewey, J., *Experience and Education*, Collier Books, New York, NY (1938).

12. Jacoby, B., *Service-Learning in Higher Education: Concepts and Practices*, Jossey-Bass Publishers, San Francisco, CA (1996).

13. Engineers Without Borders International, *EWB-I around the World* (Accessed July 30, 2015) http://www.ewb-international.org/.

14. iFoundry, *What is iFoundry?* (2012) http://ifoundry.illinois.edu/who-we-are/what-ifoundry.

15. National Academy of Engineering, *Grand Challenges for Engineering* (2008) http://www.engineeringchallenges.org/File.aspx?id=11574.

16. Longitude Prize, Longitude Prize Open (Accessed July 30, 2015) http://www.longitudeprize.org/.

CHAPTER 5:

1. Mumford, L., *Technics and Civilization*, Harcourt Brace and World, Inc., New York, NY (1934), p. 318.

2. Buxton, B., *Sketching User Experiences: Getting the Design Right and the Right Design*, Morgan Kaufmann, Burlington, MA (2007).

3. Laurel, B., *Design Research: Methods and Perspectives*, MIT Press, Cambridge, MA (2003).

4. Zimmerman, J., Forlizzi, J., and Evenson, S., Research through design as a method for interaction design research, in *Proceedings of the Conference on Human Factors in Computing Systems*, ACM Press, New York, NY (2007), pp. 493–502.

5. Wikipedia, *Design* (2015) http://en.wikipedia.org/wiki/Design.

6. Ibid.

7. Alexander, C., Ishikawa, S., and Silverstein, M., *A Pattern Language: Towns, Buildings, Construction*, Oxford University Press, Oxford (1977).

8. Schuler, D., *Liberating Voices: A Pattern Language for Communication Revolution*, MIT Press, Cambridge, MA (2008); Schuler, D., *The Pattern Language* (Accessed August 4, 2015) http://publicsphereproject.org/patterns/pattern-table-of-contents.php.

9. The University of British Columbia, Sauder School of Business, *Design Processes* (Accessed August 4, 2015) http://dstudio.ubc.ca/toolkit/processes/.

10. ISO, *ISO 13407:1999: Human-Centered Design Processes for Interactive Systems* (Accessed August 4, 2015) http://www.iso.org/iso/ iso_catalogue/catalogue_tc/catalogue_detail.htm?csnumber=21197.

11. Design Council, *A Study of the Design Process* (2005) http://www.designcouncil.org.uk/sites/default/files/asset/document/ElevenLessons_Design_Council%20%282%29.pdf.

12. Schön, D., *The Reflective Practitioner: How Professionals Think in Action*, Basic Books, New York, NY (1983).

13. Ibid., p. 40.

14. Gladwell, M., *Blink: The Power of Thinking without Thinking*, Basic Books, New York, NY (2007).

15. Dreyfuss, H., *Designing for People*, Allworth Press, New York, NY (1955; new edition, 2003).

16. Isaacson, W., *Steve Jobs*, Simon & Schuster, New York, NY (2011).

17. The Webby Awards, *The Webby Fifty Presented by Grey Goose* (2014) https://www.webbyawards.com.

18. Preece, J. and Shneiderman, B., The Reader-to-Leader Framework: Motivating technology-mediated social participation, *AIS Transactions on Human-Computer Interaction* **1**, 1 (March 2009), 13–32. Available at http://aisel.aisnet.org/thci/vol1/iss1/5/.

19. Kahneman, D. and Tversky, A. Prospect theory: An analysis of decisions under risk, *Econometrica* **47**, 2 (1979), 263–291; Kahneman, D., *Thinking, Fast and Slow*, Farrar, Straus and Giroux, New York, NY (2011); Tversky, A. and Kahneman, D., Judgment under uncertainty: Heuristics and biases, *Science* **185**, 4157 (1974), 1124–1131; Tversky, A. and Kahneman, D., The framing of decisions and the psychology of choice, *Science* **211**, 4481 (1981), 453–458.

20. Thaler, R. and Sunstein, C., *Nudge: Improving Decisions about Health, Wealth, and Happiness*, Yale University Press, New Haven, CT (2008).

21. Ariely, D., *Predictably Irrational: The Hidden Forces That Shape Our Decisions: Second Edition*, HarperCollins, New York, NY (2012).

22. Jones, P., *Design for Care: Innovating the Healthcare Experience*, Rosenfeld Media, Brooklyn, NY (2013); Rouse, W. B. and Serban, N., *Understanding and Managing the Complexity of Healthcare*, MIT Press, Cambridge, MA (2014).

23. Kimmelman, M., In redesigned room, hospital patients may feel better already, *New York Times* (August 21, 2014) http://www.nytimes.com/2014/08/22/arts/design/in-redesigned-room-hospital-patients-may-feel-better-already.html.

24. Hevner, A. R., March, S. T., Park, J., and Ram, S., Design science research in information systems, *Management Information Systems Quarterly* **28**, 1 (March 2004), 75–105; Gregor, S. and Hevner, A. R., Positioning and presenting design science research for maximum impact, *MIS Quarterly* **37**, 2 (June 2013), 337–355.

25. Alturki, A., Gable, G. C., and Bandara, W., A design science research roadmap, in H. Jain, A. P. Sinha, and P. Vitharana (Editors), *Service-Oriented Perspectives in Design Science Research*, Lecture Notes in Computer Science 6629, Springer, Berlin (2011), 107–123; Alturki, A., Gable, G. C., and Bandara, W., The design science research roadmap: In progress evaluation, Association for Information Systems, *Pacific Asia Conference on Information Systems 2013 Proceedings* (2013), Paper 160, available at http://aisel.aisnet.org/pacis2013/160; Gregor, S. and Hevner, A., The front end of innovation: Perspectives on creativity, knowledge and design, in B. Donnellan, M. Helfert, J. Kenneally, D. VanderMeer, M. Rothenberger, and R. Winter (Editors), *New Horizons in Design Science: Broadening the Research Agenda, 10th International Conference on Design Science Research in Information Systems and Technology (DESRIST 2015), Proceedings*, Lecture Notes in Computer Science 9073, Springer, Cham (2015), pp. 249–263. doi: 10.1007/978-973-319-18714-3_16.

26. Autodesk, *The Design-Led Revolution: Let's Create a Better Future through Sustainable Design* (2015) http://www.autodesk.com/sustainable-design/revolution.

27. Cooper Hewitt, *2015 National Design Awards Winners* (Accessed August 4, 2015) http://www.cooperhewitt.org/national-design-awards/2015-national-design-awards-winners/; honoring excellence, innovation and last achievement in American Design.

28. Elle Decoration, *British Design Award Winners 2014* (Accessed August 4, 2015) http://www.elledecoration.co.uk/britishdesignawards/british-design-award-winners-2014/; The Design 100, *2015 London Design Awards* (2015) http://londondesignawards.co.uk/lon15/; Japan Institute of Design Promotion, *Good Design Award* (Accessed August 4, 2015) http://www.g-mark.org/?locale=en; Good Design Australia, *Good Design Awards* (Accessed August 4, 2015) http://www.gooddesignaustralia.com/awards/other-awards/; DesignSingapore Council, *President's Design Award Singapore 2015* (2015) http://www.designsingapore.org/PDA_PUBLIC/content.aspx?sid=4; Centro Brasil Design, *Brazil Design Award* (2015) http://www.cbd.org.br/brasil-design-award/?lang=en.

29. Simon, H., *The Sciences of the Artificial: Third Edition*, MIT Press, Cambridge, MA (1996), p. 114.

30. Ibid., p. 111.

31. President's Council of Advisors for Science and Technology, *Report to the President: Realizing the Full Potential of Health Information Technology to Improve Healthcare for Americans: The Path Forward*, Washington, DC (2010).

32. Etheredge, L. M., A rapid learning health system, *Health Affairs* **26**, 2 (2007), 107–118, doi: 10.1377/hlthaff.26.2.w107; Etheredge, L. M., Rapid learning: A breakthrough agenda, *Health Affairs* **33**, 7 (2014), 1155–1162, doi: 10.1377/hlthaff.2014.0043; National Research Council, Committee on a Framework for Developing a New Taxonomy of Disease, *Toward Precision Medicine: Building a Knowledge Network for Biomedical Research and a New Taxonomy of Disease*, National Academies Press, Washington, DC (2011); available at http://www.nap.edu/catalog.php?record_id=13284.

33. Friedman, C., Rubin, J., et al., Toward a science of learning systems: A research agenda for the high-functioning Learning Health System, *Journal of the American Medical Informatics Association* **22** (2015), 43–50.

34. Learning Health Community, *How Would You Feel?* (2015) http://www.learninghealth.org.

35. Buckminster Fuller Institute, Eight Strategies for Comprehensive Anticipatory Design Science (Accessed August 4, 2015) http://www.bfi.org/design-science/primer/eight-strategies-comprehensive-anticipatory-design-science.

36. Fuller, R. B., *Operating Manual for Spaceship Earth*, Southern Illinois University Press, Carbondale, IL (1969).

37. Fuller, R. B., *Synergetics: Explorations in the Geometry of Thinking*, Macmillan, London (1982; first edition, 1976), p. 3.

38. Fuller, R. B., *Operating Manual for Spaceship Earth*, Southern Illinois University Press, Carbondale, IL (1969), front face.

39. Cross, N., Design research: A disciplined conversation, *Design Issues* **15**, 2 (1999), 5–10.

40. Cross, N., *Engineering Design Methods: Strategies for Product Design: Fourth Edition*, Wiley, New York, NY (2008).

41. Maher, M. L. and Gero, J. S., Leadership in Design Science, in W. S. Bainbridge (Editor), *Leadership in Science and Technology: A Reference Handbook*, Sage Publishers, New York, NY (2011), pp. 114–122.

42. Fischer, G. and Giaccardi, E., Meta-design: A framework for the future of end user development, in H. Lieberman, F. Paternò, and V. Wulf (Editors), *End User Development*, Kluwer Academic Publishers, Dordrecht (2006), pp. 427–457; Fischer, G., Understanding, fostering, and supporting cultures of participation, *ACM Interactions* **28**, 3 (May + June 2011a), 42–53; Fischer, G. and Herrmann, T., Meta-design: Transforming and enriching the design and use of socio-technical systems, in D. Randall, K. Schmidt, and V. Wulf (Editors), *Designing Socially Embedded Technologies: A European Challenge*, Springer, London (2014), pp. 79–109.

43. Atman, C., Chimka, J., Bursic, K., and Nachtmann, H., A comparison of freshman and senior engineering design processes, *Design Studies* **20**, 2 (1999), 131–152.

44. Stolterman, E., The nature of design practice and implications for interaction design research, *International Journal of Design* **2**, 1 (2008), 55–65.

45. Nelson, H. G. and Stolterman, E., *The Design Way: Intentional Change in an Unpredictable World: Second Edition*, MIT Press, Cambridge, MA (2012).

46. IDEO, *IDEO Helps Companies Build Businesses, Innovate, Develop Capabilities, Grow* (2015) http://www.ideo.com/; Brown, T., *Change by Design: How Design Thinking Transforms Organizations and Inspires Innovation*, HarperBusiness, New York, NY (2009).

47. SCAD, *Mission, Vision and Values* (Accessed August 4, 2015) http://www.scad.edu/about/scad-glance/mission-vision-and-values.

48. Rhode Island School of Design, *Rhode Island School of Design* (2015) http://www.risd.edu; Maeda, J., How art, technology and design inform creative leaders, *TEDGlobal* (2012) http://www.ted.com/talks/john_maeda_how_art_technology_and_design_inform_creative_leaders.

49. Rhode Island School of Design, *STEM to STEAM* (2015) http://www.risd.edu/About/STEM_to_STEAM/.

50. Stanford University Institute of Design, *Innovators, Not Innovations* (2015) http://dschool.stanford.edu/our-point-of-view.

51. Perlroth, N., Solving problems for real world, using design, *New York Times* (December 29, 2013) http://www.nytimes.com/2013/12/30/technology/solving-problems-for-real-world-using-design.html.

52. OCAD University, *The University of the Imagination* (Accessed August 4, 2015) http://www.ocadu.ca/about.

53. OCAD University, Inclusive Design Research Center (IDRC), About the IDRC (2013) http://idrc.ocad.ca/index.php/about-the-idrc.

54. Design for America, *Vision* (2015) http://designforamerica.com/vision/.

55. Ibid.

56. Shneiderman, B. and Plaisant, C., *Designing the User Interface: Strategies for Effective Human-Computer Interaction: Sixth Edition*, Addison-Wesley, Reading, MA (2016).

57. e.g., Preece, J., Rogers, Y., and Sharp, H., *Interaction Design: Beyond Human-Computer Interaction: Fourth Edition*, Wiley, New York, NY (2015); Cooper, A., Reimann, R., Cronin, D., and Noessel, C., *About Face: Essentials of Interaction Design: Fourth Edition*, Wiley, New York, NY (2014); SIGCHI, *Welcome* (Accessed August 4, 2015) http://www.sigchi.org.

58. Norman, D., *Design of Everyday Things*, Basic Books, New York, NY (1988, 2013).

59. Harper, R., Rodden, T., Rogers, Y., and Sellen, A., *Being Human: Human-Computer Interaction in the Year 2020*, Microsoft Research, Cambridge (2008) http://research.microsoft.com/en-us/um/cambridge/projects/hci2020/downloads/BeingHuman_A3.pdf, p. 9.

CHAPTER 6:

1. DataBay, *Reclaim the Bay Innovation Challenge* (Accessed August 5, 2015) http://databay.splashthat.com/.

2. Cornell University, *Cornell Lab of Ornithology* (2015) http://www.birds.cornell.edu/; Citizen Science Association, *Citizen Science Association: A Community of Practice for the Field of Public Participation in Scientific Research* (Accessed August 5, 2015) http://citizenscienceassociation.org/conference/; The Open University, iSpot: *Share Nature* (Accessed August 5, 2015) http://www.ispotnature.org/communities/global; Citizen Science Community Forum, *Policies and Citizen Science* (2013) http://www.citizenscience.org/community/blog/2013/11/11/policies-and-citizen-science/.

3. UrbanSim, *Welcome to the UrbanSim Project* (2014) http://www.urbansim.org/Main/WebHome. "UrbanSim is a software-based simulation system for supporting planning and analysis of urban development, incorporating the interactions between land use, transportation, the economy, and the environment. It is intended for use by Metropolitan Planning Organizations (MPOs), cities, counties, non-governmental organizations, researchers and students interested in exploring the effects of infrastructure and policy choices on community outcomes such as motorized and non-motorized accessibility, housing affordability, greenhouse gas emissions, and the protection of open space and environmentally sensitive habitats."

4. Miller, J. and Parker, L., *Everybody's Business: The Unlikely Story of How Big Business Can Fix the World*, Biteback Publishing, London (2013).

5. Engineers Without Borders USA, Engineers Without Borders USA (2015) http://www.ewb-usa.org/; Engineers Without Borders International, Engineers Without Borders International (Accessed August 5, 2015) http://www.ewb-international.org/.

6. Walker, Jack L., Setting the agenda in the US Senate: A theory of problem selection, *British Journal of Political Science* **7**, 4 (October 1977), 423–455.

7. Medawar, P. B., *Advice to a Young Scientist*, Harper & Row, New York, NY (1979), p. 13.

8. Alon, U., How to choose a good scientific problem, *Molecular Cell* **35**, 6 (September 25, 2009), 726–728, http://www.cell.com/molecular-cell/abstract/S1097-2765(09)00641-8.

9. Beveridge, W. I., *Art of Scientific Investigation*, W. W. Norton & Co., New York, NY (1950; 1957; Kindle edition), location 202–203.

10. Thompson, J. M. T., Advice to a young researcher: With reminiscences of a life in science, *Philosophical Transactions of the Royal Society A* **371**, 1993 (20 May 2013), 20120425.

11. National Institutes of Health, *Brain 2025: A Scientific Vision: Research through Advancing Innovative Neurotechnologies (BRAIN) Working Group Report to the Advisory Committee to the Director, NIH* (June 5, 2014) http://www.braininitiative.nih.gov/2025/BRAIN2025.pdf.

12. Thompson, J. M. T., Advice to a young researcher: With reminiscences of a life in science, *Philosophical Transactions of the Royal Society* **371**, 1993 (20 May 2013), 20120425.

13. Booth, W. C., Colomb, G. G., and Williams, J. M., *The Craft of Research: Third Edition*, University of Chicago Press, Chicago, IL (2008).

14. Turabian, K. L., Booth, W. C., Colomb, G. G., Williams, J. M., and the University of Chicago Press Staff, *A Manual for Writers of Research Papers, Theses, and Dissertations: Eighth Edition*, University of Chicago Press, Chicago, IL (2013).

15. My version is derived from Tim Finin's website: Finin, T., *Heilmeier's Catechism* (2007) http://www.csee.umbc.edu/~finin/home/heilmeyerCatechism.html; he took it from Gio Wiederhold's website: Wiederhold, G., *CS73 N Meeting 06 Notes: Project Reviews* (2005) http://infolab.stanford.edu/pub/gio/CS99I/Meet06Notes.html. However, Wikipedia has a different version: see Wikipedia, *George H. Heilmeier*, http://en.wikipedia.org/wiki/George_H._Heilmeier. The original paper: Heilmeier, G., Some reflections on innovation and invention, *The Bridge* **22**, 4 (1992), 12–16.

16. e.g., Kumar, V., 101 *Design Methods: A Structured Approach for Driving Innovation in Your Organization*, Wiley, New York, NY (2012); Schwiesow, D., *7 Research Challenges* (And How to Overcome Them) (2015) http://www.waldenu.edu/about/newsroom/publications/articles/2010/01-research-challenges.

17. Feamster, N., Research Patterns, *How to Do Great Research: Grad School Survival Advice from Nick Feamster and Alex Gray* (September 20, 2013) http://greatresearch.org/2013/09/20/research-patterns/.

18. National Science Foundation, *A–Z Index of Funding Opportunities* (Accessed August 5, 2015) http://www.nsf.gov/funding/azindex.jsp; National Institutes of Health, *Grants & Funding* (2014) http://grants.nih.gov/searchGuide/Search_Guide_Results.cfm?RFAsToo=0.

19. Engineering and Physical Sciences Research Council, *Calls* (Accessed August 5, 2015) https://www.epsrc.ac.uk/funding/calls/; European Research Council, Funding Schemes (Accessed August 5, 2015) http://erc.europa.eu/funding-and-grants/funding-schemes; Japan Society for the Promotion of Science, Grants-in-Aid for Scientific Research (2010) https://www.jsps.go.jp/english/e-grants/; Australian Research Council, Welcome to the Australian Research Council Website (2015) http://www.arc.gov.au/; Government of Canada, Natural Sciences and Engineering Research Council of Canada (2015) http://www.nserc-crsng.gc.ca/index_eng.asp.

20. Shneiderman, B., *A Short History of Structured Flowcharts (Nassi-Shneiderman Diagrams)* (2003) http://www.cs.umd.edu/hcil/members/bshneiderman/nsd/.

21. Shneiderman, B., *Rejection Letter from the Communications of the ACM* (2003) http://www.cs.umd.edu/hcil/members/bshneiderman/nsd/rejection_letter.html.

22. Wikipedia, Nassi-Shneiderman Diagram (Accessed August 5, 2015) http://en.wikipedia.org/wiki/Nassi%E2%80%93Shneiderman_diagram.

23. Dyson, F., A meeting with Enrico Fermi, *Nature* **427**, 6972 (2004), 297.

24. National Academy of Engineering, *NAE Grand Challenges for Engineering* (2015) http://www.engineeringchallenges.org/.

25. Longitude Prize, *Longitude Prize Open* (Accessed August 5, 2015) http://www.longitudeprize.org/.

26. United Nations, *Millennium Development Goals and Beyond* (Accessed August 5, 2015) http://www.un.org/millenniumgoals/.

27. United National Department of Economic and Social Affairs (Accessed October 19, 2015) https://sustainabledevelopment.un.org/?menu=1300.

28. Sobel, D., *Longitude: The True Story of a Lone Genius Who Solved the Greatest Scientific Problem of His Time*, Walker Publishing Company, New York, NY (1995).

29. Longitude Prize, *Longitude Prize Open* (Accessed August 5, 2015) http://www.longitudeprize.org/.

30. XPRIZE Foundation, *Who We Are* (2015) http://www.xprize.org/about/who-we-are. "XPRIZE is an innovation engine. A facilitator of exponential change. A catalyst for the benefit of humanity. We believe in the power of competition."

31. XPRIZE Foundation, *XPRIZE Foundation* (2014) http://xprizebenefit.org/.

32. InnoCentive, *What We Do* (2015) http://www.innocentive.com/about-innocentive. "We crowdsource innovation solutions from the world's smartest people, who compete to provide ideas and solutions to important business, social, policy, scientific, and technical challenges."

CHAPTER 7:

1. Gawande, A., *The Checklist Manifesto: How to Get Things Right*, Metropolitan Books, New York, NY (2010).

2. ISO, *ISO 9241-210:2010: Ergonomics of Human-System Interaction*, (2015) http://www.iso.org/iso/catalogue_detail.htm?csnumber=52075.

3. Brooks, F. B., *The Mythical Man-Month: Essays on Software Engineering*, Addison-Wesley Publishers, Boston, MA (1975, 1995).

4. Patterson, D., How to build a bad research center, *Communications of the ACM* **57**, 3 (March 2014), 33–36.

5. Thomson, W., Baron Kelvin (1891). *Popular Lectures and Addresses*, Vol. 1, Macmillan, London (1891), p. 80.

6. US National Institutes of Health, *ClinicalTrials.gov* (Accessed August 6, 2015) http://clinicaltrials.gov/. "ClinicalTrials.gov is a registry and results database of publicly and privately supported clinical studies of human participants conducted around the world."

7. Ioannidis, J. P. A., Why most published research findings are false, *PLoS Medicine* **2**, 8 (August 2005), e124. doi: 10.1371/journal.pmed.0020124.

8. White House Press Release, *Obama Administration Unveils "Big Data" Initiative: Announces $200 million in New R & D Investments, Washington, DC* (March 29, 2012) http://www.whitehouse.gov/sites/default/files/microsites/ostp/big_data_press_release_final_2.pdf.

9. Tukey, J. W., *Exploratory Data Analysis*, Addison-Wesley, Boston, MA (1977).

10. Tukey, J. W., The technical tools of statistics, *American Statistician* **19**, 2 (1965), 23–28.

11. Smith, M. A., Rainie, L., Himelboim, I., and Shneiderman, B., Mapping Twitter topic networks: From polarized crowds to community clusters, *Pew Research Center Report* (Feb 20, 2014) http://www.pewinternet.org/files/2014/02/PIP_Mapping-Twitter-networks_022014.pdf.

12. Börner, K., *Atlas of Science: Visualizing What We Know*, MIT Press, Cambridge, MA (2010). Börner, K., *Atlas of Knowledge: Anyone Can Map*, MIT Press, Cambridge, MA (2015).

13. Yin, R. K., *Case Study Research: Design and Methods: Fifth Edition*, Sage Publications, Thousand Oaks, CA (2013).

14. Shneiderman, B. and Plaisant, C., Strategies for evaluating information visualization tools: Multi-dimensional in-depth long-term case studies, in *Proceedings of the Workshop of the Advanced Visual Interfaces Conference*, ACM Press, New York, NY (2006), pp. 1–7.

15. Sedlmair, M., Meyer, M., and Munzner, T., Design study methodology: Reflections from the trenches and the stacks, *IEEE Transactions on Visualization and Computer Graphics* **18**, 12 (2012), 2431–2440.

16. Schön, D., *The Reflective Practitioner: How Professionals Think in Action*, Basic Books, New York, NY (1983).

17. Obrenović, Z., Doing research in practice: Some lessons learned, *ACM XRDS* **20**, 4 (Summer 2014), 15–17.

18. Palmer, E. M., Clausner, T. C., and Kellman, P. J., Enhancing air traffic displays via perceptual cues, *ACM Transactions on Applied Perception* **5**, 1 (2008), 1–22.

19. PatientsLikeMe, *patientslikeme* (2015) http://www.patientslikeme.com. "Compare treatments, symptoms and experiences with people like you and take control of your health"; Apple Inc., *iOS8: Health* (2015) https://www.apple.com/ios/whats-new/health/; Apple Inc., *Apple: ResearchKit* (2015) https://www.apple.com/researchkit. "Medical researchers are doing some of the most important work in the world, and they're committed to making life-changing discoveries that benefit us all. To help, we've created ResearchKit, an open source software framework that makes it easy for researchers and developers to create apps that could revolutionize medical studies, potentially transforming medicine forever."

20. Kohavi, R., Deng, A., Frasca, B., Walker, T., Xu, Y., and Pohlmann, N., Online controlled experiments at large scale, in *Proceedings of the 19th ACM Conference on Knowledge Discovery and Data Mining*, ACM, New York, NY (2013), pp. 1168–1176.

21. Kramer, A. D. I., Guillory, J. E., and Hancock, J. T., Experimental evidence of massive-scale emotional contagion through social networks, *Proceedings of the National Academy of Sciences* **111**, 24 (June 17, 2014), 8788–8790.

22. Bond, R. M., Fariss, C. J., Jones, J. J., Kramer, A. D. I., Marlow, C., Settle, J. E., and Fowler, J. H., A 61-million-person experiment in social influence and political mobilization. *Nature* **489**, 7415 (2012), 295–298.

23. Ioannidis, J. P. A., Why most published research findings are false, *PLoS Medicine* **2**, 8 (August 2005). doi: 10.1371/journal.pmed.0020124.

CHAPTER 8:

1. Isaacson, W., *The Innovators: How a Group of Hackers, Geniuses, and Geeks Created the Digital Revolution*, Simon & Schuster, New York, NY (2014), p. 132.

2. Cooke, N. J. and Hilton, M. L. (Editors), *Enhancing the Effectiveness of Team Science*, National Academies Press, Washington, DC (April 24, 2015, pre-publication copy) http://www.nap.edu/catalog/19007/enhancing-the-effectiveness-of-team-science.

3. Bennis, W. and Biederman, P. W., *Organizing Genius: The Secrets of Creative Collaboration*, Perseus Books, Cambridge, MA (1997). This book contains inspiring descriptions of how "Great Groups" such as the Manhattan Project, Apple Computers, and Lockheed's Skunk Works are organized and function. It closes with "15 Take-Home Lessons."

4. University of Colorado, *Leysia Palen* (Accessed August 7, 2015) https://www.cs.colorado.edu/~palen/; Leysia Palen and Project EPIC, *Project EPIC: Empowering the Public with Information in Crises* (2013) http://epic.cs.colorado.edu/.

5. Virginia Tech, *Homepage: Edward A. Fox, fox at vt.edu* (2015) http://fox.cs.vt.edu/; Virginia Tech, *Events Archive* (Accessed August 7, 2015) http://www.ctrnet.net/; this website describes the Crisis, Tragedy, and Recovery Network.

6. Olson, J. S. and Olson, G. M., *Working Together Apart: Collaboration over the Internet*, Morgan & Claypool Publishers, San Rafael, CA (2013).

7. Bietz, M. J., Abrams, S., Cooper, D. M., Stevens, K. R., Puga, F., Patel, D. I., Olson, G. M., and Olson, J. S., Improving the odds through the Collaboration Success Wizard, *Translational Behavioral Medicine* **2**, 4 (December 2012), 480–486.

8. Hall, K. L., Stokols, D., Stipelman, B. A., Vogel, A. L., Feng, A., Masimore, B., Morgan, G., Moser, R. P., Marcus, S. E., and Berrigan, D., Assessing the value of team science: A study comparing center- and investigator-initiated grants. *American Journal of Preventive Medicine* **42**, 2 (2012), 157–163.

9. Citizen Science Alliance, What is the Citizen Science Alliance? (Accessed August 7, 2015) http://www.citizensciencealliance.org/; Cornell Lab of Ornithology, Citizen Science Central (2015) http://www.birds.cornell.edu/citscitoolkit/; Encyclopedia of Life, Global Access to Knowledge about Life on Earth (Accessed August 7, 2015) http://www.eol.org.

10. Nielsen, M., *Reinventing Discovery: The New Era of Networked Science*, Princeton University Press, Princeton, NJ (2011).

11. Bonney, R., Cooper, C. B., Dickinson, J., Kelling, S., Phillips, T., Rosenberg, K. V., and Shirk, J., Citizen Science: A developing tool for expanding science knowledge and scientific literacy, *Bioscience* **59**, 11 (2009), 977–984.

12. Diamond, J., *Collapse: How Civilizations Choose to Fail or Succeed: Revised Edition*, Penguin Books, London (2011); Tomlinson, B., Blevis, E., Nardi, B., Patterson, D. J., Silberman, M. S., and Pan, Y., Collapse informatics and practice: Theory, method, and design, *ACM Transactions on Computer-Human Interaction* **20**, 4 (September 2013), Article 24.

13. Ackerman, D., *The Human Age: The World Shaped by Us*, W. W. Norton & Company, New York, NY (2014); Diamandis, P. and Kotler, S., *Abundance: The Future is Better than You Think*, Simon & Schuster, New York, NY (2012).

14. Shenk, J. W., *Powers of Two: Finding the Essence of Innovation in Creative Pairs*, Houghton Mifflin Harcourt, Boston, MA (2014).

15. HCIL Alumni Spotlight, *An Interview with HCIL Alumnus Harry Hochheiser* (Accessed August 7, 2015) https://web.archive.org/web/20100614092303/https://blog.cs.umd.edu/hcilalumnispotlight/?p=6; Harry Hochheiser commenting on Jonathan Lazar, faculty colleagues at Towson University, taken from an interview by Juan Pablo Hourcade, posted July 28, 2008.

16. Wuchty, S., Jones, B. F., and Uzzi, B., The increasing dominance of teams in production of knowledge, *Science* **316**, 5827 (2007), 1036–1039.

17. Heer, J. and Shneiderman, B., Interactive dynamics for visual analytics, *Communications of the ACM* **55**, 4 (2012), 45–54; available at http://queue.acm.org/detail.cfm?id=2146416.

18. Cooke, N. J. and Hilton, M. L. (Editors), *Enhancing the Effectiveness of Team Science*, National Academies Press, Washington, DC (April 24, 2015, pre-publication copy), pp. 1–2; available at http://www.nap.edu/catalog/19007/enhancing-the-effectiveness-of-team-science.

19. Association for Computing Machinery, KDD 2014 (Accessed August 7, 2015) www. kdd.org/kdd2014/.

20. Bear, J. B. and Woolley, A. W., The role of gender in team collaboration and performance, *Interdisciplinary Science Reviews* **36**, 2 (June 2011), 146–153.

21. Nelson, B., The data on diversity, *Communications of the ACM* **57**, 11 (November 2014), 86–95.

22. Kahneman, D., *Thinking, Fast and Slow*, Farrar, Straus and Giroux, New York, NY (2011), p. 10.

23. Watson, J. D., *The Double Helix: A Personal Account of the Discovery of the Structure of DNA*, Atheneum Publishers, New York, NY (1968), p. 31.

24. Personal email from Hornstein, November 6, 2014.

25. Calcagno, V., Demoinet, E., Gollner, K., Guidi, L., Ruths, D., and de Mazancourt, C., Flows of research manuscripts among scientific journals reveal hidden submission patterns, *Science* **388**, 6110 (November 23, 2012), 1065–1069. doi: 10.1126/ science.1227833.

26. Börner, K., Contractor, N., Falk-Krzesinski, H. J., Fiore, S. M., Hall, K. L., Keyton, J., Spring, B., Stokols, D., Trochim, W., and Uzzi, B., A multi-level systems perspective for the science of team science, *Science of Translational Medicine* **2**, 9 (Sept 15, 2010), 49cm24.

    Sokols, D., Hall, K. L., Taylor, B. K., and Moser, R. P., The science of team science: Overview of the field and introduction to the supplement, *American Journal of Preventive Medicine* **35**, 2S (2008), S77–S88.

27. Contractor, N., Some assembly required: Leveraging Web science to understand and enable team assembly, *Philosophical Transactions of the Royal Society* **371**, 1987 (2013), 20120385; Monge, P. R. and Contractor, N. S., *Theories of Communication Networks*, Oxford University Press, Oxford (2003); Cooke, N. J. and Hilton, M. L. (Editors), *Enhancing the Effectiveness of Team Science*, National Academies Press, Washington, DC (April 24, 2015, pre-publication copy); available at http://www.nap. edu/catalog/19007/enhancing-the-effectiveness-of-team-science.

28. Olson, G. M., Zimmerman, A., and Bos, N. *Scientific Collaboration on the Internet*, MIT Press, Cambridge, MA (2008).

29. Guimera, R., Uzzi, B., Spiro, J., and Amaral, L. A. N., Team assembly mechanisms determine collaboration network structure and team performance, *Science* **308**, 5722 (2005), 697–702. doi: 10.1126/science.1106340.

30. Page, S. E., *The Difference: How the Power of Diversity Creates Better Groups, Firms, Schools, and Societies*, Princeton University Press, Princeton, NJ (2007).

31. Brand, A., Allen, L., Altman, M., Hlava, M., and Scott, J., Beyond authorship: Attribution, contribution, collaboration, and credit, *Learned Publishing* **28**, 2 (April 2015), 151–155; Allen, L., Scott, J., Brand, A., Hlava, M., and Altman, M., Publishing: Credit where credit is due, *Nature* **508** (17 April 2014), 312–313. doi: 10.1038/508312a.

32. De Bono, E., *Six Thinking Hats: Second Edition*, Back Bay Books, New York, NY (1999).

33. Hall, K. L., Vogel, A., Stipelman, B. A., Stokols, D., Morgan, G., and Gehlert, S., A four-phase model of transdisciplinary team-based research: Goals, teams processes, and strategies, *Translational Behavioral Medicine* **2**, 4 (December 2012), 415–430; available at http://www.ncbi.nlm.nih.gov/pmc/articles/PMC3589144/.

34. The Collaboration Success Wizard Team, Collaboration Success Wizard (2015) http://hana.ics.uci.edu/wizard/.

35. Bietz, M. J., Abrams, S., et al., Improving the odds through the Collaboration Success Wizard, *Translational Behavioral Medicine* **2**, 4 (December 2012), 480–486.

36. Olson, J. S. and Olson, G. M., *Working Together Apart: Collaboration over the Internet*, Morgan & Claypool Publishers, San Rafael, CA (2013).

37. Tuckman, B. W., Developmental sequence in small groups, *Psychological Bulletin* **63**, 6 (June 1965), 384–399; Tuckman, B. W. and Jensen, M. A. C., Stages of small-group development revisited, *Group Organization Management* **2**, 4 (December 1977), 419–427.

38. Uzzi, B., Mukerjee, S., Stringer, M., and Jones, B. F., Atypical combinations and scientific impact, *Science* **342**, 6157 (2013), 268–472.

39. Ibid., p. 468.

40. Ibid., p. 471.

41. Cummings, J. N. and Kiesler, S., Collaborative research across disciplinary and organization boundaries, p. 114, in G. M. Olson, A. Zimmerman, and N. Bos, *Scientific Collaboration on the Internet*, MIT Press, Cambridge, MA (2008a), pp. 99–117.

42. Florida, R., *The Rise of the Creative Class: Second Edition*, Basic Books, New York, NY (2012); Johnson, S., *Where Good Ideas Come From: A Natural History of Innovation*, Riverhead Publishers, New York, NY (2010).

43. Smith, M. A., Rainie, L., Himelboim, I., and Shneiderman, B., Mapping Twitter topic networks: From polarized crowds to community clusters, *Pew Research Center Report* (Feb 20, 2014) http://www.pewinternet.org/2014/02/20/mapping-twitter-topic-networks-from-polarized-crowds-to-community-clusters/.

44. Kristof, N., Smart Minds, Slim Impact, *New York Times* (February 16, 2014).

45. Miller, J. and Parker, L., *Everybody's Business: The Unlikely Story of How Big Business Can Fix the World*, Biteback Publishing, London (2013).

46. University of Maryland Human-Computer Interaction Lab, *University of Maryland Human-Computer Interaction Lab* (2014) http://www.cs.umd.edu/hcil.

47. Association for Computing Machinery, *2014 KDD2014* (Accessed August 7, 2015) www.kdd.org/kdd2014/.

48. Borgman, C. L., *Scholarship in the Digital Age: Information, Infrastructure, and the Internet*, MIT Press, Cambridge, MA (2010); Borgman, C. L., *Big Data, Little Data, No Data: Scholarship in the Networked World*, MIT Press, Cambridge, MA (2015).

49. Boardman, C., Gray, D., and Rivers, D., *Cooperative Research Center and Technical Innovation: Government Policies, Industry Strategies, and Organizational Dynamics*, Springer, Berlin (2013).

50. American Academy of Arts and Sciences, *ARISE 2: Advancing Research in Science and Engineering, Unleashing America's Research & Innovation Enterprise*, American Academy of Arts and Sciences, Cambridge, MA (2013), p. 9.

51. Boardman, C., Gray, D., and Rivers, D., *Cooperative Research Center and Technical Innovation: Government Policies, Industry Strategies, and Organizational Dynamics*, Springer, Berlin (2013).

52. Etzkowitz, H. and Leydesdorff, L., The dynamics of innovation: From National Systems and "Mode 2" to a Triple Helix of university–industry–government relations, *Research Policy* **29**, 2 (2000), 109–123.

53. Etzkowitz, H., *Triple Helix: University, Industry Government Innovation in Action*, Routledge Publishers, New York, NY (2008).

54. US National Network for Manufacturing Innovation (NNMI), *NNMI Snapshot* (Accessed August 7, 2015) http://manufacturing.gov/nnmi.html.

55. National Center for Advancing Translational Sciences, Clinical and Translational Science Awards (CTSA) (2015) http://www.ncats.nih.gov/ctsa. "The Clinical and Translational Science Awards program addresses the development and implementation of national standards and best practices for translation, from basic discovery to clinical and community-engaged research. The program supports a national network of medical research institutions collaborating to transform how clinical and translational science is conducted nationwide."

56. CITRIS, *Center for Information Technology Research in the Interest of Society (CITRIS)* (2015) http://citris-uc.org/.

57. Gulf of Mexico Research Initiative, *Gulf of Mexico Research Initiative: Investigating the Effect of Oil Spills on the Environment and Public Health* (2013) http://gulfresearchinitiative.org/.

58. National Science Foundation, *NSF Innovation Corps* (Accessed August 7, 2015) http://www.nsf.gov/news/special_reports/i-corps/.

59. National Science Foundation, *The Innovation Ecosystem* (Accessed August 7, 2015) http://www.nsf.gov/news/special_reports/i-corps/ecosystem.jsp.

60. Blank, S., Why the lean start-up changes everything, *Harvard Business Review* **91**, 5 (May 2013), 63–72; Blank, S. and Dorf, B., *The Startup Owner's Manual: The Step-by-Step Guide for Building a Great Company*, K & S Ranch, Pescadero, CA (2012); Ries, E., *The Lean Startup: How Today's Entrepreneurs Use Continuous Innovation to Create Radically Successful Businesses*, Crown Business Publishers, New York, NY (2011).

61. The National Academies of Sciences, Engineering, and Medicine, *Government-University-Industry Research Roundtable Homepage* (2015) http://sites.nationalacademies.org/PGA/guirr/index.htm.

62. National Council of University Research Administrators, and the Industrial Research Institute, *Guiding Principles for University-Industry Endeavors* (2006) http://sites.nationalacademies.org/cs/groups/pgasite/documents/webpage/pga_044335.pdf.

63. University Industry Innovation Network (UIIN), *About UIIN* (Accessed August 7, 2015) http://www.university-industry.com/index/uiin. "The University Industry Innovation Network (UIIN) is a dynamic network of academics, practitioners and business professionals passionate about advancing university-industry interaction, entrepreneurial universities and collaborative innovation."

64. Oakland University, *Association for Interdisciplinary Studies* (2014) http://www.oakland.edu/ais/; Oakland University, *Issues in Interdisciplinary Studies* (2014) http://www.oakland.edu/ais/publications.

65. National Academies, Committee on Facilitating Interdisciplinary Research, Committee on Science, Engineering, and Public Policy, *Facilitating Interdisciplinary Research*, Washington: National Academy Press (2004), p. 16.

66. Ibid., p. 26.

67. Ibid., p. 80.

68. Ibid., p. 110.

69. American Academy of Arts and Sciences, *ARISE2: Advancing Research in Science and Engineering, Unleashing America's Research & Innovation Enterprise*, Cambridge, MA (2013).

70. National Research Council. *Convergence: Facilitating Transdisciplinary Integration of Life Sciences, Physical Sciences, Engineering, and Beyond.* The National Academies Press, Washington, DC (2014).

71. Ibid., p. 17.

72. Brint, S., Turk-Bicakci, L., Proctor, K., and Murphy, S. P., Expanding the social frame of knowledge: Interdisciplinary, degree-granting fields in American colleges and universities, 1975–2000, *The Review of Higher Education* **32**, 2 (Winter 2009), 155–183.

73. Association for Interdisciplinary Studies Listserv, INTERDIS@LISTSERV.UA.EDU.

74. Klein, J. T., *Creating Interdisciplinary Campus Cultures: A Model for Strength and Sustainability*, Jossey Bass and the Association of American Colleges and Universities, San Francisco, CA (2010), p. 2.

75. Jacobs, J., *In Defense of Disciplines: Interdisciplinarity and Specialization in the Research University*, University of Chicago Press, Chicago, IL (2014).

76. Levitt, J. M. and Thelwall, M., Is multidisciplinary research more highly cited? A macrolevel study, *Journal of the American Society for Information Science & Technology* **59**, 12 (2008), 1973–1984.

77. European Union Research Advisory Board, *Interdisciplinarity in Research* (April 2004) http://ec.europa.eu/research/eurab/pdf/eurab_04_009_interdisciplinarity_research_final.pdf, p. 2.

78. Ibid.

79. Engineering and Physical Sciences Research Council, *Themes* (Accessed August 7, 2015) http://www.epsrc.ac.uk/research/ourportfolio/themes/.

80. Patterson, D., How to build a bad research center, *Communications of the ACM* **57**, 3 (March 2014), 33–36, p. 34.

81. Jeppesen, L. B. and Lakhani, K. R., Marginality and problem-solving effectiveness in broadcast search, *Organization Science* **21**, 5 (September–October 2010), 1016–1033.

82. Kay, M., Leave me alone, *The Chronicle of Higher Education, Chronicle Review* (November 14, 2014), B20.

83. Wikipedia, *caBIG* (Accessed August 7, 2015) http://en.wikipedia.org/wiki/CaBIG. "The cancer Biomedical Informatics Grid (caBIG) was a US government program to develop an open source, open access information network."

84. Cummings, J. N. and Kiesler, S., Collaborative research across disciplinary and organizational boundaries. *Social Studies of Science* **35**, 5 (2005), 703–722, p. 704.

85. Woolley, A. and Malone, T., Defend your research: What makes a team smarter? More women, *Harvard Business Review Report* (June 2011); available at https://hbr.org/2011/06/defend-your-research-what-makes-a-team-smarter-more-women.

CHAPTER 9:

1. Warfel, T. Z., *Prototyping: A Practitioner's Guide*, Rosenfeld Media, Brooklyn, NY (2009), p. 3.

2. Spector, A., Norvig, P., and Petrov, S., Google's hybrid approach to research, *Communications of the ACM* **55**, 7 (July 2012), 34–37, p. 35.

3. see e.g., Buxton, B., *Sketching User Experiences: Getting the Design Right and the Right Design*, Morgan Kaufmann Publishers, San Francisco, CA (2007); Snyder, C., *Paper Prototyping: The Fast and Easy Way to Design and Refine User Interfaces*, Morgan Kaufmann Publishers, San Francisco, CA (2003); Warfel, T. Z., *Prototyping: A Practitioner's Guide*, Rosenfeld Media, Brooklyn, NY (2009).

4. Kohavi, R., Deng, A., Frasca, B., Walker, T., Xu, Y., and Pohlmann, N., Online controlled experiments at large scale, in *Proceedings of the 19th ACM Conference on Knowledge Discovery and Data Mining*, ACM, New York, NY (2013), pp. 1168–1176.

5. Ibid.

6. Schrage, M., *The Innovator's Hypothesis: How Cheap Experiments Are Worth More than Good Ideas*, MIT Press, Cambridge, MA (2014), p. ix.

7. Ibid., p. 5.

8. Ibid, p. 25.

9. Beveridge, W. I., *Art of Scientific Investigation*, W. W. Norton & Co., New York, NY (2012, Kindle edition; originally published 1950; later editions 1957, 2004), location 293.

10. Mayer-Schönberger, M. and Cukier, K., *Big Data: A Revolution That Will Transform How We Live, Work, and Think*, Houghton Mifflin Harcourt, New York, NY (2013).

11. Greenwald, G., *No Place to Hide: Edward Snowden, the NSA, and the U.S. Surveillance State*, Metropolitan Books, New York, NY (2014).

12. Dwoskin, E., How New York's Fire Department Uses Data Mining, *Wall Street Journal Digits: Tech News and Analysis from the WSJ* (January 24, 2014) http://blogs.wsj.com/digits/2014/01/24/how-new-yorks-fire-department-uses-data-mining/.

13. Mayer-Schönberger, M. and Cukier, K., *Big Data: A Revolution That Will Transform How We Live, Work, and Think*, Houghton Mifflin Harcourt, New York, NY (2013), p. 14.

14. National Academies, *Protecting Individual Privacy in the Struggle Against Terrorists: A Framework for Program Assessment*, National Academies Press, Washington, DC (2008) http://www.nap.edu/catalog.php?record_id=12452.

15. Ginsberg, J., Mohebbi, M. H., Patel, R. S., Brammer, L., Smolinski, M. S., and Brilliant, L., Detecting influenza epidemics using search engine query data, *Nature* **457**, 7232 (February 19, 2009), 1012–1014.

16. Lazer, D., Kennedy, R., King, G., and Vespignani, A., The parable of Google Flu: Traps in the big data analysis, *Science* **343**, 6176 (March 14, 2014), 1203–1205.

17. Witten, I., Frank, E., and Hall, M. A., *Data Mining: Practical Machine Learning Tools and Techniques: Third Edition*, Morgan Kaufmann, Burlington, MA (2011), p. xxi.

18. National Academy of Sciences, *Frontiers of Massive Data Analysis*, National Academies Press, Washington, DC (2013), p. 13.

19. Bazeley, P., *Qualitative Data Analysis: Practical Strategies*, Sage Publications, Thousand Oaks, CA (2013), p. 4.

20. Dourish, P. and Bell, G., *Divining a Digital Future: Mess and Mythology in Ubiquitous Computing*, MIT Press, Cambridge, MA (2014).

21. Yin, R. K., *Case Study Research: Design and Methods: Fifth Edition*, Sage Publications, Thousand Oaks, CA (2013).

22. Seo, J. and Shneiderman, B., Knowledge discovery in high-dimensional data: Case studies and a user survey for the rank-by-feature framework, *IEEE Transactions on Visualization and Computer Graphics* **12**, 3 (May–June 2006), 311–322.

23. Guerra-Gómez, J. A., Pack, M. L., Plaisant, C., and Shneiderman, B., Visualizing changes over time in datasets using dynamic hierarchies: TreeVersity2 and the StemView, *IEEE Transactions on Visualization and Computer Graphics* **19**, 12 (December 2013), 2566–2575.

24. Ioannidis, J. P. A., Why most published research findings are false, *PLoS Medicine* **2**, 8 (August 2005), e124. doi: 10.1371/journal.pmed.0020124.

25. Sayer, C. and Lee, T. H., Time after time: Health policy implications of a three-generation case study, *New England Journal of Medicine* **371**, 14 (October 2, 2014), 1273–1276, p. 1275; available at http://www.nejm.org/doi/pdf/10.1056/NEJMp1407153.

26. Kramer, P., Why Doctors Need Stories, *New York Times* (October 18, 2014) http://opinionator.blogs.nytimes.com/2014/10/18/why-doctors-need-stories/.

27. Warmington, A., Action research: Its methods and its implications, *Journal of Applied Systems Analysis* **7** (1980), 23–39.

28. Keim, D., Kohlhammer, J., Ellis, G., and Mansmann, G. (Editors), *Mastering the Information Age: Solving Problems with Visual Analytics*, Eurographics Association, Goslar (2010); available at http://www.vismaster.eu/wp-content/uploads/2010/11/VisMaster-book-lowres.pdf; Yau, N., *Data Points: Visualization That Means Something*, Wiley, New York, NY (2013); see Yau, N., *Data Points: Visualization That Means Something* (Accessed August 13, 2015) http://flowingdata.com/data-points/; Lima, M., *The Book of Trees: Visualizing Branches of Knowledge*, Princeton Architectural Press, New York, NY (2014); see Lima, M., *The Book of Trees: Visualizing Branches of Knowledge* (2014) http://www.bookoftrees.info/bt/.

29. Office of Science and Technology Policy, Executive Office of the President, *Obama Administration Unveils "Big Data" Initiative: Announces $200 Million in New R&D Investments* (March 29, 2012) http://www.whitehouse.gov/sites/default/files/microsites/ostp/big_data_press_release_final_2.pdf.

30. boyd, d. and Crawford, K., Critical questions for big data: Provocations for a cultural, technological, and scholarly phenomenon, *Information, Communication and Society* **15**, 5 (June 2012), 662–679; Tufekci, Z., Engineering the public: Big data, surveillance, and computational politics, *First Monday* **19**, 7 (July 7, 2014), http://firstmonday.org/ojs/index.php/fm/article/view/4901/4097.

31. Campbell, D. T. and Stanley, J. C., *Experimental and Quasi-Experimental Designs for Research*, Houghton Mifflin Company, Boston, MA (1966), p. 6.

32. Flyvbjerg, B., Five misunderstandings about case-study research, *Qualitative Inquiry* **12**, 2 (April 2006), 219–245, p. 219.

CHAPTER 10:

1. Human-Computer Interaction Lab, *Hypertext Research: The Development of Hyper-TIES* (Accessed August 11, 2015) http://www.cs.umd.edu/hcil/hyperties/; Ewing, J., Mehrabanzad, S., Sheck, S., Ostroff, D., and Shneiderman, B., An experimental comparison of a mouse and arrow-jump keys for an interactive encyclopedia, *International Journal of Man-Machine Studies* **24**, 1 (January 1986), 29–45; Koved, L. and Shneiderman, B., Embedded menus: Selecting items in context, *Communications of the ACM* **29**, 4 (April 1986), 312–318; Ostroff, D. and Shneiderman, B., Selection devices for users of an electronic encyclopedia: An empirical comparison of four possibilities, *Information Processing and Management* **24**, 6 (1988), 665–680.

2. Shneiderman, B. (Editor), *Hypertext on Hypertext*, Hyperties disk with 1Mbyte data and graphics incorporating July 1988 issue of the *Communication of the ACM*, ACM Press, New York, NY (July 1988).

3. Berners-Lee, T., *Information Management: A Proposal* (March 1989) http://www.w3.org/History/1989/proposal.html.

4. Altman, M., *10 Simple Steps to Building a Reputation as a Researcher, in Your Early Career* (September 2014) http://www.slideshare.net/drmaltman/10-simple-steps-to-building-a-reputation-as-a-researcher-in-your-early-career; Dall'Olio, G. M., Marino, J., Schubert, M., Keys, K. L., Stefan, M. I., et al., Ten simple rules for getting help from online scientific communities, *PLoS Computational Biology* 7, 9 (2011), e1002202. doi: 10.1371/journal.pcbi.1002202.

5. Schimel, J., *Writing Science: How to Write Papers That Get Cited and Proposals That Get Funded*, Oxford University Press, New York, NY (2011), p. 8.

6. Heath, C. and Heath, D., *Made to Stick: Why Some Ideas Survive and Others Die*, Random House, New York, NY (2007).

7. Milkman, K. L. and Berger, J., The science of sharing and the sharing of science, *Proceedings of the National Academy of Sciences* 111, Supplement 4 (September 16, 2014), 13642–13649, p. 13647.

8. e.g., Luey, B., *Handbook for Academic Authors: Fifth Edition*, Cambridge University Press, Cambridge (2009); Hartley, J., *Academic Writing and Publishing: A Practical Handbook*, Routledge, London (2008).

9. Harvard University, ConSciCon, About (2015) http://comscicon.com/about. "Communicating Science is a workshop series organized by graduate students, for graduate students, focused on science communication skills. Our goal is to empower future leaders in technical communication to share the results from research in their field to broad and diverse audiences, not just practitioners in their fields."

10. Gabrys, B. J. and Langdale, J. A., *How to Succeed as a Scientist: From Postdoc to Professor*, Cambridge University Press, Cambridge (2011).

11. Thomson Reuters, *The Thomson Reuters Impact Factor* (2015) http://wokinfo.com/essays/impact-factor/; Science Gateway, *Journal Impact Factors* (Accessed August 11, 2015) http://www.sciencegateway.org/impact/.

12. Borromeo, C. D., Schleyer, T. K., Becich, M. J., and Hochheiser, H., Finding collaborators: Toward interactive discovery tools for research network systems, *Journal of Medical Internet Research* 16, 11 (November 2014), e244. doi: 10.2196/jmir.3444.

13. Kuchner, M. J., *Marketing for Scientists: How to Shine in Tough Times*, Island Press, Washington, DC (2011), p. 13.

14. Washington University in St. Louis School of Medicine, Becker Medical Library, *Strategies for Enhancing the Impact of Research* (2015) https://becker.wustl.edu/impact-assessment/strategies.

15. Academia.edu, About Academia.edu (2015) http://www.academia.edu/about. "Academia.edu is a platform for academics to share research papers. The company's mission is to accelerate the world's research."

16. ResearchGate, *About Us* (2015) http://www.researchgate.net/about. "Our mission is to connect researchers and make it easy for them to share and access scientific output, knowledge, and expertise."

17. ORCID, *ORCID: Connecting Research and Researchers* (Accessed August 11, 2015) http://orcid.org/. "ORCID provides a persistent digital identifier that distinguishes you from every other researcher."

18. VIVO, *About* (2015) http://vivoweb.org/about.

19. FORCE11, *About FORCE11* (2014) https://www.force11.org/about.

20. Mendeley, *Overview* (2015) http://www.mendeley.com/features/. "The best free way to organize your research."

21. Zotero, *Home* (Accessed August 11, 2015) https://www.zotero.org/. "Zotero is a free, easy-to-use tool to help you collect, organize, cite, and share your research sources."

22. CiteULike, *General* (2010) http://wiki.citeulike.org/index.php/About. "CiteULike is a free service to help you to store, organise and share the scholarly papers you are reading."

23. Wikipedia, *Comparison of Reference Management Software* (Accessed August 11, 2015) http://en.wikipedia.org/wiki/Comparison_of_reference_management_software.

24. Jenkins, H., Ford, S., and Green, J., *Spreadable Media: Creating Value and Meaning in a Networked Culture*, NYU Press, New York, NY (2013).

25. Darling, E. S., Shiffman, D., Cote, I. M., and Drew, J. A., The role of twitter in the life cycle of a scientific publication, Online ArXiv: 1305.0435v1 (May 2, 2013); available at http://arxiv.org/abs/1305.0435.

26. Eysenbach, G., Can tweets predict citations? Metrics of social impact based on Twitter and correlation with traditional metrics of scientific impact, *Journal of Medical Internet Research* **13**, 4 (2011), e123, p. 4; available at http://www.jmir.org/2011/4/e123/.

27. Hicks, M., What Is Probabilistic Programming? *The Programming Languages Enthusiast* (September 8, 2014) http://www.pl-enthusiast.net/2014/09/08/probabilistic-programming/.

28. reddit, *About reddit* (2015) http://www.reddit.com/about/.

29. Hicks, M., personal communication.

30. Cornell University Library, arXiv.org (Accessed August 11, 2015) http://arxiv.org/.

31. PLOS, Public Library of Science (Accessed August 11, 2015) http://www.plos.org/.

32. Norris, M., Oppenheim, C., and Rowland, F., The citation advantage of open-access articles, *Journal of the American Society for Information Science and Technology* **59**, 12 (2008), 1963–1972.

33. Kuchner, M. J., *Marketing for Scientists: How to Shine in Tough Times*, Island Press, Washington, DC (2011).

34. National Science Foundation, *Discoveries* (2015) http://www.nsf.gov/discoveries/.

35. National Institutes of Health, *NIH Research Matters* (Accessed August 11, 2015) http://www.nih.gov/researchmatters/.

36. NASA, *Research Opportunities* (2013) http://www.nasa.gov/about/research/.

37. Shneiderman, B. and Preece, J., 911.gov, *Science* **315**, 5814 (February 16, 2007), 944. This article generated widespread press reports: see Human-Computer Interaction Lab, *911.gov: Community Response Grids, E-government, and Emergencies* (2014) http://www.cs.umd.edu/hcil/911gov.

38. Smith, M. A., Rainie, L., Himelboim, I., and Shneiderman, B., *Mapping Twitter Topic Networks: From Polarized Crowds to Community Clusters, Pew Research Center Report* (February 20, 2014) http://www.pewinternet.org/files/2014/02/PIP_Mapping-Twitter-networks_022,014.pdf.

39. Schimel, J., *Writing Science: How to Write Papers That Get Cited and Proposals That Get Funded*, Oxford University Press, New York, NY (2011).

40. Merton, R. K., The Matthew effect in science, *Science* **159**, 3810 (1968), 56–63.

41. Van Noorden, R., Maher, B., and Nuzzo, R., The top 100 papers: *Nature* explores the most-cited research of all time, *Nature* **514**, 7524 (October 30, 2014), 550–553. doi: 10.1038/514550a.

42. Van Noorden, R., Maher, B., and Nuzzo, R., The top 100 papers: *Nature* explores the most-cited research of all time, *Nature* (October 29, 2014) http://www.nature.com/news/the-top-100-papers-1.16224; Google, Google Scholar (Accessed August 11, 2015) http://scholar.google.com. The online version of the *Nature* article provides links to two spreadsheets containing Google Scholar Top 100 citation lists; one includes articles only, while the other includes books as well as articles (see the section entitled "An alternative ranking," http://www.nature.com/news/the-top-100-papers-1.16224#/alternative). Google Scholar collects citations based on web contents, including books, unpublished papers, slide presentations, etc. The categories from which the citations are drawn are typically broader, and therefore the number of citations is higher, than those from the Thomson Reuters Web of Science.

43. American Society for Cell Biology, *San Francisco Declaration on Research Assessment* (Accessed August 11, 2015) am.ascb.org/dora/.

44. Washington University in St. Louis School of Medicine, Becker Medical Library, Assessing the Impact of Research (2015) https://becker.wustl.edu/impact-assessment; Sarli, C. C., Dubinsky, E. K., and Holmes, K. L., Beyond citation analysis: A model for assessment of research impact, *Journal of the Medical Library Association* **98**, 1 (2010), 17–23. doi: 10.3163/1536–5050.98.1.008.

45. Churchill, E. F., Impact! *ACM Interactions* **19**, 3 (May–June 2012), 12–15.

46. Galligan, F. and Dyas-Correia, S., Altmetrics: Rethinking the way we measure, *Serials Review* **39**, 1 (2013), 56–61; Altmetrics, *About* (Accessed August 11, 2015) http://www.altmetrics.org/about: "Altmetrics is the creation and study of new metrics based on the Social Web for analyzing, and informing scholarship"; Altmetric, *About Us* (2015) http://www.altmetric.com/about.php: "Altmetric, a London-based start-up focused on making article level metrics easy. Our mission is to track and analyse the online activity around scholarly literature"; PLOS Article-Level Metrics, *Altmetrics* (Accessed August 11, 2015) http://article-level-metrics.plos.org/alt-metrics/:

"Methods of digitally disseminating research and scholarly communication continue to evolve. PLOS contributes to the broader 'Altmetrics' movement, working to create and establish metrics for analyzing the reach and impact of published research."

47. e.g., this list in Computer Science gets much attention; see Huang, J., *Best Paper Awards in Computer Science (Since 1996)* (2015) http://jeffhuang.com/best_paper_awards.html.

48. Harzing, A. W., A preliminary test of Google Scholar as a source for citation data: A longitudinal study of Nobel Prize winners, *Scientometrics* **93**, 3 (2013), 1057–1075.

49. Hirsch, J. E., Does the h-index have predictive power? *Proceedings of the National Academy of Sciences* **104**, 49 (2007), 19193–19198; Schreiber, M., *A Case Study of the Hirsch Index for 26 Non-Prominent Physicists*, ArXiv E-Print Publication (July 31, 2007), http://arxiv.org/pdf/0708.0120.pdf; Schreiber, M., *The Predictability of the Hirsch Index Evolution*, ArXiv E-Print Publication (2013), http://arxiv.org/ftp/arxiv/papers/1307/1307.5964.pdf.

50. Penner, O., Pan, R. J. K., Petersen, A. M., Kaski, K., and Fortunato, S., On the predictability of future impact in science, *Nature Scientific Reports* **3** (October 2013), Article 3052; available at http://www.nature.com/srep/2013/131029/srep03052/full/srep03052.html.

51. STAR METRICS, *Home* (Accessed August 11, 2015) https://www.starmetrics.nih.gov/. "STAR METRICS is a federal and research institution collaboration to create a repository of data and tools that will be useful to assess the impact of federal R&D investments."

52. The National Academies of Sciences, Engineering, and Medicine, *The Federal Demonstration Partnership: Redefining the University and Government Partnership* (2015) http://sites.nationalacademies.org/pga/fdp/index.htm. "The Federal Demonstration Partnership is a cooperative initiative among 10 federal agencies and 155 institutional recipients of federal funds."

53. Koizumi, K., Bertuzzi, S., and Lane, J., *STAR METRICS: Science and Technology for America's Reinvestment: Measuring the Effects of Research on Innovation, Competitiveness and Science* (Accessed August 11, 2015) http://sites.nationalacademies.org/cs/groups/pgasite/documents/webpage/pga_064814.pdf.

54. Center for Science of Science and Innovation Policy, *Workshop on Science of Science Policy* (2015) http://cssip.org/login/june-workshop-ann-arbor.

55. Greenberg, S. A., How citation distortions create unfounded authority: Analysis of a citation network, *British Medical Journal* **339** (2009), b2680. doi: http://dx.doi.org/10.1136/bmj.b2680.

CHAPTER 11:

1. Kosara, R., List of Influences: Ben Shneiderman, *eagereyes: Visualization and Visual Communication* (blog) (Accessed August 12, 2015) https://eagereyes.org/influences/ben-shneiderman. My list of influences on my thinking, as posted on Robert Kosara's blog in 2011.

2. Rogers, E. M., *Diffusion of Innovations: Fifth Edition*, Free Press, New York, NY (2003).

3. Feldman, M. P. and Graddy-Reed, A., Accelerating commercialization: A new model of strategic foundation funding, *Journal of Technology Transfer* **39**, 4 (2014), 503–523.

4. National Science Foundation, Science of Science and Innovation Policy (SSIP) (Accessed August 12, 2015) http://www.nsf.gov/funding/pgm_summ.jsp?pims_id=501084.

5. National Science Foundation, *Science of Science and Innovation Policy Doctoral Dissertation Research Improvement Grants (SciSIP-DDRIG) Program Solicitation NSF 15-583* (2006) http://www.nsf.gov/pubs/2015/nsf15583/nsf15583.htm.

6. Broad, W. J., Billionaires with big ideas are privatizing American science, *The New York Times* (March 15, 2014).

7. National Research Council, *Convergence: Facilitating Transdisciplinary Integration of Life Sciences, Physical Sciences, Engineering, and Beyond*, The National Academies Press, Washington, DC (2014), p. 81.

8. Ibid., p. 82.

9. Northeastern University, *Cooperative Education and Career Development at Northeastern University* (2013) http://www.northeastern.edu/coop/.

10. University of Maryland, Gemstone Honors Program (Accessed August 12, 2015) http://www.gemstone.umd.edu/about/about-us.html.

11. Kelsky, K. L., Here's What Goes in Your Tenure Portfolio: A Special Request Post, *The Professor Is In* (July 21, 2011) http://theprofessorisin.com/2011/07/21/your-tenure-dossier/; Faculty Focus, *Tenure Portfolios* (2015) http://www.facultyfocus.com/tag/tenure-portfolios/; University of Washington College of Engineering, *Promotion and Tenure Toolkit* (2015) https://www.engr.washington.edu/mycoe/faculty/pt-toolkit.

12. National Research Council, *Convergence: Facilitating Transdisciplinary Integration of Life Sciences, Physical Sciences, Engineering, and Beyond*, The National Academies Press, Washington, DC (2014).

13. Ibid.

14. University of Southern California Office of Research, *Creativity and Collaboration in the Academy* (Accessed August 15, 2015) https://research.usc.edu/for-investigators/creativity-and-collaboration-in-the-academy/.

15. National Science Foundation, *Algorithms in the Field (AitF) Program Solicitation NSF 15-515* (2006)http://www.nsf.gov/pubs/2015/nsf15515/nsf15515.htm.

16. National Science Foundation, *Secure and Trustworthy Cyberspace (SaTC), Program Solicitation NSF 14-599* (2006) http://www.nsf.gov/pubs/2014/nsf14599/nsf14599.htm.

17. e.g., Chesbrough, H. W., Open Innovation: Where we've been and where we're going, *Research Technology Management* **55**, 4 (2012), 20–27; Euchner, J., Two flavors of open innovation, *Research-Technology Management* **53**, 4 (2010), 7–8.

CHAPTER 12:

1. e.g., NASA, *Enduring Quests, Daring Visions: NASA Astrophysics in the Next Three Decades* (2013) http://science.nasa.gov/media/medialibrary/2013/12/20/secure-Astrophysics_Roadmap_2013.pdf; NASA, *Science Strategy* (2015) http://nasa-science.nasa.gov/about-us/science-strategy; the latter website provides links to the NASA Science Roadmaps (multiple documents).

2. Preedy, V. R. (Editor), *Handbook of Anthropometry: Physical Measures of Human Form in Health and Disease*, Springer, New York, NY (2012).

3. Maslow, A. H., A theory of human motivation, *Psychological Review* **50**, 4 (1943), 370–396, available at http://psychclassics.yorku.ca/Maslow/motivation.htm; Maslow, A. H., *Motivation and Personality*, Harper, New York, NY (1954).

4. DesignSingapore Council, *About Us* (2015) http://www.designsingapore.org/who_we_are/about_us.aspx. "The DesignSingapore Council was established in 2003 to help develop the nation's design sector. This follows from the Economic Review Committee's report which identified the creative industry as one of the three new sectors (including education and healthcare) for economic growth. The Design-Singapore Council is part of the Ministry of Communications and Information."

5. National Academy Museum and School, National Academy Museum (Accessed August 13, 2015) http://www.nationalacademy.org/; Royal College of Art, *School of Design* (Accessed August 13, 2015) http://www.rca.ac.uk/schools/school-of-design/.

6. Borys, H., Richard Florida on Technology, Talent, and Tolerance, *PlaceShakers* (blog) (November 18, 2013) http://www.placemakers.com/2013/11/18/richard-florida-on-tech-talent-and-tolerance/.

BIBLIOGRAPHY

Ackerman, D., *The Human Age: The World Shaped by Us*, W. W. Norton, New York, NY (2014).

Alexander, C., Ishikawa, S., and Silverstein, M., *A Pattern Language: Towns, Buildings, Construction*, Oxford University Press, Oxford (1977).

Allen, L., Scott, J., Brand, A., Hlava, M., and Altman, M., Publishing: Credit where credit is due, *Nature* **508**, 7496 (April 17, 2014), 312–313. doi: 10.1038/508312a

Allen, T. J., *Managing the Flow of Technology: Technology Transfer and the Dissemination of Technological Information within the R&D Organization*, MIT Press, Cambridge, MA (1977).

Alon, U., How to choose a good scientific problem, *Molecular Cell* **35**, 6 (Sept 25, 2009), 726–728; available at http://www.cell.com/molecular-cell/abstract/S1097-2765(09)00641-8.

Alturki, A., Gable, G. C., and Bandara, W., A design science research roadmap, in H. Jain, A. P. Sinha, and P. Vitharana (Editors), *Service-Oriented Perspectives in Design Science Research*, Lectures Notes in Computer Science 6629, Springer, Berlin (2011), pp. 107–123.

Alturki, A., Gable, G. C., and Bandara, W., The design science research roadmap: In progress evaluation, Association for Information Systems, in *Pacific Asia Conference on Information Systems 2013 Proceedings* (2013), Paper 160; available at http://aisel.aisnet.org/pacis2013/160.

American Academy of Arts and Sciences, *ARISE 2: Advancing Research in Science and Engineering, Unleashing America's Research and Innovation Enterprise*, American Academy of Arts and Sciences, Cambridge, MA (2013).

Anderson, T. and Shattuck, J., Design-based research: A decade of progress in education research, *Educational Researcher* **41**, 1 (2012), 16–25.

Argote, L., *Organizational Learning: Creating, Retaining and Transferring Knowledge: Second Edition*, Springer, New York, NY (2012).

Ariely, D., *Predictably Irrational: The Hidden Forces That Shape Our Decisions: Second Edition*, HarperCollins, New York, NY (2012).

Arthur, B., *The Nature of Technology: What It Is and How It Evolves*, Free Press, New York, NY (2009).

Atman, C., Chimka, J., Bursic, K., and Nachtmann, H., A comparison of freshman and senior engineering design processes, *Design Studies* **20**, 2 (1999), 131–152.

Bartneck, C. and Hu, J., Scientometric analysis of the CHI proceedings, in *Proceedings of the 27th International Conference on Human Factors in Computing Systems*, ACM Press, New York, NY (2009), pp. 699–708.

Basalla, G., *The Evolution of Technology*, Cambridge University Press, New York, NY (1988).

Basili, V. R., Shull, F., and Lanubile, F., Building knowledge through families of experiments, *IEEE Transactions in Software Engineering* **25**, 4 (April 1999), 456–473.

Bazeley, P., *Qualitative Data Analysis: Practical Strategies*, Sage Publications, Thousand Oaks, CA (2013).

Bear, J. B. and Woolley, A. W., The role of gender in team collaboration and performance, *Interdisciplinary Science Reviews* **36**, 2 (June 2011), 146–153.

Bennis, W. and Biederman, P. W., *Organizing Genius: The Secrets of Creative Collaboration*, Perseus Books, Cambridge, MA (1997).

Berners-Lee, T., Hall, W., Hendler, J. A., Shadbolt, N., and Weitzner, D. J., Creating a science of the Web, *Science* **313**, 5788 (2006), 769–771.

Beveridge, W. I., *Art of Scientific Investigation*, W. W. Norton, New York, NY (1950; later editions 1957, 2004).

Bietz, M. J., Abrams, S., Cooper, D. M., Stevens, K. R., Puga, F., Patel, D. I., Olson, G. M., and Olson, J. S., Improving the odds through the Collaboration Success Wizard, *Translational Behavioral Medicine* **2**, 4 (December 2012), 480–486.

Blank, S., Why the lean start-up changes everything, *Harvard Business Review* **91**, 5 (May 2013), 63–72; available at http://hbr.org/2013/05/why-the-lean-start-up-changes-everything.

Blank, S. and Dorf, B., *The Startup Owner's Manual: The Step-by-Step Guide for Building a Great Company*, K & S Ranch, Pescadero, CA (2012).

Boardman, C., Gray, D., and Rivers, D., *Cooperative Research Center and Technical Innovation: Government Policies, Industry Strategies, and Organizational Dynamics*, Springer, Berlin (2013).

Bond, R. M., Fariss, C. J., Jones, J. J., Kramer, A. D. I., Marlow, C., Settle, J. E., and Fowler, J. H., A 61-million-person experiment in social influence and political mobilization, *Nature* **489**, 7415 (2012), 295–298; available at http://cameronmarlow.com/media/massive_turnout.pdf.

Bonney, R., Cooper, C. B., Dickinson, J., Kelling, S., Phillips, T., Rosenberg, K. V., and Shirk, J., Citizen science: A developing tool for expanding science knowledge and scientific literacy, *Bioscience* **59**, 11 (2009), 977–984.

Booth, W. C., Colomb, G. G., and Williams, J. M., *The Craft of Research: Third Edition*, University of Chicago Press, Chicago, IL (2008).

Borgman, C. L., *Scholarship in the Digital Age: Information, Infrastructure, and the Internet*, MIT Press, Cambridge, MA (2010).

Borgman, C. L., *Big Data, Little Data, No Data: Scholarship in the Networked World*, MIT Press, Cambridge, MA (2015).

Bornmann, L., Measuring the broader impact of research: The potential of altmetrics, Online ArXiv: 1406.7091 (submitted June 27, 2014; revised September 10, 2014); available at http://arxiv.org/abs/1406.7091.

Borromeo, C. D., Schleyer, T. K., Becich, M. J., and Hochheiser, H., Finding collaborators: Toward interactive discovery tools for research network systems, *Journal of Medical Internet Research* **16**, 11 (November 2014), e244. doi: 10.2196/jmir.3444.

boyd, d. and Crawford, K., Critical questions for big data: Provocations for a cultural, technological, and scholarly phenomenon, *Information, Communication and Society* **15**, 5 (June 2012), 662–679.

Börner, K., *Atlas of Science: Visualizing What We Know*, MIT Press, Cambridge, MA (2010).

Börner, K., *Atlas of Knowledge: Anyone Can Map*, MIT Press, Cambridge, MA (2015).

Börner, K., Chen, C., and Boyack, K. W., Visualizing knowledge domains. *Annual Review of Information Science and Technology* **37**, 1 (2003), 179–255. doi: 10.1002/aris.1440370106.

Börner, K., Contractor, N., Falk-Krzesinski, H. J., Fiore, S. M., Hall, K. L., Keyton, J., Spring, B., Stokols, D., Trochim, W., and Uzzi, B., A multi-level systems perspective for the science of team science, *Science of Translational Medicine* **2**, 9 (September 15, 2010), 49cm24.

Börner, K., Klavans, R., Patek, M., Zoss, A., Biberstine, J. R., Light, R., Larivière, V., and Boyack, K. W., Design and update of a classification system: The UCSD Map of Science. *PLoS ONE* **7**, 7 (2012), e39464. doi: 10.1371/journal.pone.0039464.

Brand, A., Allen, L., Altman, M., Hlava, M., and Scott, J., Beyond authorship: Attribution, contribution, collaboration, and credit, *Learned Publishing* **28**, 2 (April 2015), 151–155.

Branscomb, L., The false dichotomy: Scientific creativity and utility, *Issues in Science and Technology* **16**, 1 (2007), 66; available at http://www.issues.org/16.1/branscomb.htm.

Brin, S. and Page, L., The anatomy of a large-scale hypertextual Web search engine, *Computer Networks and ISDN Systems* **30**, 1–7 (April 1998), 107–117.

Brint, S., Turk-Bicakci, L., Proctor, K., and Murphy, S. P., Expanding the social frame of knowledge: Interdisciplinary, degree-granting fields in American colleges and universities, 1975–2000, *The Review of Higher Education* **32**, 2 (Winter 2009), 155–183.

Broad, W. J., Billionaires with big ideas are privatizing American science, *New York Times* (March 15, 2014) http://www.nytimes.com/2014/03/16/science/billionaires-with-big-ideas-are-privatizing-american-science.html.

Brooks, F. B., *The Mythical Man-Month: Essays on Software Engineering*, Addison-Wesley, Reading, MA (1975, 1995).

Brooks, F. B., *The Design of Design: Essays from a Computer Scientist*, Addison-Wesley, Reading, MA (2010).

Brown, J. S. and Duguid, P., *The Social Life of Information*, Harvard Business School Press, Boston, MA (2002).

Brown, T., *Change by Design: How Design Thinking Transforms Organizations and Inspires Innovation*, HarperBusiness, New York, NY (2009).

Bush, V., *Science: The Endless Frontier: A Report to the President on a Program for Postwar Scientific Research*, Office of Scientific Research and Development, Washington, DC (1945).

Buxton, B., *Sketching User Experiences: Getting the Design Right and the Right Design*, Morgan Kaufmann Publishers, San Francisco, CA (2007).

Calcagno, V., Demoinet, E., Gollner, K., Guidi, L., Ruths, D., and de Mazancourt, C., Flows of research manuscripts among scientific journals reveal hidden submission patterns, *Science* **388**, 6110 (November 23, 2012), 1065–1069. doi: 10.1126/science.1227833.

Campbell, D. T. and Stanley, J. C., *Experimental and Quasi-Experimental Designs for Research*, Houghton Mifflin Company, Boston, MA (1966).

Candy, L. and Edmonds, E., *Interacting: Art, Research and the Creative Practitioner*, Libri Publishing, Faringdon (2011).

Carter, M., *Designing Science Presentation: A Visual Guide to Figures, Papers, Slides, Posters, and More*, Academic Press, New York, NY (2013).

Celeste, R. F., Griswold, A., and Straf, M. L. (Editors), *Furthering America's Research Enterprise*, National Academies Press, Washington, DC (2014).

Chen, C., Ibekwe-SanJuan, F., and Hou, J., The structure and dynamics of co-citation clusters: A multiple-perspective co-citation analysis. *Journal of the American Society for Information Science and Technology* **61**, 7 (2010), 1386–1409.

Chesbrough, H. W., Open innovation: Where we've been and where we're going, *Research Technology Management* **55**, 4 (2012), 20–27.

Churchill, E. F., Impact! *ACM Interactions* **19**, 3 (May–June 2012), 12–15.

Computer Science and Telecommunications Board, *Innovation in Information Technology*. National Academies Press, Washington, DC (2003); available at http://www.nap.edu/openbook.php?isbn=0309089808.

Contractor, N. S., Some assembly required: Leveraging Web science to understand and enable team assembly, *Philosophical Transactions of the Royal Society* **371**, 1987 (2013), 20120385.

Contractor, N. S. and DeChurch, L. A., Integrating social networks and human social motives to achieve social influence at scale, *Proceedings of the National Academy of Sciences* **111**, 4 (2014), 13650–13657.

Cooke, N. J. and Hilton, M. L. (Editors), *Enhancing the Effectiveness of Team Science*, National Academies Press, Washington, DC (April 24, 2015, pre-publication copy); available at http://www.nap.edu/catalog/19007/enhancing-the-effectiveness-of-team-science.

Cooper, A., Reimann, R., Cronin, D., and Noessel, C., *About Face: Essentials of Inter-action Design: Fourth Edition*, Wiley, New York, NY (2014).

Cross, N., Design research: A disciplined conversation, *Design Issues* **15**, 2 (1999), 5–10.

Cross, N., *Engineering Design Methods: Strategies for Product Design: Fourth Edition*, Wiley, New York, NY (2008).

Cross, N., *Design Thinking: Understanding How Designers Think and Work*, Berg, Oxford (2011).

Crow, M. M. and Bozeman, B., *Limited by Design: R&D Laboratories in the U. S. National Innovation System*, Columbia University Press, New York, NY (1998).

Crow, M. M. and Dabars, W. B., Interdisciplinarity as a design problem: Toward mutual intelligibility among academic disciplines in the American research university, in M. R. O'Rourke, S. J. Crowley, S. D. Eigenbrode, and J. D. Wulfhorst (Editors), *Enhancing Communication and Collaboration in Interdisciplinary Research*, Sage Publications, Los Angeles, CA (2013), pp. 294–322.

Crow, M. M. and Dabars, W. B., A new model for the American research university, *Issues in Science and Technology* **31**, 3 (Spring 2015), 55–62.

Crow, M. M. and Dabars, W. B., *Designing the New American University*, Johns Hopkins University Press, Baltimore, MD (2015).

Cummings, J. N. and Haas, M. R., So many teams, so little time: Time allocation matters in geographically dispersed teams, *Journal of Organizational Behavior* **33**, 3 (2012), 316–341.

Cummings, J. N. and Kiesler, S., Collaborative research across disciplinary and organizational boundaries. *Social Studies of Science* **35**, 5 (2005), 703–722.

Cummings, J. N. and Kiesler, S., Coordination costs and project outcomes in multi-university collaborations, *Research Policy* **36**, 10 (2007), 1620–1634.

Cummings, J. N. and Kiesler, S., Collaborative research across disciplinary and organization boundaries, in G. M. Olson, A. Zimmerman, and N. Bos (Editors), *Scientific Collaboration on the Internet*, MIT Press, Cambridge, MA (2008a), pp. 99–117.

Cummings, J. N. and Kiesler, S., Who collaborates successfully? Prior experience reduces collaboration barriers in distributed interdisciplinary research, in *Proceedings of the ACM Conference on Computer-Supported Cooperative Work*, ACM, New York, NY (2008b), pp. 437–446.

Dall'Olio, G. M., Marino, J., et al., Ten simple rules for getting help from online scientific communities, *PLoS Computational Biology* **7**, 9 (2011), e1002202. doi: 10.1371/journal.pcbi.1002202.

Darling, E. S., Shiffman, D., Cote, I. M., and Drew, J. A., The role of twitter in the life cycle of a scientific publication, Online ArXiv: 1305.0435v1 (May 2, 2013); available at http://arxiv.org/abs/1305.0435.

Davis, F. D., Perceived usefulness, perceived ease of use, and user acceptance of information technology, *MIS Quarterly* **13**, 3 (1989), 319–340.

De Bono, E., *Six Thinking Hats: Second Edition*, Back Bay Books, New York, NY (1999).

Dede, C., If design-based research is the answer, what is the question? *Journal of the Learning Sciences* **13**, 1 (2004), 105–114.

Design Council, *A Study of the Design Process* (2005) http://www.designcouncil.org.uk/sites/default/files/asset/document/ElevenLessons_Design_Council%20%282%29.pdf.

Dewey, J., *Experience and Education*, Collier Books, New York, NY (1938).

Diamond, J., *Collapse: How Civilizations Choose to Fail or Succeed: Revised Edition*, Penguin Books, London (2011).

Diamandis, P. and Kotler, S., *Abundance: The Future is Better than You Think*, Simon & Schuster, New York, NY (2012).

Dourish, P. and Bell, G., *Divining a Digital Future: Mess and Mythology in Ubiquitous Computing*, MIT Press, Cambridge, MA (2014).

Dreyfuss, H., *Designing for People*, Allworth Press, New York, NY (1955; new edition, 2003).

Dyson, F., A meeting with Enrico Fermi, *Nature* **427**, 6972 (2004), 297.

Edgerton, D., The linear model did not exist: Reflections on the history and historiography of science and research in industry in the twentieth century, in K. Grandin and N. Wormbs (Editors), *The Science–Industry Nexus: History, Policy, Implications*, Watson, New York, NY (2004).

Edmonds, E. A. and Candy, L., Relating theory, practice, and evaluation in practitioner research, *Leonardo* **43**, 5 (2010), 470–476.

Etheredge, L. M., A rapid-learning health system, *Health Affairs* **26**, 2 (2007), 107–118. doi: 10.1377/hlthaff.26.2.w107.

Etheredge, L. M., Rapid learning: A breakthrough agenda, *Health Affairs* **33**, 7 (2014), 1155–1162. doi: 10.1377/hlthaff.2014.0043.

Etzkowitz, H., *Triple Helix: University, Industry Government Innovation in Action*, Routledge Publishers, New York, NY (2008).

Etzkowitz, H. and Leydesdorff, L., The dynamics of innovation: From National Systems and "Mode 2" to a Triple Helix of university–industry–government relations, *Research Policy* **29**, 2 (2000), 109–123.

Euchner, J., Two flavors of open innovation, *Research-Technology Management* **53**, 4 (2010), 7–8.

European Union Research Advisory Board, *Interdisciplinarity in Research* (April 2004) http://ec.europa.eu/research/eurab/pdf/eurab_04_009_interdisciplinarity_research_final.pdf.

Eysenbach, G., Can tweets predict citations? Metrics of social impact based on Twitter and correlation with traditional metrics of scientific impact, *Journal of Medical Internet Research* **13**, 4 (2011), e123; available at http://www.jmir.org/2011/4/e123/.

Feamster, N. and Gray, A., Can great research be taught? Independent research with cross-disciplinary thinking and broader impact, in *Proceedings of the 39th ACM SIGCSE Technical Symposium on Computer Science Education*, ACM Press, New York, NY (2008), pp. 471–475.

Feldman, M. P. and Graddy-Reed, A., Accelerating commercialization: A new model of strategic foundation funding, *Journal of Technology Transfer* **39**, 4 (2014), 503–523.

Fenn, J. and Raskino, M., *Mastering the Hype Cycle: How to Choose the Right Innovation at the Right Time*, Harvard Business Press, Boston, MA (2008).

Fiore, S. M., Power and promise: Cognitive psychology and cognitive technology, *Cognitive Technology* **13**, 1 (2008), 5–8.

Fiore, S. M., Cognition and technology: Interdisciplinarity and the impact of cognitive engineering research on organizational productivity, in S. Kozlowski (Editor), *Oxford Handbook of Industrial and Organizational Psychology*, Oxford University Press, Oxford (2012), pp. 1306–1322.

Fischer, G., Understanding, fostering, and supporting cultures of participation, *ACM Interactions* **28**, 3 (May + June 2011a), 42–53.

Fischer, G., Social creativity: Exploiting the power of cultures of participation, in *2011: 7th International Conference on Semantics, Knowledge and Grids* (SKG), IEEE, Piscataway, NJ (October 2011b), pp. 1–8.

Fischer, G. and Giaccardi, E., Meta-design: A framework for the future of end user development, in H. Lieberman, F. Paternò, and V. Wulf (Editors), *End User Development*, Kluwer Academic Publishers, Dordrecht (2006), pp. 427–457.

Fischer, G. and Herrmann, T., Socio-technical systems: A meta-design perspective, *International Journal of Sociotechnology and Knowledge Development* **3**, 1 (2011), 1–33.

Fischer, G. and Herrmann, T., Meta-design: Transforming and enriching the design and use of socio-technical systems, in D. Randall, K. Schmidt, and V. Wulf (Editors), *Designing Socially Embedded Technologies: A European Challenge*, Springer, London (2014), pp. 79–109.

Florida, R., *The Rise of the Creative Class: Second Edition*, Basic Books, New York, NY (2012).

Flyvbjerg, B., Five misunderstandings about case-study research, *Qualitative Inquiry* **12**, 2 (April 2006), 219–245.

Friedman, C., Rubin, J., et al., Toward a science of learning systems: A research agenda for the high-functioning Learning Health System, *Journal of the American Medical Informatics Association* **22** (2014), 1–6.

Fuller, R. B., *Operating Manual for Spaceship Earth*, Pocket Books, New York, NY (1970).

Gabrys, B. J. and Langdale, J. A., *How to Succeed as a Scientist: From Postdoc to Professor*, Cambridge University Press, Cambridge (2011).

Galey, A. and Ruecker, S., How a prototype argues, *Literary and Linguistic Computing* **25**, 4 (2010), 405–424.

Galligan, F. and Dyas-Correia, S., Altmetrics: Rethinking the way we measure, *Serials Review* **39**, 1 (2013), 56–61.

Gawande, A., *The Checklist Manifesto: How to Get Things Right*, Metropolitan Books, New York, NY (2010).

Gertner, J., *The Idea Factory: Bell Labs and the Great Age of American Innovation*, Penguin Press, New York, NY (2012).

Gladwell, M., *Blink: The Power of Thinking without Thinking*, Basic Books, New York, NY (2007).

Greenberg, S. A., How citation distortions create unfounded authority: Analysis of a citation network, *British Medical Journal* **339** (2009), b2680; available at http://dx.doi.org/10.1136/bmj.b2680.

Greenwald, G., *No Place to Hide: Edward Snowden, the NSA, and the U. S. Surveillance State*, Metropolitan Books, New York, NY (2014).

Gregor, S. and Hevner, A. R., Positioning and presenting design science research for maximum impact, *MIS Quarterly* **37**, 2 (June 2013), 337–355.

Gregor, S. and Hevner, A. R., The front end of innovation: Perspectives on creativity, knowledge and design, in B. Donnellan, M. Helfert, J. Kenneally, D. VanderMeer, M. Rothenberger, and R. Winter (Editors), *New Horizons in Design Science: Broadening the Research Agenda,10th International Conference on Design Science Research in Information Systems and Technology (DESRIST 2015), Dublin, Ireland, Proceedings*, Lecture Notes in Computer Science 9073, Springer, Cham (2015), 249–263. doi: 10.1007/978–973-319–18714-3_16.

Guerra-Gómez, J. A., Pack, M. L., Plaisant, C., and Shneiderman, B., Visualizing changes over time in datasets using dynamic hierarchies: TreeVersity2 and the StemView, *IEEE Transactions on Visualization and Computer Graphics* **19**, 20 (December 2013), 2566–2575.

Guimera, R., Uzzi, B., Spiro, J., and Amaral, L. A. N., Team assembly mechanisms determine collaboration network structure and team performance, *Science* **308**, 5722 (2005), 697–702. doi: 10.1126/science.1106340.

Guthrie, S., Wamae, W., Diepeveen, S., Wooding, S., and Grant, J., *Measuring Research: A Guide to Research Evaluation Frameworks and Tools*. RAND Corporation, Santa Monica, CA (2013); available at http://www.rand.org/pubs/monographs/MG1217.html.

Hagel, J. III, Brown, J. S., and Davison, L., *The Power of Pull: How Small Moves, Smartly Made, Can Set Big Things in Motion*, Basic Books, New York, NY (2010).

Hall, K. L., Stokols, D., Stipelman, B. A., Vogel, A. L., Feng, A., Masimore, B., Morgan, G., Moser, R. P., Marcus, S. E., and Berrigan, D., Assessing the value of team science: A study comparing center- and investigator-initiated grants. *American Journal of Preventive Medicine* **42**, 2 (2012), 157–163.

Hall, K. L., Vogel, A., Stipelman, B. A., Stokols, D., Morgan, G., and Gehlert, S., A four-phase model of transdisciplinary team-based research: Goals, teams processes, and strategies, *Translational Behavioral Medicine* **2**, 4 (December 2012), 415–430; available at http://www.ncbi.nlm.nih.gov/pmc/articles/PMC3 589144/.

Hargittai, M., *Women Scientists: Reflections, Challenges, and Breaking Boundaries*, Oxford University Press, Oxford (2015).

Harzing, A. W., A preliminary test of Google Scholar as a source for citation data: A longitudinal study of Nobel Prize winners, *Scientometrics* **93**, 3 (2013), 1057–1075.

Haskins, R. and Margolis, G., *Show Me the Evidence: Obama's Fight for Rigor and Results in Social Policy*, Brookings Institution Press, Washington, DC (2014).

Heath, C. and Heath, D., *Made to Stick: Why Some Ideas Survive and Others Die*, Random House, New York, NY (2007).

Heilmeier, G., Some reflections on innovation and invention, *The Bridge* **22**, 4 (1992), 12–16.

Hendler, J., Shadbolt, N., Hall, W., Berners-Lee, T., and Weitzner, D., Web science: An interdisciplinary approach to understanding the Web, *Communications of the ACM* **51**, 7 (2008), 60–69.

Henry, N., Goodell, H., Elmqvist, N., and Fekete, J.-D., 20 Years of four HCI conferences: A visual exploration, *International Journal of Human-Computer Interaction* **23**, 3 (2007), 239–285; available at http://dx.doi.org/10.1080/10447310701702402.

Hevner, A. R., March, S. T., Park, J., and Ram, S., Design science research in information systems, *Management Information Systems Quarterly* **28**, 1 (March 2004), 75–105.

Hirsch, J. E., Does the h-index have predictive power? *Proceedings of the National Academy of Sciences* **104**, 49 (2007), 19193–19198.

Hooper, C. and Dix, A., Web science and human-computer interaction: When disciplines collide, in *WebSci '12, Proceedings of the 4th Annual ACM Web Science Conference*, ACM, New York, NY (2012), pp. 128–136.

Hooper, C. and Dix, A., Web science and human-computer interaction: Forming a mutually supportive relationship, *ACM Interactions* **20**, 3 (May/June 2013), 52–57.

Hooper, C. J., Millard, D. E., Fantauzzacoffin, J., and Kaye, J., Science vs. science: The complexities of interdisciplinary research, in *CHI' 13, CHI'13 Extended Abstracts on Human Factors in Computing Systems*, ACM, New York, NY (April 2013), pp. 2541–2544.

Horgan, J., *The End of Science: Facing the Limits of Science in the Twilight of the Scientific Age*, Broadway Books, New York, NY (1996).

Ioannidis, J. P. A., Why most published research findings are false, *PLoS Medicine* **2**, 8 (August 2005), e124. doi: 10.1371/journal.pmed.0020124.

Isaacson, W., *Steve Jobs*, Simon & Schuster, New York, NY (2011).

Isaacson, W., *The Innovators: How a Group of Hackers, Geniuses, and Geeks Created the Digital Revolution*, Simon & Schuster, New York, NY (2014).

ISO, *ISO 9241–210:2010: Ergonomics of Human-System Interaction*, (2015) http://www.iso.org/iso/catalogue_detail.htm?csnumber=52075.

Jacobs, J., *In Defense of Disciplines: Interdisciplinarity and Specialization in the Research University*, University of Chicago Press, Chicago, IL (2014).

Jacoby, B., *Service-Learning in Higher Education: Concepts and Practices*, Jossey-Bass Publishers, San Francisco, CA (1996).

Jacoby, B., *Service-Learning Essentials: Questions, Answers, and Lessons Learned*, Jossey-Bass Publishers, San Francisco, CA (2014).

Jenkins, H., Ford, S., and Green, J., *Spreadable Media: Creating Value and Meaning in a Networked Culture*, NYU Press, New York, NY (2013).

Jeppesen, L. B. and Lakhani, K. R., Marginality and problem-solving effectiveness in broadcast search, *Organization Science* **21**, 5 (September–October 2010), 1016–1033.

Johnson, S., *Where Good Ideas Come From: A Natural History of Innovation*, Riverhead Publishers, New York, NY (2010).

Johnson, S., *How We Got to Now: Six Innovations that Made the Modern World*, Riverhead Publishers, New York, NY (2014).

Jones, B. F., Wuchty, S., and Uzzi, B., Multi-university research teams: Shifting impact, geography, and stratification in science. *Science* **322**, 5905 (2008), 1259–1262. doi: 10.1126/science.1158357.

Jones, P., *Design for Care: Innovating the Healthcare Experience*, Rosenfeld Media, Brooklyn, NY (2013).

Kahneman, D., *Thinking, Fast and Slow*, Farrar, Straus and Giroux, New York, NY (2011).

Kahneman, D. and Tversky, A., Prospect theory: An analysis of decisions under risk, *Econometrica* **47**, 2 (1979), 263–291.

Kamenetzy, J. R., Opportunities for impact: Statistical analysis of the National Science Foundation's broader impact criteria, *Science and Public Policy* **40**, 1 (2013), 72–84.

Kay, M., Leave me alone, *The Chronicle of Higher Education, Chronicle Review* (November 14, 2014), B20.

Keim, D., Kohlhammer, J., Ellis, G., and Mansmann, G. (Editors), *Mastering the Information Age: Solving Problems with Visual Analytics*, Eurographics Association, Goslar (2010); available at http://www.vismaster.eu/wp-content/uploads/2010/11/VisMaster-book-lowres.pdf.

Kimmelman, M., In redesigned room, hospital patients may feel better already, *New York Times* (August 21, 2014). http://www.nytimes.com/2014/08/22/arts/design/in-redesigned-room-hospital-patients-may-feel-better-already.html.

Klein, J. T., *Creating Interdisciplinary Campus Cultures: A Model for Strength and Sustainability*, Jossey Bass and the Association of American Colleges and Universities, San Francisco, CA (2010).

Knapp, B., Bardenet, R., et al., Ten simple rules for a successful cross-disciplinary collaboration, *PLoS Computational Biology* **11**, 4 (April 30, 2015), e1004214. doi: 10.1371/journal.pcbi.1004214.

Kohavi, R., Deng, A., Frasca, B., Walker, T., Xu, Y., and Pohlmann, N., Online controlled experiments at large scale, in *Proceedings of the 19th ACM Conference on Knowledge Discovery and Data Mining*, ACM, New York, NY (2013), pp. 1168–1176.

Kramer, A. D. I., Guillory, J. E., and Hancock, J. T., Experimental evidence of massive-scale emotional contagion through social networks, *Proceedings of the National Academy of Sciences* **111**, 24 (June 17, 2014), 8788–8790; available at http://www.pnas.org/content/111/24/8788.full.pdf.

Kramer, P., Why Doctors Need Stories, *New York Times* (October 18, 2014) http://opinionator.blogs.nytimes.com/2014/10/18/why-doctors-need-stories/.

Kristof, N., Smart Minds, Slim Impact, *New York Times* (February 16, 2014).

Kuchner, M. J., *Marketing for Scientists: How to Shine in Tough Times*, Island Press, Washington, DC (2011).

Kuhn, T., *The Structure of Scientific Revolutions*, University of Chicago Press, Chicago, IL (1962; third edition 1996).

Kumar, V., *101 Design Methods: A Structured Approach for Driving Innovation in Your Organization*, Wiley, New York, NY (2012).

Lane, J., Assessing the impact of science funding. *Science* **324**, 5932 (2009), 1273–1275.

Lane, J., Let's make science metrics more scientific. *Nature* **464**, 7288 (2010), 488–489; available at http://dx.doi.org/10.1038/464488a.

Lane, J. and Bertuzzi, S., Measuring the results of science investments, *Science* **331**, 6810 (2011), 678–680.

Laurel, B., *Design Research: Methods and Perspectives*, MIT Press, Cambridge, MA (2003).

Lawson, B., *How Designers Think: The Design Process Demystified: Fourth Edition*, Architectural Press, Oxford (2005).

Lazer, D., Kennedy, R., King, G., and Vespignani, A., The parable of Google Flu: Traps in the big data analysis, *Science* **343**, 6176 (March 14, 2014), 1203–1205.

Lazowska, E., Envisioning the future of computing research, *Communications of the ACM* **51**, 8 (August 2008), 28–30.

Lazowska, E. and Patterson, D., An endless frontier postponed. *Science* **308**, 5723 (2005), 757.

Levitt, J. M. and Thelwall, M., Is multidisciplinary research more highly cited? A macro-level study, *Journal of the American Society for Information Science and Technology* **59**, 12 (2008), 1973–1984.

Lewin, K., *Field Theory in Social Science*, Basic Books, New York, NY (1951).

Liang, B. C., *Managing and Leading for Science Professionals (What I Wish I'd Known While Moving Up the Management Ladder)*, Academic Press, New York, NY (2013).

Lima, M., *The Book of Trees: Visualizing Branches of Knowledge*, Princeton Architectural Press, New York, NY (2014).

Lungeanu, A. and Contractor, N. S., The effects of diversity and network ties on innovations: The emergence of a new scientific field, *American Behavioral Scientist* **59**, 5 (2014), 548–564. doi: 10.1177/0002764214556804.

Lungeanu, A., Huang, Y., and Contractor, N. S., Understanding the assembly of interdisciplinary teams and their impact on performance, *Journal of Informetrics* **8**, 1 (2014), 59–70. doi: 10.1016/j.joi.2013.10.006.

Maher, M. L. and Gero, J. S., Design science, in W. S. Bainbridge (Editor), *Leadership in Science and Technology: A Reference Handbook*, Sage Publishers, New York, NY (2011), pp. 114–122.

Malina, R. F., Strohecker, C., LaFayette, C., and Ione, A., *Steps to an Ecology of Networked Knowledge and Innovation: Enabling New Forms of Collaboration among Sciences, Engineering, Arts, and Design, Volume I: Synthesis Report* (2013a) https://seadnetwork.files.wordpress.com/2014/01/volume_i_print_final.pdf.

Malina, R. F., Strohecker, C., LaFayette, C., and Ione, A., *Steps to an Ecology of Networked Knowledge and Innovation: Enabling New Forms of Collaboration among Sciences, Engineering, Arts, and Design, Volume II: Meta-Analyses, Abstracts and White Papers* (2013b) https://seadnetwork.files.wordpress.com/2014/01/volume_ii_print.pdf.

Maslow, A. H., A theory of human motivation, *Psychological Review* **50**, 4 (1943), 370–396; available at http://psychclassics.yorku.ca/Maslow/motivation.htm.

Maslow, A. H., *Motivation and Personality*, Harper, New York, NY (1954).

Mayer-Schönberger, M. and Cukier, K., *Big Data: A Revolution That Will Transform How We Live, Work, and Think*, Houghton Mifflin Harcourt, New York, NY (2013).

McLuhan, M., *Understanding Media: The Extensions of Man*, McGraw-Hill, New York, NY (1964).

Medawar, P. B., *Advice to a Young Scientist*, Harper & Row, New York, NY (1979).

Merton, R. K., The Matthew effect in science, *Science* **159**, 3810 (1968), 56–63.

Milkman, K. L. and Berger, J., The science of sharing and the sharing of science, *Proceedings of the National Academy of Sciences* **111**, Supplement 4 (September 16, 2014), 13642–13649.

Miller, J. and Parker, L., *Everybody's Business: The Unlikely Story of How Big Business Can Fix the World*, Biteback Publishing, London (2013).

MIT Committee to Evaluate the Innovation Deficit, *The Future Postponed: Why Declining Investment in Basic Research Threatens a U. S. Innovation Deficit* (2015) http://dc.mit.edu/sites/default/files/innovation_deficit/Future%20Postponed.pdf.

Monge, P. R. and Contractor, N. S., *Theories of Communication Networks*, Oxford University Press, Oxford (2003).

Moore, G. A., *Crossing the Chasm*, HarperCollins, New York, NY (1991).

Morris, S. and Martens, B., Mapping research specialties, *Annual Review of Information Science* **42**, 1 (2007), 213–295.

Morris, S. A., Yen, G., Zheng, W., and Asnake, B., Time line visualization of research fronts. *Journal of the American Society for Information Science and Technology* **54**, 5 (2003), 413–422.

Mumford, L., *Technics and Civilization*, Harcourt Brace and World, Inc., New York, NY (1934).

Mumford, L., *The Myth of the Machine*, Harcourt Brace Jovanovich, Inc., New York, NY (1967).

Narayanamurti, V., Odumosu, T., and Vinsel, L., RIP: The basic/applied research dichotomy, *Issues in Science and Technology* **29**, 2 (2013), 31–36.

National Academies, *Guiding Principles for University-Industry Endeavors*, Washington, DC (2006) http://sites.nationalacademies.org/cs/groups/pgasite/documents/webpage/pga_044335.pdf.

National Academies, *Protecting Individual Privacy in the Struggle Against Terrorists: A Framework for Program Assessment*, National Academies Press, Washington, DC (2008); available at http://www.nap.edu/catalog.php?record_id=12452.

National Academies, Committee on Facilitating Interdisciplinary Research, Committee on Science, Engineering, and Public Policy, *Facilitating Interdisciplinary Research*, National Academy Press, Washington, DC (2004).

National Academies, Science of Science and Innovation Policy, *Principal Investigators' Conference Summary*, National Academy Press, Washington, DC (2014).

National Academy of Sciences, *Beyond Productivity: Information Technology, Innovation and Creativity*, National Academies Press, Washington, DC (2003).

National Academy of Sciences, *Frontiers of Massive Data Analysis*, National Academies Press, Washington, DC (2013).

National Academy of Sciences, National Academy of Engineering, and Institute of Medicine, *On Being a Scientist: A Guide to Responsible Conduct in Research: Third Edition*, National Academies Press, Washington, DC (2009).

National Institutes of Health, *Brain 2025: A Scientific Vision: Research through Advancing Innovative Neurotechnologies (BRAIN) Working Group Report to the Advisory Committee to the Director*, NIH (June 5, 2014) http://www.braininitiative.nih.gov/2025/BRAIN2025.pdf.

National Research Council, Committee on a Framework for Developing a New Taxonomy of Disease, *Toward Precision Medicine: Building a Knowledge Network for Biomedical Research and a New Taxonomy of Disease*, National Academies Press, Washington, DC (2011); available at http://www.nap.edu/catalog.php?record_id=13284.

National Research Council, *Convergence: Facilitating Transdisciplinary Integration of Life Sciences, Physical Sciences, Engineering, and Beyond*. The National Academies Press, Washington, DC (2014).

National Science Foundation, *Investing in America's Future: Strategic Plan 2006–2011*, National Science Foundation, Arlington, VA (2006).

National Science Foundation, *Proposal and Award Policies and Procedures Guide*, National Science Foundation, Arlington, VA (2014).

Nelson, B., The data on diversity, *Communications of the ACM* **57**, 11 (November 2014), 86–95.

Nelson, H. G. and Stolterman, E., *The Design Way: Intentional Change in an Unpredictable World: Second Edition*, MIT Press, Cambridge, MA (2012).

Nielsen, M., *Reinventing Discovery: The New Era of Networked Science*, Princeton University Press, Princeton, NJ (2011).

Nilsson, L., How To Attract Female Engineers? *New York Times* (April 27, 2015) http://www.nytimes.com/2015/04/27/opinion/how-to-attract-female-engineers.html.

Norman, D., *Design of Everyday Things*, Basic Books, New York, NY (1988, 2013).

Norris, M., Oppenheim, C., and Rowland, F., The citation advantage of open-access articles, *Journal of the American Society for Information Science and Technology* **59**, 12 (2008), 1963–1972.

Obrenović, Ž., Design-based research: What we learn when we engage in design of interactive systems, *ACM Interactions* **18**, 5 (2011), 56–59.

Obrenović, Ž., Doing research in practice: Some lessons learned, *ACM XRDS* **20**, 4 (Summer 2014), 15–17.

Office of Science and Technology Policy, Executive Office of the President, *Obama Administration Unveils "Big Data" Initiative: Announces $200 Million in New R&D Investments* (March 29, 2012) http://www.whitehouse.gov/sites/default/files/microsites/ostp/big_data_press_release_final_2.pdf.

Ogle, R., *Smart World: Breakthrough Creativity and the New Science of Ideas*, Harvard Business School Press, Boston, MA (2007).

Olson, G. M., Zimmerman, A., and Bos, N., *Scientific Collaboration on the Internet*, MIT Press, Cambridge, MA (2008).

Olson, J. S. and Olson, G. M., *Working Together Apart: Collaboration over the Internet*, Morgan & Claypool Publishers, San Rafael, CA (2013).

Olson, J. S., Hofer, E. C., Bos, N., Zimmerman, A., Olson, G. M., Cooney, D., and Faniel, I., Interdisciplinarity as a design problem: Toward mutual intelligibility among academic disciplines in the American research university, in G. M. Olson, A. Zimmerman, and N. Bos, *Scientific Collaboration on the Internet*, MIT Press, Cambridge, MA (2008), pp. 73–97.

Onarheim, B. and Friis-Olivarius, M., Applying the neuroscience of creativity to creativity training, *Frontiers in Human Neuroscience* **7**, (October 16, 2013), Article 656. doi: 10.3389/fnhum.2013.00656.

Page, S. E., *The Difference: How the Power of Diversity Creates Better Groups, Firms, Schools, and Societies*, Princeton University Press, Princeton, New Jersey (2007).

Pahl, G., Beitz, W., Feldhusen, J., and Grote, K., *Engineering Design: A Systematic Approach: Third Edition*, Springer, London (2007).

Palmer, E. M., Clausner, T. C., and Kellman, P. J., Enhancing air traffic displays via perceptual cues, *ACM Transactions on Applied Perception* **5**, 1 (2008), 1–22.

Papanek, V., *Design for the Real World: Human Ecology and Social Change*, Chicago Review Press, Chicago, IL (1971; revised edition, 2005).

Patterson, D., How to build a bad research center, *Communications of the ACM* **57**, 3 (March 2014), 33–36.

Penner, O., Pan, R. J. K., Petersen, A. M., Kaski, K., and Fortunato, S., On the predictability of future impact in science, *Nature Scientific Reports* **3** (October 2013), Article 3052; available at http://www.nature.com/srep/2013/131029/srep03052/full/srep03052.html.

Pentland, A., *Social Physics: How Good Ideas Spread: The Lessons from a New Science*, Penguin Press, New York, NY (2014).

Perrow, C., *Normal Accidents: Living with High-Risk Technologies*, Basic Books, New York, NY (1984).

Perrow, C., *The Next Catastrophe: Reducing Our Vulnerabilities to Natural, Industrial, and Terrorist Disasters*, Princeton University Press, Princeton, NJ (2007).

Petroski, H., *To Engineer is Human: The Role of Failure in Successful Design*, Vintage, New York, NY (1992).

Petroski, H., *The Essential Engineer: Why Science Alone Will Not Solve Our Global Problems*, Knopf, New York, NY (2010).

Pinker, S., *The Sense of Style: The Thinking Person's Guide to Writing in the 21st Century*, Viking Adult, New York, NY (2014).

Preece, J., Rogers, Y., and Sharp, H., *Interaction Design: Beyond Human-Computer Interaction: Fourth Edition*, Wiley, New York, NY (2015).

Preece, J. and Shneiderman, B., The reader-to-leader framework: Motivating technology-mediated social participation, *AIS Transactions on Human-Computer Interaction* **1**, 1 (March 2009), 13–32; available at http://aisel.aisnet.org/thci/vol1/iss1/5/.

Preedy, V. R. (Editor), *Handbook of Anthropometry: Physical Measures of Human Physical Form in Health and Disease*, Springer, New York, NY (2012).

President's Council of Advisors on Science and Technology, *Report to the President: Realizing the Full Potential of Health Information Technology to Improve Healthcare for Americans: The Path Forward*, Washington, DC (2010).

President's Council of Advisors on Science and Technology, *Transformation and Opportunity: The Future of the U. S. Research Enterprise*, Washington, DC (November 2012); available at http://www.whitehouse.gov/administration/eop/ostp/pcast/docsreports.

Rainie, L. and Wellman, B., *Networked: The New Social Operating System*, MIT Press, Cambridge, MA (2012).

Ries, E., *The Lean Startup: How Today's Entrepreneurs Use Continuous Innovation to Create Radically Successful Businesses*, Crown Business Publishers, New York, NY (2011).

Roco, M. C., Bainbridge, W. S., Tonn, B., and Whitesides, G. (Editors), *Convergence of Knowledge, Technology, and Society: Beyond Convergence of Nano-Bio-Info-Cognitive Technologies*, Springer, New York, NY (2013).

Rogers, E. M., *Diffusion of Innovations: Fifth Edition*, Free Press, New York, NY (2003).

Rogers, Y., *HCI Theory: Classical, Modern, and Contemporary*, Morgan & Claypool Publishers, San Rafael, CA (2012).

Rouse, W. B. and Serban, N., *Understanding and Managing the Complexity of Healthcare*, MIT Press, Cambridge, MA (2014).

Sandstrom, P. E., Scholarly communication as a socioecological system, *Scientometrics* **51**, 3 (2001), 573–605.

Sayer, C. and Lee, T. H., Time after time: Health policy implications of a three-generation case study, *New England Journal of Medicine* **371**, 14 (October 2, 2014), 1273–1276; available at http://www.nejm.org/doi/pdf/10.1056/NEJMp1407153.

Schimel, J., *Writing Science: How to Write Papers That Get Cited and Proposals That Get Funded*, Oxford University Press, New York, NY (2011).

Schön, D., *The Reflective Practitioner: How Professionals Think in Action*, Basic Books, New York, NY (1983).

schraefel, m. c. and Churchill, E., Wellth creation: Using computer science to support proactive health, *IEEE Computer* **47**, 11 (November 2014), 70–72.

Schrage, M., *The Innovator's Hypothesis: How Cheap Experiments Are Worth More than Good Ideas*, MIT Press, Cambridge, MA (2014).

Schreiber, M., *A Case Study of the Hirsch Index for 26 Non-Prominent Physicists*, ArXiv E-Print Publication (July 31, 2007) http://arxiv.org/pdf/0708.0120.pdf.

Schreiber, M., *The Predictability of the Hirsch Index Evolution*, ArXiv E-Print Publication (2013) http://arxiv.org/ftp/arxiv/papers/1307/1307.5964.pdf.

Schuler, D., *Liberating Voices: A Pattern Language for Communication Revolution*, MIT Press, Cambridge, MA (2008).

Sedlmair, M., Meyer, M., and Munzner, T., Design study methodology: Reflections from the trenches and the stacks, *IEEE Transactions on Visualization and Computer Graphics* **18**, 12 (2012), 2431–2440.

Seo, J. and Shneiderman, B., Knowledge discovery in high-dimensional data: Case studies and a user survey for the rank-by-feature framework, *IEEE Transactions on Visualization and Computer Graphics* **12**, 3 (May–June 2006), 311–322.

Shadbolt, N. and Berners-Lee, T., Web science emerges, *Scientific American* **299**, 4 (October 2008), 32–37.

Shadbolt, N., Hall, W., and Berners-Lee, T., The semantic Web revisited, *IEEE Intelligent Systems* **21**, 3 (2006), 96–101.

Shenk, J. W., *Powers of Two: Finding the Essence of Innovation in Creative Pairs*, Houghton Mifflin Harcourt, New York, NY (2014).

Shneiderman, B., *Leonardo's Laptop: Human Needs and the New Computing Technologies*, MIT Press, Cambridge, MA (2002).

Shneiderman, B., Web science: A provocative invitation to computer science. *Communications of the ACM* **50**, 6 (June 2007), 25–27. doi: 10.1145/1247001.1247022.

Shneiderman, B., Creativity support tools: Accelerating discovery and innovation, *Communications of the ACM* **50**, 12 (December 2007), 20–32.

Shneiderman, B., et al., Creativity support tools: Report from a U. S. National Science Foundation sponsored workshop. *International Journal of Human-Computer Interaction* **20**, 2 (2006), 61–77.

Shneiderman, B., Dunne, C., Sharma, P., and Wang, P., Innovation trajectories for information visualization: A comparison of treemaps, cone trees, and hyperbolic trees, *Information Visualization Journal* **11**, 2 (2011), 87–105.

Shneiderman, B. and Plaisant, C., Strategies for evaluating information visualization tools: Multi-dimensional in-depth long-term case studies, in T. Catarci and M. F. Costabile, *Proceedings of the Workshop of the Advanced Visual Interfaces Conference*, ACM Press, New York, NY (2006), pp. 1–7.

Shneiderman, B. and Plaisant, C., *Designing the User Interface: Strategies for Effective Human-Computer Interaction: Sixth Edition*, Addison-Wesley, Reading, MA (2016).

Simon, H., *The Sciences of the Artificial: Third Edition*, MIT Press, Cambridge, MA (1996).

Smith, M. A., Rainie, L., Himelboim, I., and Shneiderman, B., *Mapping Twitter Topic Networks: From Polarized Crowds to Community Clusters, Pew Research Center Report* (Feb 20, 2014) http://www.pewinternet.org/2014/02/20/mapping-twitter-topic-networks-from-polarized-crowds-to-community-clusters/.

Snyder, C., *Paper Prototyping: The Fast and Easy Way to Design and Refine User Interfaces*, Morgan Kaufmann Publishers, San Francisco, CA (2003).

Sobel, D., *Longitude: The True Story of a Lone Genius Who Solved the Greatest Scientific Problem of His Time*, Walker Publishing Company, New York, NY (1995).

Spector, A., Norvig, P., and Petrov, S., Google's hybrid approach to research, *Communications of the ACM* **55**, 7 (July 2012), 34–37.

Stokes, D., *Pasteur's Quadrant: Basic Science and Technological Innovation*, Brookings Institution, Washington, DC (1997).

Stokols, D., Hall, K. L., Taylor, B. K., and Moser, R. P., The science of team science: Overview of the field and introduction to the supplement, *American Journal of Preventive Medicine* **35**, 2S (2008), S77–S88.

Stolterman, E., The nature of design practice and implications for interaction design research, *International Journal of Design* **2**, 1 (2008), 55–65.

Swaby, R., *Headstrong: 52 Women Who Changed Science—and the World*, Broadway Books, New York, NY (2015).

Thaler, R. and Sunstein, C., *Nudge: Improving Decisions about Health, Wealth, and Happiness*, Yale University Press, New Haven, CT (2008).

Thomas, J. C., Facilitating global intelligence, *IEEE Computer Graphics and Applications* **19**, 6 (1999), 70–74.

Thomas, J. C., An HCI agenda for the next millennium: Emergent global intelligence, in R. Earnshaw, R. Guedj, A. van Dam, and J. Vince (Editors), *Frontiers of Human-Centered Computing, Online Communities, and Virtual Environments*, Springer-Verlag, London (2001), pp. 198–219.

Thomas, J. J. and Cook, K. A. (Editors), *Illuminating the Path: Research and Development Agenda for Visual Analytics*, IEEE, Piscataway, NJ (2005).

Thompson, C., *Smarter than You Think: How Technology is Changing Our Minds for the Better*, Penguin Press, New York, NY (2013).

Thompson, J. M. T., Advice to a young researcher: With reminiscences of a life in science, *Philosophical Transactions of the Royal Society* **371**, 1993 (May 20, 2013), 20120425.

Tomlinson, B., Blevis, E., Nardi, B., Patterson, D. J., Silberman, M. S., and Pan, Y., Collapse informatics and practice: Theory, method, and design, *ACM Transactions on Computer-Human Interaction* **20**, 4 (September 2013), Article 24.

Tuckman, B. W., Developmental sequence in small groups, *Psychological Bulletin* **63**, 6 (June 1965), 384–399.

Tuckman, B. W. and Jensen, M. A. C., Stages of small-group development revisited, *Group Organization Management* **2**, 4 (December 1977), 419–427.

Tufekci, Z., Engineering the public: Big data, surveillance, and computational politics, *First Monday* **19**, 7 (July 7, 2014), http://firstmonday.org/ojs/index.php/fm/article/view/4901/4097.

Tukey, J. W., *Exploratory Data Analysis*. Addison-Wesley, Reading, MA (1977).

Turabian, K. L., Booth, W. C., Colomb, G. G., Williams, J. M., and the University of Chicago Press Staff, *A Manual for Writers of Research Papers, Theses, and Dissertations: Eighth Edition*, University of Chicago Press, Chicago, IL (2013).

Tversky, A. and Kahneman, D., Judgment under uncertainty: Heuristics and biases, *Science* **185**, 4157 (1974), 1124–1131.

Tversky, A. and Kahneman, D., The framing of decisions and the psychology of choice, *Science* **211**, 4481 (1981), 453–458.

Uren, V., Buckingham Shum, S., Bachler, M., and Li, G., Sensemaking tools for understanding research literatures: Design, implementation and user evaluation, *International Journal of Human-Computer Studies* **64**, 5 (2006), 420–445.

Uzzi, B., Mukerjee, S., Stringer, M., and Jones, B. F., Atypical combinations and scientific impact, *Science* **342** (2013), 268–472.

Uzzi, B. and Spiro, J., Collaboration and creativity: The small world problem, *American Journal of Sociology* **111**, 2 (September 2005), 447–504.

Valiela, I., *Doing Science: Design, Analysis, and Communication of Scientific Results: Second Edition*, Oxford University Press, Oxford (2009).

Van Noorden, R., Maher, B., and Nuzzo, R., The top 100 papers: Nature explores the most-cited research of all time, *Nature* **514**, 7524 (October 30, 2014), 550–553. doi: 10.1038/514550a.

Vansteenkiste, M. and Sheldon, K. M., There's nothing more practical than a good theory: Integrating motivational interviews with self-determination theory, *British Journal of Clinical Psychology* **45**, 1 (2006), 63–82.

Venkatesh, V., Morris, M. G., Davis, G. B., and Davis, F. D., User acceptance of information technology: Toward a unified view, *MIS Quarterly* **27**, 3 (2003), 425–478.

Walker, J. L., Setting the agenda in the US Senate: A theory of problem selection, *British Journal of Political Science* **7**, 4 (October 1977), 423–455.

Wang, P., Popular concepts beyond organizations: Exploring new dimensions of information technology innovations, *Journal of the Association for Information Systems* **10**, 1 (2009), 1–30.

Wang, P. and Ramiller, N. C., Community learning in information technology innovations, *MIS Quarterly* **33**, 4 (2009), 709–734.

Wang, P. and Swanson, E. B., Launching professional services automation: Institutional entrepreneurship for information technology innovations, *Information and Organization* **17**, 2 (2007), 59–88.

Warfel, T. Z., *Prototyping: A Practitioner's Guide*, Rosenfeld Media, Brooklyn, NY (2011).

Warmington, A., Action research: Its methods and its implications, *Journal of Applied Systems Analysis* **7** (1980), 23–39.

Watson, J. D., *The Double Helix: A Personal Account of the Discovery of the Structure of DNA*, Atheneum Publishers, New York, NY (1968).

Whitesides, G. M. and Deutch, J., Let's get practical, *Nature* **469**, 7328 (2011), 21–22.

Winograd, T., *Bringing Design to Software*, Addison-Wesley, Reading, MA (1996).

Witten, I., Frank, E., and Hall, M. A., *Data Mining: Practical Machine Learning Tools and Techniques: Third Edition*, Morgan Kaufmann, Burlington, MA (2011).

Woolley, A. and Malone, T., Defend your research: What makes a team smarter? More women, *Harvard Business Review Report* (June 2011); available at https://hbr.org/2011/06/defend-your-research-what-makes-a-team-smarter-more-women.

Wuchty, S., Jones, B. F., and Uzzi, B., The increasing dominance of teams in production of knowledge. *Science* **316**, 5827 (2007a), 1036–1039. doi: 10.1126/science.1136099.

Wuchty, S., Jones, B. F., and Uzzi, B., Why do team-authored papers get cited more? Response. *Science* **317**, 5844 (2007b), 1497–1498.

Yau, N., *Data Points: Visualization That Means Something*, Wiley, New York, NY (2013).

Yin, R. K., *Case Study Research: Design and Methods: Fifth Edition*, Sage Publications, Thousand Oaks, CA (2013).

Zachary, G. P., *Endless Frontier: Vannevar Bush, Engineer of the American Century*, MIT Press, Cambridge, MA (1999).

Zimmerman, J., Forlizzi, J., and Evenson, S., Research through design as a method for interaction design research, in *Proceedings of the Conference on Human Factors in Computing Systems*, ACM Press, New York, NY (2007), 493–502.

NAME INDEX

SUBJECT INDEX

Figures are indicated by an italic *f* following the page number.